THE PHILOSOPHY OF
DAVID CRONENBERG

THE PHILOSOPHY OF DAVID CRONENBERG

Edited by Simon Riches

UNIVERSITY PRESS OF KENTUCKY

Copyright © 2012 by The University Press of Kentucky

Scholarly publisher for the Commonwealth,
serving Bellarmine University, Berea College, Centre
College of Kentucky, Eastern Kentucky University,
The Filson Historical Society, Georgetown College,
Kentucky Historical Society, Kentucky State University,
Morehead State University, Murray State University,
Northern Kentucky University, Transylvania University,
University of Kentucky, University of Louisville,
and Western Kentucky University.
All rights reserved.

Editorial and Sales Offices: The University Press of Kentucky
663 South Limestone Street, Lexington, Kentucky 40508-4008
www.kentuckypress.com

16 15 14 13 12   5 4 3 2 1

Cataloging-in-Publication data is available from the Library of Congress.

ISBN 978-0-8131-3604-2 (hardcover : alk. paper)
ISBN 978-0-8131-3617-2 (ebook)

This book is printed on acid-free paper meeting
the requirements of the American National Standard
for Permanence in Paper for Printed Library Materials.

Manufactured in the United States of America.

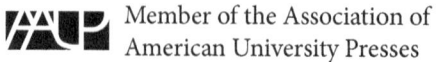 Member of the Association of
American University Presses

Contents

Introduction 1
Simon Riches

Part 1. Body Horror and Bodily Transformation

The Fly and the Human: Ironies of Disgust 9
Colin McGinn

Tragedy and Terrible Beauty in *A History of Violence* and *Eastern Promises* 24
Cynthia Freeland

Cronenberg as Scientist: Antiessentialism, Sex as Remixing, and the View from Nowhere 36
Peter Ludlow

What Happens to Brundle? Problems of Teleportation and Personal Identity in *The Fly* 53
Paul F. Snowdon

Part 2. Psychology, Skepticism, and the Self

eXistenZial Angst 69
Duncan Pritchard

"Freaks of Nature": Extrasensory Perception and the Paranormal in the Films of David Cronenberg 77
Keith Allen

Deception and Disorder: Unraveling Cronenberg's Divided Minds   91
Simon Riches

Psychological Determinism in the Films of David Cronenberg   113
Daniel Shaw

Self-Creation, Identity, and Authenticity: A Study of *A History of Violence* and *Eastern Promises*   125
Daniel Moseley

Part 3. Words and Worldviews

The Fiction of Truth in Fiction: Some Reflections on Semantics and *eXistenZ*   143
Graham Stevens

Re(ct)ifying Empty Speech: Cronenberg and the Problem of the First Person   155
Brook W. R. Pearson

The Politics of Mad Science in *The Fly* and *Dead Ringers*   175
R. Barton Palmer

From "Impassioned Morality" to "Bloodless Agnosticism": A Philosophy of David Cronenberg through the Burroughs/Ballard Axis   197
Jones Irwin

List of Contributors   217

Index   221

Introduction

Simon Riches

There can be no doubt that the widely renowned and influential Canadian filmmaker David Cronenberg (1943–) has produced a diverse contribution to modern cinema. With his propensity to create imagery that is at once disturbing and provocative, Cronenberg has come to mainstream prominence with a striking collection of films. There were the breakthrough shockers, like *Shivers* (1975) and *Scanners* (1981); subversive media critiques, like *Videodrome* (1983); and mainstream hits, like *The Fly* (1986), which were both horrifying and appealing in equal measure. These early films revealed Cronenberg's pioneering employment of the concept of "body horror," but perhaps more significantly, they raised an abundance of questions for critics and viewers alike.

In subsequent years, Cronenberg has continued to pose questions in his films, adapting supposedly unfilmable cult literature, such as William S. Burroughs's *Naked Lunch* (1991) and J. G. Ballard's *Crash* (1996). And even more recently, he has created perceptive and detailed depictions of the criminal underworld with his critically acclaimed *A History of Violence* (2005) and *Eastern Promises* (2007), which expose the conflicted psychology and morality of such lifestyles. For a long time regarded as a cult figure with a following predominantly among sci-fi and horror film fans, Cronenberg has now emerged as a major and commercially viable filmmaker, producing such recent mainstream successes, but he has always stayed true to the aim of making thought-provoking cinema.

A constant throughout these various endeavors, and a project that has remained at the heart of Cronenberg's cinematic output, is a predilection to engage with philosophical questions about human beings and the world that they inhabit. There is evidently an interest in the physical human form, but there is also interest in human psychology. The seventeenth-century

1

French philosopher René Descartes famously made a distinction between the mind and the body, a view known as "dualism." The two sides to this dualism are prominent in Cronenberg's work. In interviews, Cronenberg has often spoken of his interest in "the human condition," and of this aspect to his interest in philosophy. He once said:

> Many of the peaks of philosophical thought revolve around the impossible duality of mind and body. Whether the mind aspect is expressed as soul or spirit, it's still the old Cartesian absolute split between the two. There seems to be a point at which they should fuse and it should be apparent to everyone. But it's not. It really isn't. The basis of horror—and difficulty in life in general—is that we cannot comprehend how we can die. Why should a healthy mind die, just because the body is not healthy? How can a man die a complete physical wreck, when his mind is absolutely sharp and clear? There seems to be something wrong with that. It's very easy to see why many philosophers detach the mind from the body and say, "The answer is that after the body dies the mind continues to work somehow." But I don't believe that. All cultures try to come to some kind of accord with this reality. But I don't think anybody's really successfully done it to the extent that men walk around completely integrated.[1]

Although it is true to say of many filmmakers that they have philosophical interests, or that their films present philosophical ideas, Cronenberg stands out for the extent and the degree to which he presents some of the most well-known philosophical ideas on the screen. It is no exaggeration to say that a Cronenberg film wears its philosophical interests clearly on its sleeve. Throughout his films we encounter a wide variety of philosophical problems, including personal identity and bodily transformation, the nature of the self, skepticism about the external world, and the nature of reality. It is the aim of this book to draw out these themes and to show *how* his films are able to present these philosophical problems.

The volume includes contributions from various academic philosophers. Some are specialists in the philosophy of film, and others are leading experts in philosophical fields that Cronenberg addresses in his films. All of the contributors are unified by their interest in Cronenberg's work and the philosophical issues it raises. Where chapters overlap, it is interesting to see where the different contributors agree and where they disagree, and how they have interpreted various scenes differently. All the essays are intended to be accessible to the general reader who seeks to learn about philosophy issues through Cronenberg's films; but they are also intended to be of interest to academic philosophers and students of philosophy who are interested in the philosophical views of the contributors.

The book is split into three sections that capture some of the broad philosophical domains in which Cronenberg has directed his attention through his films. Part 1, "Body Horror and Bodily Transformation," focuses predominantly on the body, a subject that figures heavily in Cronenberg's work. Cronenberg regularly poses questions about the boundaries of the human body—"I see technology as being an extension of the human body," he has said[2]—and he sees the body as fundamental to our sense of identity: "For me, the first fact of human existence is the human body. That is the most real fact we have. The further from your own body you get, the less real everything is, the less verifiable, the less you connect with it. But if you embrace the reality of the human body, you are embracing your own mortality."[3] In developing these themes of the body, this section looks at aesthetic issues in Cronenberg's treatment of the human body, his signature theme of body horror, and the prevalent theme of bodily transformation, in particular the way this impacts on issues like identity and our ordinary distinction between the organic and the inorganic. To begin the section, Colin McGinn analyzes our relationship with the subject of disgust, and argues that while we may look at other creatures as repellent, the real monster lies within ourselves. Then Cynthia Freeland delves into the tragedy of *A History of Violence* and *Eastern Promises* and sees a "terrible beauty" within the violence. Picking up on Cronenberg's rejection of key distinctions like organic and inorganic, Peter Ludlow views Cronenberg as an antiessentialist and humanist who challenges us to alter our perception of what is human. Lastly, Paul Snowdon looks at the classic philosophical problem of personal identity insofar as it figures in the ill-fated life of scientist Seth Brundle (Jeff Goldblum) in *The Fly*. He argues that deep philosophical issues related to personal identity and to teleportation arose when Brundle decided to step inside his machine.

Part 2, "Psychology, Skepticism, and the Self," takes us away from issues that relate to the body and on to philosophical problems of the mind. It focuses on the way that Cronenberg has engaged with issues that relate to psychology and with the theme of the self. In this regard, Cronenberg has said that "every film for me is just an exploration of the human condition. That's really it. And of course it is in heightened dramatic form, but that sort of illuminates the nature of the human beast."[4] The section begins with Duncan Pritchard, who introduces the popular philosophical idea of radical skepticism, which is vividly captured by *eXistenZ* (1999), and shows how the uncertainty that this scenario creates can leave one in a state of existential angst. Returning to some of Cronenberg's earlier work, such as *Stereo* (1969) and *Scanners,* Keith Allen observes how extrasensory perception has been a recurring theme in Cronenberg's cinema and considers the questions that this raises in epistemology and the philosophy of mind. Then, my chapter describes the theme of deception that pervades Cronenberg's films and uses this as a context within which to discuss the changing way that Cronenberg has looked at the topic of mental disorder. Following on from this, Daniel Shaw develops the Freudian position to argue that Cronenberg presents an overtly deterministic and pessimistic view of human nature. In doing so he places particular emphasis on *Dead Ringers* (1988). Finally, Daniel Moseley continues the examination of identity and shows how *A History of Violence* and *Eastern Promises* constitute a profound meditation on self-creation, practical identity, and authenticity.

Part 3, "Words and Worldviews," broadens the area of focus outside of the individual and considers topics like language, reality, the literary adaptations, and the Cronenbergian worldview, particularly insofar as this leads to the examination of moral and political themes. In this section, Graham Stevens considers what it means for a statement to be true in a fiction and argues that the uncertainty over the nature of reality in *eXistenZ* makes it a particularly interesting and unusual case. Brook W. R. Pearson develops the theme of the self or the first person but with particular attention to the role of speech. In doing so he intertwines the views of Jacques Lacan, Ludwig Wittgenstein, and Gilles Deleuze and Félix Guattari. R. Barton Palmer provides a survey of how Cronenberg's work constitutes a critique of modern science, and draws a fascinating comparison between Cronenberg's mad scientists and Robert Louis Stevenson's *Strange Case of Dr. Jekyll and Mr. Hyde.* Lastly, Jones Irwin provides an analysis of the way Cronenberg negotiated his adaptations of Burroughs's *Naked Lunch* and Ballard's *Crash* and places this in the broad context of subjects like the nature of morality and the distinction between the social and the individual.

Finally, I would like to use this opportunity to thank all the contributors for their involvement and their hard work on the project. I would also like to thank series editor Mark Conard and the University Press of Kentucky, especially Anne Dean Watkins, Liz Smith, David Cobb, and Cameron Ludwick.

Notes

1. Quoted in Chris Rodley, ed., *Cronenberg on Cronenberg,* rev. ed. (London: Faber and Faber, 1997), 79.

2. Quoted in Rob Blackwelder, "David Cronenberg Interview," *Contactmusic.com*, http://www.contactmusic.com/interview/cronenberg.
3. Quoted in "The Mixing of Blood: An Interview with David Cronenberg," *Filmthreat.com*, http://www.filmthreat.com/interviews/6/.
4. Quoted in Lewis Wallace, "Body Language: An Interview with David Cronenberg," *Wired.com*, December 29, 2007, http://www.wired.com/underwire/2007/12/body-language-a/.

Part 1

Body Horror and Bodily Transformation

The Fly and the Human
Ironies of Disgust

Colin McGinn

The Hermeneutics of the Fly

Different animal species evoke distinctive emotional reactions in human beings. On the positive side, we feel affection, admiration, attraction, and aesthetic pleasure. On the negative side, we feel fear, contempt, revulsion, and aesthetic displeasure. Pandas, elephants, whales, cats, dogs, birds, butterflies, turtles, and kangaroos are examples that tend to fall on the positive side. Sharks, bears, worms, rats, mice, spiders, bacteria, bats, snakes, mosquitoes, and lice are apt to fall on the negative side. With some animals we smile; with others we shudder. Toward a small minority (or is it a majority?) we feel something like envy: this is particularly true of birds, whose aerial abilities we marvel at and covet. Sometimes, perhaps, we envy animals their mindlessness, their freedom from angst, their spontaneity. I don't think we ever hate an animal species, as opposed to fearing it, because to hate something requires that you believe it has wronged you (or another person), and animals, not being moral agents, can't wrong you—though they can obviously harm you.[1] (If some primates are to be accorded the status of moral agents, this generalization needs to be restricted; in any case, it is true for the vast majority of animals.) Yet we are capable of extremely strong aversive reactions to certain animal species: they make our flesh creep, they "gross us out," they inspire dread and fear. What the number one most disliked species may be is debatable: some say the rat, others the tapeworm, yet others the mosquito. In any case, we simply can't stand certain animals; their extinction would not sadden us a bit.

The humble fly ranks high here. Of the order Diptera (two winged), flies proper are distinct from other flying insects, such as dragonflies, fireflies, and butterflies, in possessing only a single pair of wings and in other anatomical respects; and we have notably different attitudes toward these categories of insects. Flies in the narrow sense include mosquitoes, gnats, and midges, as well as the common housefly. They are born as eggs, develop into legless maggots, and finally metamorphose into the buzzing nuisances we know them to be. They are short lived, surviving a matter of days, consume only liquid food, and are adept at the art of clinging to things by using spongy pads on their feet; they are also agile and flummoxed by panes of glass. They breed prodigiously ("like flies") and are quite hard to kill without employing low-level chemical warfare (a rolled newspaper is a notably blunt weapon). With their zigzag flight, protuberant compound eyes, and tiny bristles—conspicuous under a microscope—they strike us as alien and vaguely reprehensible; not pretty, to be sure. Moreover, they exhibit a kind of driven stubborn determination, taking all manner of risks, not afraid to settle in the most dangerous places. They are surprisingly difficult to get rid of. To make matters worse, they often bite—and some even suck blood. They are invasive of human space—taking up residence in our houses, eating our food, seemingly drawn by our orifices, especially the mouth. They will settle on your face without so much as a by-your-leave, and even lick your lips if they get the chance.

But none of that comes close to their most notorious trait: their penchant for human garbage, rotting flesh, and feces. The things we find most disgusting seem to excite their ravenous little appetites the most. They love places of death, exposed human waste, and garbage dumps. They like to stick their little feet into such revolting material and then suck on it. Our hell is their heaven (pigs have nothing on flies). Thus they strike as supremely dirty, avatars of filth. They are themselves units of dirt, a measure of how mucky a place is. They are saturated with the filth they so relish, we feel. If anything, the maggots are worse: corpses are their dining hall and playground. Squirming, senseless, hideously pale—not many things revolt us as maggots do. The caterpillar we can tolerate, we love the butterfly, but the fly and its maggot progeny excite only nausea and disdain. Note that our reaction is not one of fear: with the exception of disease-carrying mosquitoes, we are not afraid of flies, since they cannot really harm us; rather, they are objects of our disgust. Flies are perceived as contaminating, as agents of defilement, not as dangerous to life and limb (nothing like sharks, say).[2] It is their invasiveness combined with their fecal and putrescent proclivities that generate our extreme reaction of disgust: not only are flies in constant contact with the filthy and revolting; they also bring it to us, *on* us, with their rapid flight and nimble landings on human skin. We can't keep the fecal and putrescent away if flies carry traces of it on their feet and mandibles and then transfer it to us. What is so disturbing (and heartbreaking) about those pictures of African children with dozens of flies buzzing around their face, settling on their eyes, nose, and mouth, is the thought that those very flies have recently been wallowing in feces and filth. Flies represent in concentrated form the invasion of filth on the human domain. They are not just one species among many, going about its own business, oblivious to human beings; they are enmeshed in our human life, surviving on what we reject and then bringing it back to us. They are so much a part of human life, such a dependable nuisance, yet at the same time they are so alien to us; with us but not *of* us, so present and so shunned.

Flies, then, exist in close proximity to humans. I mean this in the spatial sense, that they take up residence in our houses and buzz around our kitchen tables, but also in the sense that they make contact with substances close to our nature as biological organisms: our food, our excrement, our dead bodies. They want to be near what we are near to, whether *we* want to be near it or not (death, decay, foul matter). They survive in relation to the most distasteful of biological facts. Indeed, they thrive on what we produce in the way of filth and waste. After all, the feces they so gleefully perch on are often those we humans have only recently released from our own appendage for perching, and the rotting corpses they delight in may be the bodily remnants of a lately deceased conscious human being. They touch us in our most degraded and shameful state. Inevitably, then, they remind us of certain disagreeable facts about ourselves—facts that naturally excite shame and loathing. The fly is an emblem of our mortal organic condition, our connection to the world of biological processes: digestion, dying, the soft and slimy. To be or become food for flies and worms—that is the most base level of human existence.

And there is one other fact about flies and humans that is worth mentioning: the vulnerability that is common to both. Flies live a very short time, yet they thrust and strive like tiny packets of pure will. Their lives seem to us a paradigm of meaninglessness, mere mechanical contrivances for mindless genes to perpetuate themselves: nasty, brutish, short—but also filthy and degraded. They can also, despite their agility, be squashed by the random thwack of a newspaper, or poisoned by a jet of chemicals; the end comes abruptly and unfairly. Flies die easily. That is an uncomfortable mirror of our own mortality: our lives too are short and strenuous, with sudden death always a heartbeat away. We are easily squashed, quickly choked. And then there is the threat of the powerful other—the unbeatable enemy. We may dislike flies, but the sight of one of them caught in a spider's web, trussed up, still breathing, waiting its torturous end—that is a sight to engage our sympathies, our queasy recognition of vulnerability. The fly caught in the spider's web is a symbol of all imprisonment, subjugation, despair, and hopelessness. The fly is vulnerable and so are we; our kinship is as undeniable as our difference. Our emotional relationship to flies is thus a multifaceted and complex one: they touch us at many points, carrying a weight of meaning disproportionate to their size. Sometimes they seem to exist at the opposite pole from us; sometimes they seem our intimates and counterparts, symbols of our own destiny. They disgust us and yet they reflect us. They are a fact of human life that cannot be denied or remedied, as well as being repellent and tragic in themselves. Inescapability, repugnance, queasy sympathy—these are the contours of our human feeling about flies.

Cronenberg's Hymn to the Fly

In his 1986 *The Fly,* itself a remake of a 1958 film based on a short story by George Langelaan, David Cronenberg made a film with a fly as its star. Seth Brundle (Jeff Goldblum), an eccentric but brilliant scientist, is working on teleportation and making great strides. In one of his experiments he successfully transports himself between two telepods, emerging jubilant, anxious to tell his new girlfriend Veronica (Geena Davis) all about it. After a short while, however, signs that something may have gone wrong emerge: he has abnormal amounts of energy, feels strong and invulnerable, and is sexually potent to an alarming degree. As it turns out, a common housefly had flown into the container with Seth, and the computer then genetically fused the two organisms. As the film progresses, this hybrid status becomes increasingly evident as Seth becomes more physically like a fly. The transformations are grotesque in the extreme: first just bristles on the back, but then loss of fingernails and teeth, blotching of the skin, facial disfigurement, bodily deformation, nasty fluids, twitching of the head, limbs replaced by clawlike structures, and finally a complete metamorphosis into a giant human-fly hybrid, with the fly decidedly in the ascendant. The pathos and horror of this transformation are made vivid to the audience, the emerging creature a disgusting assemblage of sticky, suppurating, deformed tissue, at once soft and bony—biological matter at its most repulsive. In the end Seth is put out of his misery by his former girlfriend, by a gunshot that explodes his fly-like head. Our prior horror of the fly is magnified, refracted, as Seth's body takes on the texture and shape of a fly's body. Many animals could have played this role, but somehow the despised fly seems the most inspired choice: to become a creature we regard with such revulsion, such disdain, strikes us as the most terrible of tragedies, the most horrifying of outcomes. A bee would have been so much more bearable; a butterfly might even have been quite nice. But to turn into a *fly*—that is utter degradation, and cruel comeuppance for the scientist's hubris.

Two interpretations of this powerful story seem available. The superficial interpretation is that Seth begins as a fine healthy specimen of lovely humanity and then deteriorates into an alien creature existing at the opposite aesthetic pole. The tragedy then is that the beautiful and desirable, the noble and godlike, metamorphoses into the ugly, disgusting, and contemptible: the sublime mutates to the sordid—rather as the fairy-tale prince turns into the frog. The deep interpretation is that the visible transformation we witness is not really a crossing of ontological boundaries at all: the human being was *already* a loathsome monster, a revolting hybrid, *before* his DNA and that of the hapless fly were joined accidentally together. The tragedy then is not the end result but the starting point—the tragedy is the tragedy of *being human*. The transformation into a giant fly serves only to dramatize our given ontological predicament. In effect, we *are* what Seth becomes. I will explain and defend this interpretation in what follows.

But first let me bring in another famous monster—the one created by another brilliant but incautious young scientist, Victor Frankenstein. (Cronenberg makes the comparison himself, in the commentary to the DVD of *The Fly*—though he makes the common mistake of supposing that it is the monster that is called Frankenstein not his creator; importantly, the monster has no name.[3]) Once again, we have an ugly and disgusting creature created by human hubris, whose basic tragedy is to offend the human senses. Does this unfortunate creature stand apart from us, our polar opposite, as a wholly alien form; or is he really the human being writ large and loathsome? As I have argued elsewhere, the latter is the better interpretation: he is made from human materials; he suffers the same physical and social insecurities as humans, especially in their adolescent years; he is stung by the same loneliness and rejection that can afflict us; his idealism turns to bitterness as he ages.[4] Thus we identify with the monster, seeing our own reflection in his predicament. It is human perfection that is the myth, not the fact of human monstrosity (just look beneath the skin's surface, as Frankenstein's monster invites us to, with his scars and seams). And it is much the same story with other well-known monsters, such as vampires and werewolves. It is what they tell us about ourselves, physically and psychologically, that commands our attention. It is the gods who are truly alien, not the monsters. The sexual, in particular, is never far away from these canonical monsters—as with Brundlefly, whose sexual powers are radically enhanced by his incipient transformation. Our eating habits, too, in their violence and gore, their biochemical crudity, are put under the magnifying glass. The monster lurks *within*—not in a place far, far away.

Then there are those traduced human beings on whom an accusation of monstrosity is unfairly pinned. Not merely the deformed and diseased, who make ready targets, but also ethnic and social groups that offend the majority: these are regularly stigmatized by allegations of culpable disgustingness. At different times such treatment has been meted out to Jews, blacks, women, poor people, Gypsies, and homosexuals.[5] Such classification is politically motivated, of course, but it also seems to involve a kind of displacement of repressed knowledge: the majority's own self-disgust, which cannot be fully acknowledged, is projected onto others as if they were alien, not continuous with the majority. The human body as such, its evil secretions and excretions, its dark urges and dank recesses, its hairy animal-like surface, its hellish interior, its involuntary smells and sounds—all these are repellent to their possessors. Unable to accept the reality of our organic existence, we project it outward onto groups that are held to exhibit it to a strong (and pungent) degree. But the insistence on otherness that accompanies such projection is just a mask for self-insecurity—for recognition that we are *all* monstrous, loathsome, and disgusting. We aggressively displace our revoltingness onto others because we cannot bear to accept it in ourselves. The ideal of the perfect male, white, invulnerable body, so prized by the Nazis, but not only by them, is as much a myth as that of the inferior flabby and smelly alien other. In general, wherever you find the strident assertion of alien monstrosity, look to see the cringing normal human thinly disguised.

Now let's return to Brundlefly, twitching and expectorating in his lab. At first no sign of his new Dipteral DNA is present; indeed, the results of his recent teleportation seem all good, at least from Seth's point of view. He feels exhilarated, exuberant, and full of life; nothing can stop him now. His strength has been greatly increased: expert gymnastic moves come easy, he shatters the arm of an arm-wrestling bruiser, he punches through walls. Sexually he is confident and tireless. Even the bristles that appear on his back give him a strange thrill, physical evidence of his transformation—Superman with a hairy back. At this stage he is like a developing adolescent, fired up, more powerful, sprouting hair—not the naive childlike nerd he was at the start of the movie. He likes himself this way, and so does Veronica. Clearly, he represents us here, at least in our dreams. But as time passes, a metamorphosis sets in, and it is not a pleasant one. This is presented as inevitable, a simple working out of the logic of DNA; there is no way back, no cure. As Cronenberg himself has remarked, the story is a metaphor for aging and with it the diseases of aging: the discolored, lumpy skin; the loss of teeth and hair; the reduced mobility and use of crutches. Seth is aging rapidly before our eyes, as he hurtles toward flyhood. We all know what aging is like (eventually, anyway), and disease is a constant anxiety and curse. And these human transformations have their share of the disgusting, which only adds to their tragedy. We identify with Seth as he suffers these indignities and miseries and diminutions. All human life is metamorphosis, from fertilized egg to fetus, from baby to child, then the spurt of adolescence, adulthood, and then the long decline into old age, infirmity, and finally the rapidly decaying corpse. Being equipped with memory and self-consciousness, we are always aware of our own inevitable metamorphoses, of the body's temporal convulsions and rebirths. In the creature Brundlefly we see our own lives speeded up, caricatured, but not falsely represented. As Seth examines his face in the mirror, noting each new bulge and blotch, the dance of the grotesque trampling on his ever-changing face, we see ourselves and our appalled fascination with mirrors—the incredulity, the shock, the revulsion. *This* is what I have become—and the sure knowledge that things only get a lot worse down the road. The fly's DNA is doing it to Seth; our DNA is doing it to us (with a little help from outside).

And it is significant and resonant that it is a fly that spells Seth's deterioration, because of the proximity of flies to humans. They were always invasive, buzzing around us, landing on us, giving us a friendly nip, entranced by our bodily waste, present even in death; now a fly has penetrated human DNA, invaded the very soul of a human, inserted itself into our essential biological nature. They seemed to want to get inside us, by any available orifice, and now one of them really has. The fly has merged with the human and has come out on top. If a human nightmare is to be covered with flies and be unable to brush them off, then Seth has taken it one stage further: he is covered with fly on the *inside*. Seth has embraced his inner fly, willingly at first, unwillingly later. He is no longer the Lord of the Flies; the Fly is Lord of him. He has reached biological maturity, and that, it turns out, is to be a fly. Embryologists have taught us that the human fetus contains the traces of earlier life-forms that still haunt our human DNA: thus there is a stage at which gills appear in the neck area of the fetus, evidence of our piscine ancestry. In Seth's case, middle age reveals the genetic imprint of the fly, an ancient order. We are ape and fish and fly and wolf and bird and . . . We are, in short, evolved animals, creatures of the churning biological world, carrying traces of all that came before. We may not literally be flies, but we are of the same ilk.

Imagine a story in which a brilliant scientist fly suffers the same fate as human Brundle: he merges accidentally with a human who has sneaked into his telepod. At first there is no external change in the fly's appearance, just a feeling of melancholy, some poetry, much self-pity, maybe an enhanced fashion sense; but then the human DNA starts to assert itself, turning our handsome, sturdy, intelligent fly into a soft and fleshy humanoid *thing*. Imagine his horror, his disgust, and his despair! He loses his wings, his clinging ability, his mental toughness; his girlfriend can no longer stand the sight of him (but his sexual potency is shot anyway). He is not a happy fly, indeed hardly a fly at all. (It's all relative, like they say.) Well, real-life Brundle is just the converse of that: he has merged with the despised fly, symbol of all that's unholy. But he was never that holy to begin with. His eyes darted a bit too quickly, his mouth was on the fleshy side, his mop of hair seemed excessive; and this is before we get to his genitals, anus, and internal organs. Let's face it: he was a pretty nasty piece of work already (and Jeff Goldblum is quite a handsome guy, humanly speaking). Objectively, is he any more appealing than a fly? Intelligent flies wouldn't think so. In fact, he is at his most repellent when his human body is falling apart, not when his fly body finally emerges—that is more scary than disgusting. The loose fingernails, rotting teeth, detached ear, bulging eyes, drooling mouth, ripped-off jaw—these are all human anatomy. It is when his human body is cleft and punctured that our disgust is at its height—and that reflects its antecedent clandestine nature. He makes manifest what we intrinsically are. The fly in him reveals our inherent disgustingness; it doesn't constitute it.[6]

Mind and Body

Watching Seth's physical transformation also reminds us of a deep fact about our nature: that the connection between mind and body is tenuous, contingent. Even when he fully turns into a fly, and despite his psychological alterations, it is still Seth in there, not the soul of a fly (if there could be such a thing). This tells us something deeply disturbing: *that we could have had the body of a fly.* That is, our minds are only contingently connected to the specific body type we have: there could have been a species much like us mentally that had the body type characteristic of an insect like a fly (think here of Kafka's tale of the beetle man). Would we have loathed that body type as we now loathe that of a fly? That seems doubtful, since habituation is a powerful force. But the deeper point is that we are not all that thrilled with the bodies we actually (but contingently) have: they offend our aesthetic sense in all sorts of ways. Still, the contingency of the connection underlines the uneasy relation between the human as a psychological being and the human as a biological being. We are not simply identical to our bodies, mere biological stuff, but we transcend them (at any rate, that is our self-conception). That is our existential predicament and the source of much of our mortal unease (I will come back to this shortly).

If the deep interpretation of *The Fly* is right, then we might expect the film to show some awareness of it. I believe it does, in the way it sets up the viewer for the scenes of transformation. The plot is a basic love story, involving Seth, Veronica (a journalist), and Stathis (John Getz), her ex-boyfriend (and boss). The story revolves around this love triangle, with Stathis trying to wrest Veronica back from Seth. In a late scene Seth actually melts off Stathis's hand and foot with his super-corrosive saliva-stuff, causing great agony, and is about to do the same to his face before Veronica steps in. Here we see the human body at its most vulnerable and fleshy, easily turned to messy foam. I have already mentioned the scene in which Seth snaps a man's arm so that the bone protrudes through the skin. Also, scenes of avid eating, bloody steaks, human nakedness, animalistic sex, and so on frame the depiction of a man's body suffering a terrible transformation. How different, the film asks, is human eating and sex from the kind engaged in by animals, even flies? The sex scene between Seth and a bar slut he picks up works as a transition from the more civilized kind between Seth and Veronica—here he is on the borderline between human and insect. The movement from human to insect thus appears seamless, smooth, not a sudden jump into the wildly alien. It is more amplification than transmutation. Nature was already doing its grisly work even before Seth went completely rogue. He wasn't yet a full-fledged fly, but he was of a particular biological species, with all that that implies. In addition, there is a notably gross scene in which Veronica dreams of giving birth to Seth's child—the baby coming out as a giant writhing maggot, glistening white and bathed in blood. She screams, as who wouldn't? But the scene is uncomfortably reminiscent of actual childbirth, with its terror of deformity in the baby, its bodily fluids, its bloodiness, the squirming of the glistening newborn, the horror of the bodily interior becoming exterior. Giving birth to a giant maggot is a pretty nasty idea, but giving birth to a human is not exactly a bowl of cherries. And someone has to do it—give birth to maggots, I mean. One supposes that a mother fly loves her precious little maggots too. It's really all of a piece, the biological world—all muck and guts, as the saying goes.

I mentioned just now the contingent relation between mind and body. Seth's eventual fate is to be a brilliant scientist (and artist—he plays the piano) trapped inside the body of a giant fly. This seems incongruous, tragic, absurd, and even grimly comical. What is a fine mind like Seth's doing inside the body of a fly? That seems like some sort of massive miscalculation, a fracture at the heart of being—preposterous, paradoxical. We feel he is trapped in there, betrayed by his body, misrepresented by it—let down, shamed, embarrassed, angered. It seems like an ultimate existential cruelty to have such a soul stuck inside such a vehicle, unable to break free, its very survival dependent on this grotesque shell. (But would a fly scientist and artist feel the same about his fly body?) On reflection, though, isn't that our fate as things actually stand? Brundlefly is a metaphor for our existential predicament as incongruous dualities—transcendent egos trapped inside organic shells. He is a hybrid of man and fly, but aren't we all hybrids of soul and organism? And isn't the organism an ontological level down from the soul—a hunk of gunk encasing a fine and noble spirit? As has been remarked, we are the "god who shits": we are quasi-divine beings that happen to inhabit a lump of moist organic matter.[7] Seth just dramatizes our situation as biologically embodied beings: his incongruity is our incongruity, his dismay is ours—and his anger too. His fate also mirrors ours: no soul can survive the blowing apart of its head, human or fly. We are hostage to the organism that houses us.

Not only are we such hybrids, but we are also self-aware, so that we are conscious of our split being—we have to live with it, day in and day out. We are inescapably aware of our own absurdity. We are like beings made of two parts that have not properly merged—just like Seth. We lack unity, and we are conscious of this lack. In Seth, the pain of disunity becomes too much and only death offers release. When humans age and deteriorate, the disunity becomes ever more apparent, the body ever more traitorous; we become victims of our biological nature. Like Veronica, we want to scream. But only death offers any solution to the conundrum, when unity and disunity no longer matter. Thus the film epitomizes primal anxieties that reach into our basic nature. In this sci-fi horror flick our existential predicament is laid painfully bare.

There are other metaphorical expressions of our hybrid nature, in dream and myth. Typically these involve cross-species fusion: the centaur who is half horse and half man, the mermaid who is half fish and half woman. To be such a being would involve an awareness of a radically dual nature, one part deemed "higher" than the other. Here the duality is woodenly literal, with two species spliced physically together. Other types of merging have been envisaged, but the literal type of the mermaid and centaur provides the most vivid illustration of the theme. Spiderman is perhaps the closest thing to Brundlefly, though here the merging has no untoward side effects to speak of. Fusion of the two sexes is another rich theme of duality. Clearly, humans are onto their own hybrid nature, giving it poetic and mythical expression. (Living with it is another matter.) The point I want to highlight here is that our reaction to Brundlefly is not an affective anomaly, a piece of pure science fiction, but part of our nature as self-conscious biologically embodied beings. We feel the same way about ourselves; he just heightens the perception. Like many another horror film, *The Fly* speaks to our secret fears and anxieties about ourselves, enabling us to experience them in refracted form. Horror begins at home.

Love Story

One of the clever things about Cronenberg's version of the original fly story is linking it to a burgeoning love affair. Once Seth's DNA gets scrambled the affair is doomed, though initially it gets a positive jolt. We see Seth's deterioration through the eyes of Veronica: a man she once found attractive and seductive turns repellent and monstrous—and in pretty short order. The monster emerges gradually from within, literally coming to Seth's surface and bursting through. Here two themes are interwoven: one epistemological, the other existential. Epistemologically, we don't really know when we fall in love with someone exactly who he or she will turn out to be: a monster might lie beneath the surface. This ignorance often dooms the relationship. Existentially, the original love is doomed by the facts of human existence: first, the beloved is a kind of monster just by being a biological human; second, time will bring aging and disease, which only accentuate the monstrosity. Love must be blind, to shield us from harsh reality. Love may work heroically against disgust and its sidekicks, but it cannot wholly overcome them.[8] The seamier side of humanity must be kept decently cloaked if love is to thrive; but it will come seeping (if not roaring) through in the end, and then love has its work cut out. Veronica's love, originally classically romantic, turns into something closer to pity, as well as sheer revulsion; and it must be true that a similar transformation occurs in those who have to deal with aging and disease in those they once loved in the romantic sense. I don't mean to say that love cannot survive the ravages of time, or the realities of organism, but it is necessarily challenged by these things and cannot retain its original innocent form—and in that sense, it is doomed. If you married someone who turned out to be a fly (suppose he or she fooled you by use of good makeup), you would have a problem no matter how much you loved that individual. Well, everyone in effect turns out to be a fly, sooner or later, and the love must find a way to adapt. Maybe it can, but it must change in the process.

Self-love is not so different. Seth is initially a cocky, self-assured young man, despite his nerdiness—he is not short on self-esteem. In fact, he is a bit of a narcissist (he's tall, handsome, gifted, charismatic, proud of his muscles). But by the end of the film all that narcissism has turned to bitter self-loathing, and with good reason. Self-love has given way to self-hatred, self-disgust, shame. He is a complete wreck—a shuffling, lisping, vile heap of putrescent flesh: definitely not someone to take home to show your mother. Here again the metaphor leaps out: our self-love is doomed too. Maybe we can sustain it for a while, if we avert our eyes (and nose) enough, but age and disease will kick holes in it. Narcissism does not survive a handful of decades on this earth and a clean mirror (hence all the plastic surgery). Nor, in fact, is it particularly robust even during those periods in which the body is at its most appealing: even in the best of health the body is always leaking, spewing, bulging, heaving, squawking. Burps, farts, shit, piss, sweat, snot, blood, and earwax—all of that is always there, and much else besides. You can't deny it, you can't escape it, and you can't hide from it. It is difficult to be too much in love with yourself with all that to contend with. Narcissism, though potent, has its limits, its no-go areas. Seth's self-love is swiftly punctured, but that too is our common lot.

Risky Science

I do not mean to suggest that self-disgust and our mortal condition is the only theme of *The Fly*. One theme that stands out plainly is the responsibility of the scientist and the unforeseen consequences of technology. Brundle's work was going well until the mishap with the fly, though there was that nasty incident with the baboon—turned inside out into a twitching bloody mass and still alive. The scientist had invented teleportation! So thrilled with success was he that he failed to take proper precautions in the use of his telepods; he didn't scour them for alien organisms—and you should always scour your telepods for alien organisms before using them. That fly was a piece of bad luck, but the responsible scientist should be on the lookout for bad luck. Frankenstein had shown the perils of not thinking things through, and you would have thought that Brundle would have borne his cautionary tale in mind. And messing with people's DNA is always a risky business. Cronenberg says in his DVD commentary that he is by no means against scientific innovation, despite its attendant risks; he makes things go badly wrong for Brundle for dramatic effect, not in order to discourage innovative science. But it is clear that the kind of science Brundle is engaged in is totally unregulated, perilous, and subject to the law of unforeseen consequences. In a deleted scene, a monkey and a cat are accidentally fused by the apparatus, an appalling event that should have alerted Brundle to other potential fusion catastrophes.[9] Driven by curiosity and the thirst for fame, Brundle (maybe we should rename him Bungle) will not be deterred—and, like Frankenstein, bears the brunt of his own tunnel vision. Many real human inventions illustrate the same lesson. Who would have thought that the motorcar would so transform human life? Who could predict that human technology would cause the planet to heat up to dangerous levels? Where will genetic engineering take us? Will computers eventually replace us? What about nanotechnology? Nuclear weapons? All good questions, and ones that should be in the forefront of the scientist's mind—yet seldom are.

Film and Disgust

I want to make a final point about disgust and the cinematic image. The cinematic image transforms the body into a two-dimensional patch of light.[10] This image can be neither touched nor smelled. It thus tends to bleach the disgusting from its object: the affective and sensory impact of a cinematically pictured disgust object cannot equal the actual presence of such an object. Certainly, we do not fear contamination by such a pictured object, since we are well aware that it cannot come into contact with us. Accordingly, we never feel that Seth's suppurating body will intrude on our own body, leaving its revolting trace on us. Thus the cinematic image is itself an agent of transformation, away from the disgusting. This is why the human body appears so idealized on the big screen, its blemishes removed by the magic of movies. Correlatively, the spiritual or psychological side of the human being comes into the foreground in the film-watching experience: we feel the force of the character's inner life, as we perceive the transformed image of his or her body. I would say, then, that movies are intrinsically an antidisgust medium, in that they mitigate the impact of the disgusting stimulus. (Much the same might be said about the written word.) This is not to say that the emotion of disgust cannot be aroused by movies—it clearly can. But the effect is muted, transformed, refracted through the artistic medium of film.

In watching a movie like *The Fly,* then, we are made aware of two transformations proceeding simultaneously: the transformation in the subject matter of the film, in this case the man Seth Brundle, which is toward the disgusting; and the transformation effected by the medium of film itself, which is away from the disgusting. We are brought close to the disgusting, but we are also kept at a distance from it. Our perception of Seth's awful appearance is importantly not the same as Veronica's, and we are well aware of the difference. Our aesthetic experience is simultaneously mired in the disgusting and free of it. I conjecture that horror films in general achieve this ambiguous relation to the horrifying and disgusting: we wallow in it, but it never actually touches us. The experience is certainly nothing like actually experiencing the events and situations depicted. In *The Fly*, events of the utmost revoltingness occur, and the camera catches them in all their gory detail, but we never find ourselves wanting to flee the scene for fear of contamination. Our emotion is actually not that of disgust proper but only an artistically transformed simulacrum of it—quasi-disgust, as we might call it.[11] It is all an elaborate make-believe. Cronenberg makes us understand our disgustingness in *The Fly*, but he does not make us actually feel it—for that we must experience human bodies directly. Still, he does unlock a prevalent repression—causing us to acknowledge what we already know, if only implicitly. Maybe watching his film might even soften our habitual genocidal attitude toward actual flies, by prompting us to recognize the commonality between us.[12]

Notes

1. Aurel Kolnai discusses the difference between hate, fear, and disgust in his seminal monograph *On Disgust*, ed. Barry Smith and Carolyn Korsmeyer (Chicago: Open Court, 2004; orig. pub. 1929 in German). Some of my later treatment of disgust is influenced by Kolnai's discussion.

2. See William Ian Miller, *The Anatomy of Disgust* (Cambridge, Mass.: Harvard University Press, 1997), for a good general discussion of disgust, in which contamination is emphasized.

3. David Cronenberg, "Commentary," disc 1, *The Fly: Collector's Edition* (20th Century Fox, 2005), DVD.

4. I discuss the case of Frankenstein's monster in *Ethics, Evil and Fiction* (Oxford: Oxford University Press, 1997), chapter 7.

5. This is well treated in Martha Nussbaum, *Hiding from Humanity* (Princeton, N.J.: Princeton University Press, 2004), chapter 2.

6. I deal with the question of species self-disgust at much greater length in my book *The Meaning of Disgust* (New York: Oxford University Press, 2011), from which I draw in this essay.

7. The phrase occurs in Ernest Becker's classic *The Denial of Death* (New York: Free Press, 1973), chapter 2. My discussion of man's inherent duality has been influenced by this book.

8. See Miller, *The Anatomy of Disgust*, especially chapter 6, for a discussion of love and disgust.

9. "Deleted Scenes," disc 2, *The Fly: Collector's Edition* (20th Century Fox, 2005), DVD.

10. I investigate the transformative power of the cinematic image in *The Power of Movies* (New York: Pantheon Books, 2005), especially chapter 3.

11. Kendal Walton discusses the emotions aroused by fictional works in his important book *Mimesis as Make-Believe* (Cambridge, Mass.: Harvard University Press, 1990).

12. In general, *The Fly* shows some sensitivity toward animals, despite the mangling they endure; no sharp line between humans and nonhumans is drawn. Our ethical duty toward hybrids of humans and other species is worth pondering, and the question puts pressure on lazy forms of speciesism.

Tragedy and Terrible Beauty in *A History of Violence* and *Eastern Promises*

Cynthia Freeland

Many of David Cronenberg's films highlight, and even relish, images of violence done to the human body. Heads explode and parasites crawl around under people's skin. A man develops a vaginal opening in his abdomen, a sexy woman is equipped with a knifelike appendage under her arm, a pregnant woman births multiple freakish mutant babies. In Cronenberg's films, the body develops new orifices or abilities to engage in physical relations with the rest of the world, in ways that are often shocking and disgusting. In *Crash* (1996) the characters find sexual fascination with wounds and scars created by automobile parts during horrific accidents. *The Fly* (1986) and *Shivers* (1975) explore disgust to the maximum. Sometimes the changes to a person are mental transformations with real-world effects, as in *Scanners* (1981) and *The Dead Zone* (1983), or in the drugged-out scenes of *Naked Lunch* (1991). Sometimes the play with identity is more subtle. In *Spider* (2002) a man searches for a murderer who turns out to be himself. In *Dead Ringers* (1988) one actor portrays twin brothers who enact each other's lives. In *eXistenZ* (1999) there are multiple levels of animated game playing with identities uncoiling until the last moments of the film.

Tragedy or Mere Spectacle?

Few of these movies would be countenanced as tragedies, instead falling prey to Aristotle's criticism of works that pander to the audience's interest in mere spectacle. Still, some do employ two key aspects of a tragic plot, at least according to Aristotle's characterization: recognition and reversal. "Recognition" (or "discovery") is a translation of his term "anagnorisis," coming to know. "Reversal" is a direct and complete change in fortune. The combination of the two makes a tragic plot count as complex in a particular sense explicated in Aristotle's *Poetics*.[1] These two plot features do seem to apply well to some of Cronenberg's more recent films. They characterize *Spider*, for example, which has a plot much like that of Sophocles's *Oedipus Rex* (or *Oedipus Tyrannos*). Instead of unknowingly killing his father and seeking the murderer, it turns out that the protagonist (played by Ralph Fiennes) has killed his mother. In *The Fly* the hero (Jeff Goldblum) is a mad scientist who, experimenting too soon with his teleportation machine, finds he has incorporated a fly into his own DNA and is inevitably decaying into insect morality (only, of course, there isn't any such thing). Both Seth Brundle, the scientist of this movie, and his girlfriend (Geena Davis) must acknowledge that he is undergoing an extreme shift of identity that brings with it the tragic turn of fortune from happiness and optimism to misery and death. In fact, at the film's conclusion, the creature that Brundle has become begs for its own death at the hands of the sobbing woman.

The Tragic Hero's Reversal of Fortune

Aristotle tellingly noted that the recognition in a complex tragic plot is emotionally powerful and brings with it love or hate that is connected to the tragic hero's reversal of fortune. Cronenberg's films *A History of Violence* (2005) and *Eastern Promises* (2007) both feature a plot that involves crucial moments of recognition and reversal that engage the emotions of both viewers and the film's female protagonists. Besides having the same lead actor, Viggo Mortensen, these films share the structure of a revelation of identity that has deep emotional consequences for audience empathy and allegiance, and is cued by similar challenges to allegiance for the romantic partner in the film. For the earlier film, the plot threatens to force the hero, Tom Stall (Mortensen), to lose the love of his wife, Edie (Maria Bello), as she becomes aware of who he really is, the gangster Joey Cusack with a violent past. This threat seems abated, although it still lurks, at the film's conclusion. The direction of emotional engagement is the opposite in *Eastern Promises*. Here, the heroine, Anna Ivanovna (Naomi Watts), begins by hating and distrusting the seeming mobster Nikolai Luzhin (Mortensen) but becomes more and more puzzled by his behavior, beginning to trust him and ultimately seeking his help to rescue the endangered baby she has come to love. He does help her, but poignantly does not reveal his true identity to her. The audience's hopes for a romantic affiliation are raised, though, by the fact that we are shown who he is—an undercover police agent who has infiltrated the mob in order to bring its reign of terror to an end. Here the hoped-for familial alliance that would unite Anna, Nikolai, and the baby Christina is not achieved by the film's conclusion. This may, however, be the reason that Cronenberg has expressed an interest in making a sequel to *Eastern Promises*—the only film for which he has said he would like to add such an extension.[2] He comments that we are not quite finished with Nikolai's story. Whether such a sequel would actually provide an idealized happy ending or, more likely, some sort of tragic denouement, remains anyone's guess. The latter seems more likely since the Nikolai character may have become too emotionally damaged for love by his simulation of the mob members he is studying. His constant claims to Anna about being "only a driver" and his remarks to the other mob leaders about having "died" may wind up being the truth about Nikolai.

Sex, Violence, Death, and Empathy

Each of these two movies also includes extended scenes depicting morally questionable sex and extreme violence and death. I will examine some of those scenes here, in part to explore how issues of identity affect audience emotional responses of empathy. The key sex scenes I will discuss are the "rough sex on the stairs" scene between husband and wife from *A History of Violence* and the voyeuristic scene in which Kirill (Vincent Cassel) forces Nikolai to have sex with a prostitute in *Eastern Promises*. The violent scenes are the climactic fight between Joey Cusack and his brother Richie (William Hurt) and his henchmen in Philadelphia near the conclusion of the earlier film, and the extended scene in which a naked Nikolai in the steam bath is attacked by two Chechen thugs in the later film.

The relation between tragedy and horror has been explored by other authors, such as Noël Carroll in his 1990 book *The Philosophy of Horror*.[3] Carroll there developed a parallel to explain or justify an audience's interest in the violence and monsters of horror by arguing that the specific aesthetic effect aimed at in this genre is the elicitation of something he dubbed "art horror." This is a response combining appreciation of the intricacies of plot and plot resolution with the negative aspects of feeling disgusted or terrified in the face of monsters. Digging deeper, Angela Curran has argued that there can actually be a blend of the genres—that some films qualify as belonging to both horror and tragedy.[4] In Curran's account, certain works of art such as *An American Werewolf in London* (1981) or *The Sixth Sense* (1999) elicit the sorts of emotions Carroll described as well as the key Aristotelian emotional responses of tragedy: pity and fear. Thus it is likely that viewers respond with pity and fear to the fate of the protagonists of these two films, given that David Kessler (David Naughton) in *Werewolf* knows his fate and cannot escape it, hence seeks an escape in death, and that Dr. Malcolm Crowe (Bruce Willis) in *Sixth Sense* does not know but only gradually comes to recognize his true status as a dead person. Interestingly, in both of these films—as in the two Cronenberg movies I am discussing—the deepest responses of pity are prompted by the romantic loss that is portrayed, as the hero/werewolf must give up his beloved partner, the nurse, and Dr. Crowe in *Sixth Sense* must allow his wife to grieve without being able to comfort or contact her.

"Terrible Beauty"

Before going on, it will be useful to say more about the concept of "terrible beauty." This notion has been articulated as playing a role in aesthetics by contemporary philosopher Carolyn Korsmeyer.[5] As she explains it, terrible beauty is a positive aesthetic response in which we find beauty in something that is not superficially at all lovely or pretty. To the contrary, what we find beauty in may be shocking, devastating, and horrific. Beauty has to do with the moral insights gained by contemplating such horrific truth, as well as with the presentation of the insight within a medium that enables us to appreciate the insight rather than turn away from it, hiding our eyes. This medium might be poetry or beautiful language, and, I suggest, it also might be film. Korsmeyer mentions the example of certain visual artists such as Goya. She describes the nature of terrible beauty as follows: "One way to note the emergence of the beautiful out of the merely pretty is in terms of the intensification of the experience. Emotions can intensify experience without colliding with some notional 'opposite' which is the case with pleasure and pain." She explains further that the strong emotional response to something disturbing in art can itself be edifying and also aesthetic, even if not specifically "pleasurable." Not all aesthetic response, in other words, is distanced or "pure" in some positive way. As she puts it, "Emotions . . . are sometimes set aside as merely sentimental engagement. But some of them . . . pity, terror and dread . . . are recognized for their own aesthetic weight and the understanding they afford. Insight often demands that one face truths that one would rather were otherwise."[6]

Let me offer an example to help clarify Korsmeyer's concept. Near the beginning of *Eastern Promises* we witness the birth of an infant that coincides with the death of its young mother. This is the young woman who appears briefly in the opening scene of the film before collapsing in a pool of her own blood. She appears to be a heroin addict, thus heightening the contrast between her death and the birth and new life she has created. The scene showing the newborn infant is shot to highlight the little baby's exquisite delicacy—particularly the curve of its tiny ear—as it lies coated in blood. We might tell ourselves all babies are born amid gore, but this particular baby's blood is linked to that of her mother's death. And we soon learn that the death was not of her own doing—that is, it did not stem from her own choice to become a drug addict. Rather, this was something forced on her at a too-young age since she is a victim of trafficking; and furthermore, her pregnancy was a result of rape. This, I submit, is a scene of terrible beauty.

Violence and the Hero's Identity

Another issue dealt with in *A History of Violence* and *Eastern Promises* is how the male hero's identity is affected by violence. In *A History of Violence*, the issue is whether the protagonist can renounce violence and achieve a new identity. On the one hand, the film hints that he cannot, since his violent past comes back to revisit and haunt him and he must endorse his former tendencies in order to try to protect his new life and family. There are, however, indications that he has finally cleansed himself of violence and can become integrated back into his family with his true past now revealed to them. Thus in the film's final scene he is invited to rejoin the family at their classic Midwestern meal of meatloaf and mashed potatoes.

In *Eastern Promises*, the violence is not actually committed by the hero but suffered by him. He has been in prison for unstated crimes, and there he gained his identifying tattoos but lost his identity—"I died then," he says. He shows no emotional response to nasty aspersions against his own father and mother. Nikolai, in the physical embodiment of Viggo Mortensen, is subjected to forced sex (almost as much as the prostitute is) and also, of course, to the brutal attack against him in the bathhouse where his naked body is especially vulnerable to the sinister black-leather-clad, carpet-knife-wielding Chechen thugs.

"Natural" Violence

It is striking to a Cronenberg fan or admirer that these films are almost entirely naturalistic in their portrayals of violence. That is, the violence here involves everyday implements such as fists, guns, razors, and knives rather than the supernatural or magical realist violence of new bodily orifices or capacities (like the abdominal opening the hero of *Videodrome* [1983] develops or the armpit appendage the heroine of *Rabid* [1977] uses to kill men).

I say "almost" wholly naturalistic because there is perhaps one episode in *Eastern Promises* that is characteristically over the top in a Cronenbergian way (when the Chechens grab the young man in a cemetery and slice open his throat). Cronenberg has said at least of *A History of Violence* that he wanted the violence to be somewhat primitive, with an emphasis on direct bodily consequences that would force viewers to confront their own engagement with it and excitement over it. He says in the DVD commentary:

> I wanted the audience to see the results of the violence. The violence in this movie is very, very intimate. It's very physical. The kind of violence that we're most worried about is the violence done to the human body, and in this movie all the violence that's done happens to the human body. So in this movie are no car crashes, no explosions, it's all physical violence to the human body. And in each instance of violence in the movie I have a shot or two that emphasizes that, so that right in the middle of their exhilaration and their cheering of the violent act the audience finds itself looking at something particularly disturbing in terms of the effect of the violence, and that's really what I wanted. The audience is complicit in the violence and then they have to be complicit in the results of it as well. If you're gonna like the violence then you have to accept the consequences, and that of course has a lot to do with the theme of the movie here.[7]

And in fact, the director eventually cut from the film a more characteristic sort of scene in which the murdered man Carl Fogarty (Ed Harris) appears to rise from the dead, his chest still smoking from bullets that have pierced it, to shoot back at Tom in the diner—a dream sequence that was so exaggerated in style that the director apparently decided it did not fit with the ambience of the film as a whole. (It can be seen in the extra materials available on the DVD.[8])

Sexual Violence

The violent sex scenes in the two films are very different in tone and implication. First, in *A History of Violence,* the sex is consensual, despite elements of force. That is, Edie begins the interaction by slapping Tom hard. As audience members we sense that this is probably the first time she has ever done such a thing. They both look shocked at her behavior. We observe that her knowledge of her husband's violent past, added to his deep deception, has unleashed new emotions and behaviors in her. She had previously become extremely ill to the point of vomiting after questioning him on his true identity. Edie's behavior now is far from normal for her. Tom grabs back at her roughly and pushes her down onto the stairs. What looks like it may become a brutal fight is transformed into a scene of sexual exploration, with each one trying to reconnect. The two grapple somewhat desperately for each other (so much so that we are subsequently shown the bruises on her back from the hard floors). Cronenberg in his director's commentary says: "It's not a rape scene. People who are inattentive might think that. I wanted the music to address that. There's a moment where the music is telling you that this is a much more complex thing than a scene of rape or violence." The music functions by adding a layer of emotional closeness and romantic intensity rather than by pulsing beats that would accentuate violence. Sex with a stranger can be exciting and also frightening—indeed this is the theme of the couple's earlier sex scene in which Edie dresses up as a teenage cheerleader to seduce her husband, prompting Tom to ask jokingly, "What have you done with my wife?"

By comparison, the sex scene in *Eastern Promises* involving Nikolai and the Russian woman forced into being a sex slave is alienating and not arousing. Nikolai has obviously tried to put off his promise to Kirill to "choose a woman to fuck," and now he no longer can do so. He seems to select this particular woman in part because she is the oldest one there. The scene indicates how Nikolai's undercover work with the gangsters forces him into engaging in violent behavior. It is shot in a voyeuristic way that places the audience in the same position as the prurient Kirill. Since we have been given hints that Kirill is homosexual, there is an added element of male voyeurism that makes the scene very uncomfortable. Nikolai is "fucking" the woman from behind, a position that both emphasizes his distance from her and allows the camera operator to conceal some of the action that in fact everyone becomes curious to see. He finishes off in a way that conveys more of a mechanical and forced exercise rather than actual pleasure—again, a point highlighted by Kirill's slow, limp clapping, as though Kirill has seen through Nikolai's performance. Certainly the woman victimized here, who has been tricked into coming to England like the girl shown at the film's start, is being subjected to rape, but then so too is Nikolai, in the sense that his sexual performance is compelled against his will. He tries to make up for what he has done both by leaving the woman a thick wad of money and by, soon enough, managing to have her removed from the brothel and returned to her home in Russia (something Kirill is briefly suspicious about).

Realistic Gore

I turn now to the most extended and graphic violent scene in *A History of Violence:* Tom/Joey's trip to Philadelphia, the attempt to garrote him, and his killing of his brother Richie's guards along with Richie himself. Various aspects of this sequence are extremely brutal, with close attention to details of realistic gore. In his DVD commentary, Cronenberg says he wanted the movie to be personal and direct, realistic rather than artistically designed for expressive purposes. He says, "The violence in this movie, which is very intimate, very physical, was basically developed when I was looking at some DVDs that tell you how to kill people on the street. You can find them on the Net, there's quite a few. Because I wanted it to be very realistic in this movie, the violence, and not balletic, but like a street fight." Various aspects of the situation, dialogue, casting, and acting make the sequence oddly cartoon-like and humorous, such as Richie's berating of the already beat-up guards. This is also something the director intended. He comments, "I think all of my movies are funny. I don't think I've ever made a movie without humor. Except maybe *The Brood,* that may be the only one that's not funny."

The scene clearly elicits empathy with Joey, but does this empathy require identification with him? Berys Gaut has tried to redeem this often-maligned notion, arguing that identification in film is based on four aspects: perceptual, affective, motivational, and epistemic.[9] In the scene where Joey is first attacked at Richie's house, we do *not* identify with him because we as viewers have perceptual awareness of something he can't see, the bodyguard behind him preparing a garrote. Affective identification will arise because the film has built up enough solidarity with Joey for us to begin to share some of his feelings.

Narratively, throughout *A History of Violence* viewers are led to empathize with Tom/Joey.[10] He appears to be a good man: he runs a nice family diner and has an attractive, smart, loving wife and cute kids. He resorts to violence only to protect his employees from two evil men whom we have already watched kill a family and small child. Joey denies being the man that the disfigured gangster Fogarty is looking for. When Fogarty and his men threaten his family it is easy to take sides against these menacing outsiders in their enclosed black limousine. Even in deciding to kill his own brother, Joey seems justified, since it is in self-defense, and he is threatened by a gang that outnumbers him. Getting a viewer to identify with a character involves more than empathy: I could empathize with an attack victim without feeling just the same as he does—say, without wanting revenge. But Cronenberg encourages such an identification of motivation. He eggs the viewer on to want violence because the attackers are so evil and callous. This might be what makes some of the scenes here uncomfortable to watch.

Carl Plantinga has noted the role of close-ups of the human face in scenes of empathy. *A History of Violence* concludes with numerous such close-ups, including faces of those who fight and other people's reaction shots. After killing his brother, Joey falls to his knees and cleanses himself in the pond behind Richie's mansion. Because he removes his shirt, the scene highlights both his own wounded Christlike body (others have noted his initials are "J.C.") and the small crucifix dangling from his neck. The scene cuts directly to his return home, in which he enters the house after dark with visible trepidation about his welcome. If the family unit can be reunited, it will have to be on new terms that include a more complex recognition by Joey's wife and children of his actual identity.

Choreographed Violence

In comparison, the most extended scene of violence in *Eastern Promises* is much more choreographed. It required rehearsal and took two full days to shoot.[11] The most chilling aspect of the sequence is the fact that Nikolai is entirely nude throughout the entire scene. The bathhouse setting explains this, in terms of plot, but emotionally the scene highlights his vulnerability. The contrast between Nikolai's naked skin and the leather-clad powerful bodies of the men who attack him makes the threat against him very intense. Here again Cronenberg appears to have pursued the aim of showing violence that is personal, intimate, and physical—not distanced like the machine-gun sequences in Arthur Penn's *Bonnie and Clyde* (1967) or the conclusion of Sam Peckinpah's *The Wild Bunch* (1969). (Of course, it is also shown in real time and not slow motion.) Cronenberg explains, "I have a very existential approach to the human body. I take bodies seriously, [as if] I'm actually photographing the essence of this person."[12] The narrative also creates tension by revealing that Nikolai is being set up by the man who invited him there. The betrayal is complex and shows the audience that Nikolai is not as fully a part of the *Vory v Zakone* mob as previously appeared. The imminent danger is heightened by the fact that as the men approach him, Nikolai is relaxing, head down and unaware until polished shoes appear before him, shown in his point-of-view shot. As with the previous scene I discussed, the hero is outnumbered, which is likely to prompt the audience to root for him. The only other men present in the bathhouse run for cover rather than trying to help. At various points Nikolai is sliced with the razor-sharp carpet knives, socked in the gut, and kicked. These are strong, viscerally felt moves. Just when it appears he has finally defeated the second man, and he crawls to the first one to retrieve his weapon, that man awakens and tries to stab him (despite the knife sticking in his chest). Here the director plays with the element of surprise and uses the startle effect, in an apparent throwback to his horror background (à la Brian De Palma's *Carrie* [1976]). It is also significant that the scene immediately following this one shows Nikolai being taken on a gurney into a hospital, where an accidental encounter with Anna (who works there as a nurse) will carry the plot forward. Her recognition of Nikolai prompts her curiosity and empathy and paves the way for their future cooperation.

Violence and Identity Changes

The two sequences of violence I have just described play a specific role in their films. They both precede the protagonist's move away from violence and deceit and instead toward greater levels of honesty, revelation, and intimacy with the female lead. Joey may now, perhaps, finally rid himself of his violent past by closing off all links to it, particularly by killing his brother. His symbolic cleansing of himself in the pond behind the great home is crucial. After this, as I noted, he returns directly to his family.

Similarly, the attack on Nikolai, as I noted, propels his romantic reunion with Anna. She visits him in the hospital, again asking who he really is and why he has helped her family. It is important that only at this moment of the plot is information provided to viewers about Nikolai's identity as an undercover agent, a fact revealed when the Scotland Yard investigator visits him. Although Nikolai never reveals this information to Anna, she still seems to sense that he has deeper layers. At first she suspects him of helping Kirill abduct baby Christina from the hospital, but she immediately sees by his reaction that he has not been involved and trusts him to help rescue the baby. His crucial role in this leads to the one romantic moment in the film as they kiss, but then he bids her good-bye. Why has Nikolai changed?

Nikolai's infiltration of the gang appears to be succeeding when he is awarded the coveted star tattoos on his knees and upper chest. To pass the test of being worthy of such an honor he has to face scrutiny by a council of leaders who examine his past by reading his previous tattoos, and test his character and allegiance by insulting his father and mother. Nikolai responds not only that they meant nothing to him but adds, "I died when I was fifteen." This is an intriguing statement that seems to shed light on this man's somewhat elusive, empty character. Although, like Anna, we might sense that he is not who he first appears to be, it is hard to tell who he really is and what he wants. He keeps denying that he has any deeper identity by insisting, "I'm just a driver." When he tells Anna he has helped her because "to be the king you must kill the king," it is hard for her and us to know how truthful this statement is. Nikolai is a person who seems to have erased or denied his own identity. The tragedy here is that he may have been too successful at it. Thus in the film's concluding scene we watch him sitting alone in the Russian restaurant with an ambiguous expression. It seems that his remark to Anna earlier was on target when he said she belonged in the world of "nice people," not the world of the Russian mob, and she should go away and forget it all. This romantic pair, unlike Tom and Edie Stall, appears to have no prospects of achieving union, even if she does learn of his actual identity.

Conclusion

I have argued here that Cronenberg's films *A History of Violence* and *Eastern Promises* can both be regarded as tragedies. Each film narrates an arc of action within which we experience a sort of pity and fear—the classic tragic emotions—for the tragic hero. Each film also foregrounds some moments of violence, whether in a sexual context or in a male physical fight, with occasional flashes of what I have described, using Korsmeyer's term, as "terrible beauty." The two films raise difficult questions about the need for violence in a good person's life. Tom Stall has sought to escape his violent past but events, including direct threats to his family and his life, appear to force him back into its use in order to survive and protect his more innocent new way of life. Nikolai in *Eastern Promises* appears immured in violence, but he can still elicit our pity and sympathy because of his helpful behavior and his ultimately virtuous aim of eliminating the Russian mob's evil leader. These films work in much the way Aristotle argued that tragedy can, to educate our moral emotions and prompt activity of moral reflection. Cronenberg takes viewers through a complex process of being both attracted and repelled by the hero's violence in each film. If I am right that the female romantic lead in each film offers viewers a surrogate who can guide our ultimate assessment and response, then in both cases there is room for hope, though it is not simple. Like the hero of an Aristotelian tragedy, both Joey Cusack and Nikolai Luzhin have committed a fundamental hamartia, or error, through their acceptance of violence. Although we may sympathize, we might also not consider them eligible any longer for happiness. Or if they are, the path toward that end is far from straightforward. But no one can be sure that life will be simple with a happy ending.

Notes

1. See Aristotle, *Poetics*, trans. I. Bywater, in *Complete Works of Aristotle*, ed. Jonathan Barnes (Princeton, N.J.: Princeton University Press, 1984), 2324.

2. Eric Ditzian, "David Cronenberg Making Plans for 'Eastern Promises' Sequel," *MTV Movies Blog*, March 30, 2009, http://moviesblog.mtv.com/2009/03/30/exclusive-david-cronenberg-making-plans-for-%E2%80%98eastern-promises%E2%80%99-sequel/ (accessed November 9, 2010).

3. Noël Carroll, *The Philosophy of Horror, or Paradoxes of the Heart* (Cambridge, Mass.: Harvard University Press, 1990).

4. Angela Curran, "Aristotelian Reflections on Horror and Tragedy in *An American Werewolf in London* and *Sixth Sense*," in *Dark Thoughts: Philosophical Reflections on Cinematic Horror*, ed. Steven Jay Schneider and Daniel Shaw (Lanham, Md.: Scarecrow, 2003), 47–64.

5. Carolyn Korsmeyer, "Terrible Beauties," in *Contemporary Debates in Aesthetics and the Philosophy of Art*, ed. Matthew Kieran (Malden, Mass.: Blackwell, 2006), 51–63.

6. Korsmeyer, "Terrible Beauties," 60.

7. David Cronenberg, "Commentary," *A History of Violence* (New Line, 2006), DVD.

8. "Deleted Scenes," *A History of Violence* (New Line, 2006), DVD. See also Bart Beaty, *David Cronenberg's A History of Violence* (Toronto: University of Toronto Press, 2008).

9. Berys Gaut, "Identification and Emotion in Narrative Film," in *Passionate Views: Film, Cognition, and Emotion*, ed. Carl Plantinga and Greg M. Smith (Baltimore, Md.: Johns Hopkins University Press, 1999), 200–216.

10. My account draws on Gaut's discussion of identification, as well as Carl Plantinga's "The Scene of Empathy and the Human Face on Film," in *Passionate Views*, ed. Plantinga and Smith, 239–55.

11. Gina Piccalo, "'Their History of Violence," *Los Angeles Times*, September 11, 2007, http://articles.latimes.com/2007/sep/11/entertainment/et-eastern11 (accessed November 9, 2010).

12. Quoted in Piccalo, "Their History of Violence."

Cronenberg as Scientist

Antiessentialism, Sex as Remixing, and the View from Nowhere

Peter Ludlow

Much of the writing on Cronenberg's work has focused on his literary influences and the literary quality of his screenplays.[1] And to be sure, Cronenberg has spoken of being deeply influenced by writers J. G. Ballard, William S. Burroughs, and Henry Miller, among others.[2] There is less attention paid to the fact that Cronenberg began his undergraduate career in the sciences (with a special interest in biochemistry) at the University of Toronto. Of this, Cronenberg once said:

> If I had stayed the course, I would have been in biochemistry. I was never interested in hardware sciences. Chemistry was more interesting because it related to the body; not just the human body, but the planet's body. I loved botany. I loved the interchange of fluids and plants; the chemistry of plants. All that stuff. So it was biochemistry in a broader sense; because there's biochemistry in the brain, getting at the physical basis of thought and imagination. I think it is natural that I should try to draw those parts of myself [literary and scientific] together and integrate them, finally, in film-making.[3]

Cronenberg found that path of study stifling and left it early in his undergraduate career, but I will make the case that his background in the sciences has deeply influenced his work and that it provides the X factor that powers the more unsettling and provocative aspects of his work. Crucially, my point will be that it is not the scientific facts and technologies larded throughout his work that power it, so much as three important attitudes at the foundation of modern science.

The first attitude is the suspicion (if not outright rejection) of essential properties in natural systems. Essential properties are those properties that the system has by virtue of metaphysical necessity. Sometimes philosophers explain this by saying that the system has the properties in every metaphysically possible world. Consider biological kinds, for example. From Aristotle until Charles Darwin science offered taxonomies of organisms and systems that pegged them as essentially different from each other—for example, that there are properties like rationality that distinguish humans from all other creatures. But work in biology from Darwin onward has shown these taxonomies to be less than rigid (different species have common ancestors, after all), and in important cases the taxonomies have collapsed altogether. How could they not collapse given the basic tenets of evolution introduced by Darwin in *The Origin of Species,* including the idea of common ancestry, and the idea that genetic variation takes place via mutation and recombination?[4] I'll make the case that this assault on neat biological taxonomies is expressed in many of Cronenberg's films, including *The Fly* (1986), *Scanners* (1981), and *Shivers* (1975).

Similarly, we traditionally suppose that there are important differences between organic and inorganic systems (biological systems and machines), but fusions of such systems are clearly possible. For example, work on Artificial Life (or "A-life") has shown that mechanical and computational systems can reproduce and evolve in a way that is mathematically parallel to the way biological organisms do.[5] Meanwhile, technologies for the enhancement of the human body have collapsed the neat distinction between organic and inorganic systems—a theme common in Cronenberg's work (*The Fly, eXistenZ* [1999], *Videodrome* [1983])—and work on virtual reality and virtual worlds has put the distinction between virtual life and real life under pressure (a theme that dominates *eXistenZ,* for example).

The second attitude is the notion that sex is not the expression of love one finds in Shakespearean sonnets, but is in fact a process that is ubiquitous in the organic world and not so very different from information processing. Although much has been written about the sexual content of Cronenberg's work, and critiques of it come in every flavor (from feminist to Freudian to Marxist/queer theorist to traditional moralist[6]), I'll make the case that these efforts badly miss the target. The key perspective of Cronenberg on sex (and a plausible perspective in biology) is simply this: Sex is a process by which information is not directly copied but is recombined and synthesized from multiple sources, and the process exploits whatever coupling mechanism is effective in accomplishing this information exchange and synthesis. It is a process analogous to remixing in music.

The third scientific attitude is the idea that we might call the nonperspectival nature of scientific explanation and understanding. For example, science does not consider Earth's position in the universe to be special. The position of the sun is no more special—the heliocentric picture of the universe was rejected long ago. Similarly, relativistic physics gives us no reason to suppose that our temporal perspective is special. What counts as happening "now" is relative to an inertial frame, and there is nothing special about our inertial frame. In the same way, when we move from a cosmological perspective to a biological perspective we understand that we are not more successful or better adapted than other primates or even cockroaches.

From the scientific perspective there is nothing special about us at all. We, like the other organisms and systems, are merely here because we are, for the moment, well adapted to our environments. Some of the creatures and diseases coevolved with us. And although mutants are almost always "bad guys" in the horror and science fiction genres, from a scientific point of view we humans are simply the product of generation after generation of mutations. When you are the descendant of an endless parade of mutants, it hardly seems fair to dismiss the new mutants.

Cronenberg's work, of course, does not follow the common formulae of the horror and science fiction genres. Are the mutants in *Scanners* the good guys or the bad guys? By the end it is not clear. Is the parasite in *Shivers* a body-snatching foreign creature or is it a symbiont that pairs up with our bodies to form a third creature? Again, at the end of the movie it is far from clear.

Some commentators have suggested that Cronenberg tells his stories from the perspective of the disease, but this isn't quite right. He is telling the story from the perspective of the scientist. The story is "the view from nowhere"—that is, he is describing natural processes from a third-person position that is not from our temporal, spatial, and personal perspective—and this, ultimately, is why Cronenberg's work is so frightening and unsettling.

Standard horror and science fiction almost always indulges the fiction that human beings are special. Even if the other creatures get the best of the human beings and slaughter them, we at least have the consolation that we are different from them and indeed are special. What is truly horrifying, however, is not the rise of the mutants and diseases and rogue machines, no matter how hideous they may be, or how much slime they secrete, or how violent their interactions with us. What is truly horrifying is the realization that we are not in a special place in the universe and that we are of a kind with the mutants and machines that frighten us so. And this is more frightening than anything from the pages of *Fangoria* will ever be.

My claim is provocative, of course, and calls for a detailed defense. Accordingly, I will go into detail on Cronenberg's "horrifying ideas," making the case that his cinematic oeuvre is fraught with these three ideas and that the three ideas are scientifically sound, and explaining why we find the ideas so horrifying.

The Rejection of Essentialism

Before Darwin, the biological taxonomies were taken to be immutable—they were with us from the creation, and the elements of the taxonomies were not just different, but *essentially* different from each other. That is to say, these differences were not just contingent but would continue to hold in every possible world. In other words, no matter how much we might permute the state of the world, we would not get a world in which biological taxonomies are violated. If a bear is really different from a panda (or a human is different from a fly) then they are different in every possible world. There are bearlike properties that only bears have and panda-like properties that only pandas have. On the traditional view they are thus necessary differences and not merely contingent differences.

While many writing in the humanities are on board with some of the concepts of evolution, they have a hard time letting go of the essentialism. Don't humans have properties that make us essentially different from other creatures? Rationality? Love? Something?

Essentialism has been under pressure not only in biology but in philosophy as well. Some philosophers, such as W. V. O. Quine, find the whole distinction between essential and contingent properties baffling:

> Perhaps I can evoke the appropriate sense of bewilderment as follows. Mathematicians may conceivably be said to be necessarily rational and not necessarily two-legged; and cyclists necessarily two-legged and not necessarily rational. But what of an individual who counts among his eccentricities both mathematics and cycling? Is this concrete individual necessarily rational and contingently two-legged or vice versa? Just insofar as we are talking referentially of the object, with no special bias towards a background grouping of mathematicians as against cyclists or vice versa, there is no semblance of sense in rating some of his attributes as necessary and others as contingent. Some of his attributes count as important and others as unimportant, yes, some as enduring and others as fleeting; but none as necessary or contingent.[7]

Quine famously went on to propose a "regimented" language for scientific inquiry—one in which it would simply be impossible to make essentialist claims (the language would be "extensionalist" in Quine's terminology). Quine thought that talk of essences simply got in the way of good science; it kept us locked in dogmas and tone deaf to new empirical discoveries. This is a point that is also emphasized in biology by David L. Hull, who argued that essentialism in biology led to two thousand years of stasis in the field.[8]

While contemporary philosopher Saul Kripke has subsequently defended a version of essentialism, his defense cuts the link between something having a property essentially (e.g., a mineral sample being nephrite) and our knowing that it does.[9] That is to say, on Kripke's defense of essentialism, essences are discovered not by philosophical reflection from the armchair, but rather by empirical investigation. This means that you can believe that things have essential properties without being a Scholastic philosopher. It also means you had best not be dogmatic about the essential properties you propose because you can be refuted by the right empirical data.

Now, you might think that Kripke has given us enough to get the ball rolling for a defense of essential properties among species, but this is actually not the case. In the first place, some recent work in philosophy and biology has shown that species should not be thought of as natural kinds;[10] other work has pointed out that there is no consistent notion of species,[11] and still others have rejected the idea that there are species altogether.[12] For the record, Darwin himself seemed to have doubts about the very idea of species as evinced by these remarks in a letter to botanist Joseph Dalton Hooker: "It is really laughable to see what different ideas are prominent in various naturalists' minds, when they speak of 'species'; in some, resemblance is everything and descent of little weight—in some, resemblance seems to go for nothing, and Creation the reigning idea—in some, sterility an unfailing test, with others it is not worth a farthing. It all comes, I believe, from trying to define the indefinable."[13]

We used to think that the notion of species was stable, at least. For example, one view of species is that two creatures are of the same species if they have fertile offspring when they mate, but an alternative dominant view in biology is that species are to be individuated by a common lineage. This leaves open plenty of possibility for species fusion. Indeed, strictly speaking, it allows that different species could be morphologically and genetically identical (for example, they could, by a combination of chance and environmental pressure, converge on the same genetic makeup and still be distinct species).

One alternative view of species, for example, American philosopher Richard Boyd's theory of species as "homeostatic property clusters," doesn't lean on common lineage, but rather defines species in terms of whether they share functional properties—that is, that they look and function alike (even if coming from distinct lineages).[14] But notice that even on this view there still are no essential biological properties that are required to belong to a species. The right combination of contingent properties is all that is needed.

Of course, the real issue is not whether there are species or how they are individuated, but whether there are properties that are essential to a fly and properties that are essential to a person, and whether those properties are fundamentally distinct. That is certainly the Aristotelian view, but it is not the view of contemporary biology. We share plenty of genetic material with flies and other animals. Indeed, in some cases we share genetic material with other species that we do not share with some of our conspecifics. Popular science writer Matt Ridley illustrates the point as follows: "Some of these polymorphisms are astonishingly ancient. They have persisted for aeons. For example, there are genes that have several versions in mankind, and the equivalent genes in cows also have several versions, but what is bizarre is that the cows have the very same version of the genes as mankind. This means that you, reader, might have a gene that is more like the gene of a certain cow than it is like the equivalent gene in your spouse."[15]

What does all this have to do with Cronenberg? The genius of Cronenberg is in his ability to illustrate the porous and contingent nature of our traditional taxonomies in biology and elsewhere. You might think that a human and a fly are fundamentally different in kind, but *The Fly* suggests the possibility of a genetic fusion. From a biological point of view there is already a kind of common genetic link between us and a fly. For that matter, you might not even need to rely exclusively on swapping genetic material to become more fly-like—it might be enough to activate certain genes that you already share with flies. Crucially, radical gene swapping (and gene activation), while apt to lead to unfortunate consequences for the subject, is possible and does not require that essential properties of the subject organism be breached. Indeed, we don't actually have evidence that there *are* essential properties.

The result of the teleporter accident in *The Fly* is something for the pages of *Fangoria,* but is the gore the source of the horror? Is it really just that someone messed with Mother Nature and the result was a monster? I don't think so. In the first place, the monstrous character of the resulting creature is not obviously contributed by the fly, but by the human side, flush with delight in its new powers. The really unnerving thing is that there is nothing essentially different about us and the fly—the way in which the scientist Seth Brundle (Jeff Goldblum) easily adapts to his new form suggests that there is something not entirely foreign about it. That we are not so very far apart from common houseflies.

Darwin broke down the essentialism in biology, but we can extend the point to the very distinction between biological and mechanical systems. The basic principle underlying evolution, after all, is algorithmic (that is, it is a kind of very dumb mechanical process—much like following a recipe to the letter) and not tied to biological tissue.[16] Recent work in A-life suggests that lifelike processes can be realized not just in carbon-based systems but in software and in hardware. Accordingly, fusions of organic systems with mechanical systems may well result in a very messed-up creature (consider Seth Brundle after his final teleportation), but not one that is ruled out by the biological and physical world having different essences.

The barrier between the biological and the physical is collapsed elsewhere in Cronenberg's work. Consider, for example, the insertion of the videocassette into the cavity in Max Renn's (James Woods) stomach in *Videodrome*. Or consider the fusion of Renn's hand and gun. We understand, of course, that the human body can be equipped with prosthetics, but these images from Cronenberg suggest something else—a collapse of the very distinction between flesh and machine. Although it is never clear whether it is happening in reality (or whether there is a fixed reality at all), in *eXistenZ* the game pods are gaming platforms in which the electronics are replaced with parts harvested from biological organisms. Implausible? Not at all, since of course biological systems can be used to carry out computations, and work progresses on this front in laboratories today.[17]

Cronenberg's goal is not simply to introduce us to the possibility of organic computing, nor is it to offer some sort of judgment of the evil that could ensue from the development of such technologies. Rather it is to get us to focus on just how unsettling this is. Of course, the special effects are unsettling in themselves (the guts of the game pods and the opening in Max Renn's stomach are certainly grotesque), but the really frightening thing is that yet another safe distinction has collapsed on us. The organic and inorganic worlds are of a piece, and the future of our descendants does not really lie exclusively in either of them.

The theme is extended even further in *eXistenZ*, since the really interesting idea is not the collapse of the physical and the biological, but rather the collapse of the virtual and the real. And of course, the distinction between real and virtual has been under pressure for some time. Many of the goods that we buy and sell today are virtual—Bill Gates's fortune comes from the sale of a virtual product, after all (we aren't paying for the disks or boxes they come in). In virtual worlds such as *World of Warcraft* and *Second Life,* robust economies have emerged that eclipse those of many real-world governments.[18] People's online lives come to be at least as important as their physically mediated lives, leading to virtual partnerships and suicides when the virtual partnerships fail.[19] Could virtual reality become so robust that we fail to see the distinction between the real and the virtual? The question is wrongly put. The real question is whether there is a distinction there at all. Is there any reason to think that a piece of software is less real than a car fender? Is there any reason to think that the currency in an online world is less real than that of a terrestrial government? Not really.

This is not merely a theme of *eXistenZ,* but of *Videodrome* as well. Cronenberg scholar Serge Grünberg suggests that the tumors afflicting Renn and Dr. O'Blivion (Jack Creley) are caused by radiation, but this isn't correct; they are "caused" by being exposed to a certain signal—in effect, by being exposed to information.[20]

Is it implausible to think that environmental information flow can have an impact on our physical bodies? Can it lead to the formation of a tumor—or as Dr. O'Blivion puts it, a new organ? Well, not exactly, but the story line is not far from a thesis about the language faculty articulated by linguist and cognitive scientist Noam Chomsky.[21] In Chomsky's view we are endowed with an innate language acquisition device (a "mental organ" in Chomsky's terminology). The interesting thing is that if the language faculty is not exposed to environmental linguistic data during a critical period of a child's development, it effectively goes fallow, or, if you prefer, does not develop into a functioning language organ. In this case, the information (linguistic data in the environment) does not strictly speaking cause the language faculty to exist, but it certainly activates it and contributes to its development into something that can serve as a language acquisition device.

Elsewhere Chomsky has suggested that the language faculty may have been a mutation that lay fallow for tens of thousands of years before it was activated and pressed into use. Certainly, a similar story could be told about Dr. O'Blivion's and Renn's new organs. But are they helpful new organs, or malfunctions and tumors? I will return to this question later, but from the perspective of science there need not be a real distinction. The only test of goodness of the mutation is whether it survives. (Parenthetically, it is interesting to note that the opening in Max Renn's stomach is not just an opening for the introduction of a physical object—it is also a port for information transfer. The videotapes reprogram Renn. It is a docking port.)

Now, again, the visual imagery provided by Cronenberg makes all of this disturbing, but the really disturbing aspect is not what the special effects provide but rather the underlying philosophical/scientific premise—that the organic, the physical, and the virtual collapse. Our bodies are not insulated from the physical world and the information flow that they are exposed to, but rather they are plastic and change and morph in response to the flow of information in our environment—so much so that it may well be information flow all the way down (a possibility suggested at the very end of *eXistenZ*—"Are we still in the game?"). This is at least as frightening as the philosopher's scenario of us as brains in vats. Even the scenario described in *The Matrix* (1999) didn't go this far, since the material constitution of our bodies remained more or less constant in the face of information flow (modulo possible damage and death if things go too badly in the matrix).

Cronenberg's war against essentialism is not limited to grand distinctions between species, between the biological and the physical, or between the real and the virtual. He has also extended it to neat distinctions that we like to make in our folk psychology—for example, between the sane and insane, and between good guy and criminal. There is a point in *Spider* (2002) in which young Dennis Cleg (Bradley Hall) seems normal enough, and we can understand how his mental illness could be caused by the apparent horrific betrayal by his father. That far into the movie we feel safe, because it would take a horrific event to turn a seemingly normal boy into a broken schizophrenic. But by the end of the movie we come to understand that there was no betrayal—it was a simple case of an Oedipus complex triggering his mental collapse. But this is the horrifying and unsettling part—we suppose that monsters come about from monstrous events, but we learn that needn't be so, that the line between us and Cleg is very thin indeed. The story line in *Dead Ringers* (1988) is similar; something as simple as an emotional separation sets into motion a chain of events that lead the Mantle doctors (Jeremy Irons) from being respected medical professionals to madmen.

And indeed, what is the difference between us and a madman? Psychopaths in the cinema (whether Norman Bates or Jason or Hannibal Lecter) are usually the product of extreme circumstances. Cronenberg shows us that this needn't be the case—that the essentialism we posit in our distinction between the sane and the mad is dishonest. If we are sane, it is a contingent fact that we are so. We are not safely sane.

What applies to madness applies also to the distinction between good and evil. *A History of Violence* (2005) shows how the line between a non-violent upstanding citizen and a killing machine is also thin. This is true not just for Tom Stall (Viggo Mortensen), who is successfully hiding his violent past, but also for his son, who morphs from a self-effacing pacifist to someone capable of harm and killing just by having violence come into his orbit. The fact that Tom Stall can successfully hide his violent nature merely highlights the deep, unsettling truth: there is no essentialism in human personality; the violent and the pacifist are not so very far apart, and whether we are one or the other is fundamentally a contingent fact. Similarly, in *Eastern Promises* (2007), Nikolai Luzhin (Viggo Mortensen), the driver/FSB agent (and British government informant) who ends up as the head of a criminal organization, sits on the blurred line between good and evil. We could argue about whether Luzhin is good or evil, but in Cronenberg's world he is really neither.

Summing up this section, it is my view that the most horrific aspects of Cronenberg's work—and it is a theme throughout his work—is not that uncontrolled science leads to monsters. It is rather that the lines between monster and human, human and nonhuman, biological and mechanical, real and virtual, sane and mad, good and evil all collapse. And this is not merely unsettling, but deeply frightening. We want to cling to our essentialism, but Cronenberg simply will not let us.

Sex as Remixing

Sex is a theme throughout Cronenberg's work, and it has led to all manner of postmodern and traditional critique, censorship, and disgust.[22] The sex isn't limited to obvious cases of human intercourse, but nearly anything can and will be sexualized by Cronenberg. There are the game pods (and bioports) of *eXistenZ*, the phallic hand/gun and vaginal VCR slot in Renn's stomach in *Videodrome*, the half slug/half penis-shaped parasites of *Shivers*, the phallic underarm growth in *Rabid* (1977), and the list could go on.

Usually we think of sex as being an activity that animals engage in to procreate, but of course at a conceptual level it is something rather different. Sex isn't needed for procreation. Many species in the world are asexual (dandelions, for example). Ridley synthesizes a great deal of work in contemporary biology and makes the case that sex evolved in nature as a solution to the problem of parasites (broadly understood to include viruses and bacteria).[23] How does sex help? Sex is a process by which genetic material can be recombined in each generation. Parasites can mutate rapidly, but sexual organisms in nature can change rapidly as well. Each coupling yields a new combination of genetic material (making for radically different genetic makeups across the population), leaving the parasites racing to catch up. In effect, in each generation we remix to keep the parasites locked out.[24]

Indeed, Richard Dawkins has observed, "Eavesdrop [over] morning coffee at any major center of evolutionary theory today, and you will find 'parasite' to be one of the commonest words in the language. Parasites are touted as the prime movers in the evolution of sex, promising a final solution to that problem of problems."[25]

Dr. Hobbes (Fred Doederlin) in *Shivers* proclaims that "sex is the invention of a clever venereal disease." From the perspective of modern biology, Dr. Hobbes is wrong, but he is actually close to the mark. It would be more accurate to say that sex is nature's solution to the presence of parasites. (Of course, it is worth noting that many parasites reproduce sexually as well.)

This kind of strategy is not just a biological strategy, it is a more general strategy for any system subject to evolutionary dynamics. For example, ecologist Thomas S. Ray constructed a computer program in which he planted sexual and asexual "organisms" and then sprinkled "parasites" within the population.[26] What he discovered is that the sexual organisms were more successful. You can think of this as modeling biological processes, but you can also think of the evolutionary dynamics in play as being the more basic fact. If you were interested in computer programs that fought viruses, you might make them "sexual"—in that each generation recombined with other programs, yielding offspring that shared bits of code of the parents. Cloning the same programs over and over leads to vulnerability because it allows the virus makers to catch up.

But sex isn't just about combining male and female organisms to yield an offspring. There are many ways to be sexual, both in the abstract and in biological systems. All that is really required is that reproduction involves mixing genetic material (or information) from systems carrying different information structures. There are lots of ways to accomplish this. Some fungi, like toadstools, have a good ten thousand sexes. That is great news if you are a toadstool interested in reproduction, because your potential reproductive partners are not just half the population, but 99.99 percent of the population. Other organisms are hermaphrodites (allowing them to have sex with anyone but themselves).

Now, let's take this basic picture about the nature of sex and combine it with the lessons from the previous section. If sex is about combining with systems that have different genetic (information-theoretic) makeups, and if we reject essentialism about species and other natural systems, then it is possible to have a form of sex between all kinds of systems. We don't even need to think in terms of genes in the traditional sense. Genes, after all, simply use four basic proteins to code information. Sex provides a way of encrypting our biological information to lock out the parasites. The key word here is "information," since that is what is really being transmitted between generations and that is what sex is designed to protect, in effect by re-encrypting the information in each generation.

Elsewhere I've argued that language works this way.[27] The traditional view about the nature of language is that one learns a language like English or French and uses that to communicate. But I think that a more accurate alternative picture is that when two or more people get together to have a conversation they "build" a little microlanguage on the fly, using bits and pieces of the linguistic backgrounds they bring with them. We don't "learn" languages; we "build" them, and we do it in a way that rewires our new shared language so as to avoid group-think, and to some extent to thwart those who attempt to co-opt our language, and perhaps most importantly to lock out eavesdroppers and outsiders (think of the rapidly shifting nature of street language). Linguist Mark C. Baker is illuminating on this point:

> The way human languages differ can be compared to cryptographic techniques of the 16th century. Sixteenth century cryptographers used a variety of techniques: they both replaced and rearranged symbols in systematic ways, and they performed these transformations both at the level of letters and at the level of words and phrases. This layered complexity evolved over time with the explicit purpose of defeating particular code-breaking strategies (such as frequency analysis). Natural languages also differ from one another in ways that show layered complexity, using substitutions and arrangement at multiple levels. Many of the specific tricks of the early cryptographers have striking analogies in natural language. This gives credence to the notion that natural languages have the same concealing function as man-made ciphers.[28]

All of our cultural products work in this way. Music is successful when it remixes traditions, as in Danger Mouse's *Grey Album,* which mixed the Beatles' "White Album" with Jay-Z's *Black Album.*[29] Remixing allows us to preserve our cultural products but in a way that freezes out the cultural "parasites"—those who would co-opt artistic products.

Again, what does all this have to do with Cronenberg? Very simply, Cronenberg is absolutely correct to sexualize many of the forms of information transfer in his movies because it just is a form of sex in the sense I've been articulating. Implanting a VCR cassette in Max Renn is a form of sex because it takes information from the tape and uses it to rewire (reprogram) Renn. Similarly, the sexual nature of the game pods in *eXistenZ* is not about the bioports but really inheres in the fact that the game pod and the player share bits of information with each other and effectively reprogram each other into something altogether new (the player and the pod form a new entity that is a synthesis of the two).

Even in a movie like *Crash* (1996), the sexuality is much deeper than we might suppose. The car crashes are simply the point of contact at which the human body and the machine engage each other and transfer information. When James Ballard (James Spader) asks Vaughan (Elias Koteas) what his project is, the answer is telling: "It's something we're all intimately involved in: the reshaping of the human body by modern technology."

This too should be unsettling. It is not just that there is sex or that at times it can be grotesque. The really unsettling feature of sex in Cronenberg's films is that he shows that it is ubiquitous and that it is a process by which we become something else. Humans are not fixed creatures. We have no essence. Sex is a system by which we recombine into something new. The recombination need not even be limited to biological change. A form of sexual intercourse takes place between us and our technologies, and us and our information processing systems—even our games. The technologies do not enhance us. We combine with them to form something new.

The View from Nowhere

The most stunning thing about Cronenberg's movies is that they don't follow the usual formula of horror and science fiction. In the fictional world of *Star Trek,* for example, it is our essential humanity that makes us special and that allows us to triumph. We will not be borged. Even in science fiction scenarios where we do not triumph, we are still distinct. We lose to the mutants, and some evil scientist is doubtless to blame. There is always a judgment that the human position is superior, even if at risk. The only thing up for grabs is whether humanity will triumph.

In Cronenberg's view, we are being borged all the time, and Cronenberg, at least as a director, does not judge. When the population of the high-rise apartment in *Shivers* is infected by the parasite, Cronenberg does not let on whether this is good or bad. It just is what it is. When the "mutants" in *Scanners* triumph, there is no judgment. Again, it just is what it is.

Missing from Cronenberg's work, then, is the familiar trope of the evil scientist deserving of our scorn. Commentators like William Beard often read a critique of science into his work, but so far as I can tell, that is more from habit than something actually in the films.[30] There is an interesting passage in Cronenberg's interview with Chris Rodley in which this comes up:

> I feel a lot of empathy for doctors and scientists. I often feel they are my persona in my films. Although they may be tragic and demented, I don't subscribe to the view that they are playing with things that shouldn't be played with. You have to believe in God before you can say there are things that man was not meant to know. I don't think there's anything man wasn't meant to know. There are just some stupid things that people shouldn't do. In another way, everybody's a mad scientist, and life is their lab. We're all trying to experiment to find a way to lie, to solve problems, to fend off madness and chaos.[31]

This is the part of Cronenberg that commentators have the most difficult time trying to wrap their minds around. Grünberg, for example, seems to miss the point at every step. First, he supposes that the "heroes" in Cronenberg are flawed or sick in some sense: "The Cronenberg hero is sick: attacked by parasites that he vomits into toilets (*Shivers*), victim of an unfortunate implant (*Rabid*), afflicted with a monstrous psychosomatic illness (*The Brood*), poisoned by a futuristic version of Thalidomide (*Scanners*), exposed to lethal rays (*Videodrome*), plunged into a coma for several years (*The Dead Zone*), dislocated by drugs (*Dead Ringers, Naked Lunch* of 'The Italian Machine'), he is dysfunctional; his biological 'programme' has been accidentally disturbed, he has been diverted from the 'normal' road of existence."[32] The problem is that sickness suggests that a norm (health) has been breached, but I don't see any reason to suppose this. Pregnant women vomit into toilets too, but we don't consider this to be a sickness per se. It is part of the natural process of being pregnant. So too with the parasites in *Shivers*. There are physical side effects, but these are the natural product of human-parasite union.

Grünberg is more importantly off the mark when he supposes that these kinds of illnesses are part of some advance of the human condition—a march toward "perfection": "Finally, it is sickness that makes the human body advance towards foreseeable perfection; it is sickness that has led to the revolutions in medical knowledge that have ensured the future of our species."[33] This is simply incorrect. Sickness does not drive the human body toward perfection or even something better. Clearly, we have evolved strategies for dealing with illness (if Ridley is right, the evolution of sex is one such strategy), but the result is not something better—it is either something that survives or something that does not. When the parasite-infected humans of *Shivers* drive off, it is not obviously good or obviously bad. It just is what it is.

Grünberg's confusions are similar to misconceptions about evolution in popular culture. We suppose that evolution leads to something better—to us, for example. But from an evolutionary perspective there is nothing more special about us than any other organism. We all happen to be adapted to the world that we live in at the moment, but we have achieved this by changing rapidly. For sexual creatures like us, the change takes place every generation, as we remix genetic material (information) that will keep parasites at bay for a while. Ridley calls it the "Red Queen theory" because, like the Red Queen in *Alice in Wonderland,* organisms must keep running (changing) just to stay in place (to survive).

Here I think is where the humanities have failed us over the past two hundred years. Science has shown that we are not special, but the humanities continually try to deny this fundamental truth. Most humanists want to tell us that we are the capstone of evolution, or that we are different from other animals because we are rational, or that we have uniquely human emotions. This is self-deception, and it is intellectually dishonest.

Cronenberg is one of the few honest humanists. His great gift is to show us the view from nowhere. We are not special. We have no essential nature. We are rapidly mutating creatures sexually combining with other creatures and systems to form something different. This isn't good and it isn't bad, but of course it is deeply horrifying. It is not monsters that should scare us, but this frightening truth. Cronenberg's films force us to confront this truth with unflinching honesty. *This* is the human condition.

Notes

1. For an overview, see Mark Browning, introduction to *David Cronenberg: Author or Film-Maker?* (Chicago: University of Chicago Press, 2007).

2. Chris Rodley, ed., *Cronenberg on Cronenberg,* rev. ed. (London: Faber and Faber, 1997), 4.

3. Rodley, *Cronenberg on Cronenberg,* 8.

4. Charles Darwin, *The Origin of Species,* 150th anniversary ed. (New York: Penguin, Signet Classics, 2002).

5. Christopher G. Langon, *Artificial Life: An Overview* (Cambridge, Mass.: MIT Press, 1995); Steven Levy, *Artificial Life: A Report from the Frontier Where Computers Meet Biology* (New York: Random House, 1992).

6. For an example, see Robin Wood, "Cronenberg: A Dissenting View," in *The Shape of Rage: The Films of David Cronenberg,* ed. Piers Handling (Toronto: Academy of Canadian Cinema, 1983), 115–35.

7. W. V. O. Quine, *Word and Object* (Cambridge, Mass.: MIT Press, 1960), 199.

8. David L. Hull, "The Effect of Essentialism on Taxonomy: Two Thousand Years of Stasis," *British Journal for the Philosophy of Science* 15 (1965): 314–26, and 16 (1965): 1–18.

9. Saul Kripke, *Naming and Necessity* (Cambridge, Mass.: Harvard University Press, 1980).

10. See Michael T. Ghiselin, "A Radical Solution to the Species Problem," *Systematic Zoology* 23 (1974): 536–44, and David L. Hull, "A Matter of Individuality," *Philosophy of Science* 45 (1978): 335–60.

11. For example, M. F. Claridge, H. A. Dawah, and M. R. Wilson, eds., *Species: The Units of Biodiversity* (London: Chapman and Hall, 1997) observed that there are a dozen notions of species in play in biology.

12. B. D. Mishler and M. J. Donoghue, "Species Concepts: A Case for Pluralism," *Systematic Zoology* 31 (1982): 491–503.

13. December 24, 1856, in Francis Darwin, ed., *The Life and Letters of Charles Darwin, including an Autobiographical Chapter*, vol. 2 (London: John Murray, 1877/1887), 88.

14. Richard Boyd, "Homeostasis, Species, and Higher Taxa," in *Species: New Interdisciplinary Essays*, ed. Robert A. Wilson (Cambridge, Mass.: MIT Press, 1999), 141–85.

15. Matt Ridley, *The Red Queen: Sex and the Evolution of Human Nature* (London: Penguin, 1993), 70.

16. See Richard Dawkins, "Universal Darwinism," in *Evolution from Molecules to Men*, ed. D. S. Bendall (Cambridge: Cambridge University Press, 1983), 403–25; Daniel C. Dennett, *Darwin's Dangerous Idea: Evolution and the Meaning of Life* (New York: Simon and Schuster, 1995); and Martin A. Nowak, *Evolutionary Dynamics: Exploring the Equations of Life* (Cambridge, Mass.: Harvard University Press, 2006).

17. Phillip A. Laplante, ed., *Biocomputing* (Hauppauge, N.Y.: Nova Science, 2003).

18. See Peter Ludlow and Mark Wallace, *The Second Life Herald: The Virtual Tabloid That Witnessed the Dawn of the Metaverse* (Cambridge, Mass.: MIT Press, 2007), chapter 4.

19. See Mark Stephen Meadows and Peter Ludlow, "A Virtual Life. An Actual Death," *H+*, September 2, 2009, http://hplusmagazine.com/articles/virtual-reality/virtual-life-actual-death.

20. Serge Grünberg, *David Cronenberg: Interviews with Serge Grünberg* (London: Plexus, 2006), 9.

21. Noam Chomsky, *Knowledge of Language* (New York: Praeger, 1986).

22. For a survey, see Handling, *The Shape of Rage*.

23. Ridley, *The Red Queen*.

24. See also W. D. Hamilton, R. Axelrod, and R. Tanese, "Sexual Reproduction as an Adaptation to Resist Parasites (a Review)," *Proceedings of the National Academy of Sciences of the USA* 87 (1990): 3566–73.

25. Richard Dawkins, "Parasites, Desiderata Lists and the Paradox of the Organism," *Parasitology* 100 (1990): S63–S73.

26. Thomas S. Ray, "Evolution and the Optimization of Digital Organisms" (Manuscript, University of Delaware, 1992).

27. Peter Ludlow, "The Myth of Human Language," *Croatian Journal of Philosophy*

18 (2006): 385–400, and "Cheap Contextualism," *Nous. Philosophical Issues 16: Annual Supplement,* ed. Ernest Sosa and Enrique Villanueva (2007): 104–29.

28. Mark C. Baker, "Linguistic Differences and Language Design," *Trends in Cognitive Science* 7 (2003): 352.

29. This is a point emphasized in Lawrence Lessig, *Remix: Making Art and Commerce Thrive in the Hybrid Economy* (New York: Penguin, 2008).

30. William Beard, *The Artist as Monster: The Cinema of David Cronenberg* (Toronto: University of Toronto Press, 2006), 32–33.

31. Rodley, *Cronenberg on Cronenberg,* 5.

32. Grünberg, *David Cronenberg,* 9.

33. Grünberg, *David Cronenberg,* 9.

What Happens to Brundle?
Problems of Teleportation and Personal Identity in *The Fly*

Paul F. Snowdon

What is there in *The Fly* (1986) of interest to philosophy? Sometimes films deliberately aim to stimulate philosophical reflection by manifestly engaging with philosophical themes. I will argue that *The Fly* does not do that. Rather, philosophy engages with *The Fly* when we stand back from our natural involvement in, and reaction to, the plot and ask what sense, if any, can be made of the story. Considering the plot brings us face to face with two large philosophical debates. The result of this encounter is that it is very difficult to say what happens in *The Fly*; in particular, what happens to Brundle.

The Fly is a film that produces sharply different reactions in different viewers. Aficionados of nasty surprises and gore love it and assign it, probably rightly, an important place in the development of the genre they admire. Those of us with less of a taste for blood and guts can see it as a film with a fairly simple plot that moves quickly to its messy conclusion. It tells the tale of an experiment that goes sadly wrong in the context of—and *because* it is in the context of—that old-fashioned dramatic structure, the eternal triangle. Seth Brundle's (Jeff Goldblum) fatal and unwitting decision to step into the teleporter device along with what we might call the fly in the ointment is inspired by drink and a jealousy he feels about Veronica Quaife's (Geena Davis) involvement with her boss, Stathis Borans (John Getz). (This sentence reveals one very curious aspect of the film—its totally absurd names!) Of course Brundle, being the emotional incompetent that he is, has completely misinterpreted Quaife's motives and behavior. The rest is history, with Brundle's life (or, perhaps, not strictly *Brundle's* life, as we will see) going (as one might put it with pardonable understatement) from bad to worse.

Who is Brundle?

Brundle is the central character, and any consideration of the film must start and end with him. He is a scientist to whom something truly awful happens. Quite how we should describe that awful thing is something of a mystery. But Brundle himself is also a mystery. He is a genius and a man, but apart from that he is very hard to describe, and our reaction to him is simply to ask questions. Is he an innocent? Is he autistic? Does he have emotions? How does he feel about his own fate? I will return to Brundle, but first I want to ask what else there is in the film.

Within the film there are undoubtedly real pluses that anyone would recognize. There is plenty of humor—some is fairly low grade, but nonetheless it's definitely funny. For example, when Brundle leaps through the glass to steal Veronica from the planned abortion, there is real shock, but the effect is also comic and absurd. Cronenberg also uses humor to define his main characters. Brundle jokes in an ironic and somewhat detached way as his bodily parts drop off and he puts them in his "natural history museum." This conveys his dispassionate and scientific nature. In contrast, Stathis's humor is vulgar and sexual, like his character, but nonetheless still funny. Another comic aspect is the equipment that Brundle employs. The pods look like the products of a nineteenth-century foundry. Cronenberg seems remarkably taken with the little revolving wheel that turns whenever the doors close, and we are repeatedly shown it. The computer that Brundle types into is, no doubt intentionally, laughable. The really major plus, it seems to me, is Geena Davis's performance, in which she very effectively conveys the emotions that the evolving drama inspires in her character. Her emotional conflict at the end is undoubtedly highly moving. Somewhat oddly, the consequence is that although the real tragedy is Brundle's, it is Quaife's reactions and feelings that affect the audience.

It is also undeniable that the film generates a growing and real tension. Cronenberg employs standard devices to produce this. Thus, for example, when teleportation occurs, the receiving pod fills with steam (or something like it), and so we must wait, with mounting tension, to see what it contains. Brundle's warehouse apartment is in such a run-down area that whenever someone arrives there is a feeling of doom generated by the general dilapidation. Another device is the dream birth sequence (in which Cronenberg himself appears), which projects into the drama the tensions and feelings that birth induces in us. And, of course, as the drama evolves, the audience waits to see how even more grotesque Brundle (or something closely related to Brundle) has become.

On the other side, though, there are incongruities and oddities in the plot, leaving aside the remarkable events in the main story. Why does Brundle play the piano to Veronica when she first goes to his flat, the displayed music revealing that Brundle plays Beethoven and Bach? I cannot imagine what reaction that is meant to generate. Brundle horrifically snaps a man's arm in a wrestling bout in a bar, revealing bones and blood, but then just walks away (with a trophy girl). Is that an occupational hazard for arm wrestlers, which they and their audience simply take in their stride? Wouldn't one expect them rather to detain or even lynch him?

Back now to Brundle. We really have no idea about his life and what type of person he is. Is he meant to be a total innocent, who has devoted himself to science, and so cannot handle the new feelings that Veronica inspires? Why, in fact, does he invite her to his apartment? He drops hints about his own ignorance of the flesh. But what, really, does that mean? Or is he, as it were, the mad scientist from the word go? Is he not, as one might say, properly human even as the film begins? We simply do not know, and Jeff Goldblum's performance hints at nothing one way or the other. So, at the center of the drama there is a large and, for me, mildly unsatisfactory hole.

It is, of course, hard not to think that these oddities about Brundle, generated both by the plot and Goldblum's manner of portraying him, in contrast to the much more rounded presentation of Veronica by Davis, are deliberate. What, then, might be Cronenberg's point?[1] We can only speculate. One possibility is that he wants the audience to be somewhat detached from Brundle before the awful things start to happen so that the events are not too upsetting. Another possibility is that he wishes to present Brundle as psychologically abnormal in a way that creative geniuses can be. Still another possibility is that Cronenberg wishes the audience to wonder what manner of thing Brundle is before the changes start; that is, to wonder about Brundle's nature and identity before events highlight the question. We do not know, but I suggest that the final idea is dubious. The oddities about Brundle do not lead us to doubt that he is one of us, a human being. They lead us, rather, to view him as simply an odd human being. The real uncertainties concern what actually happens to this rather odd human.

Teleportation and Identity

Brundle's fate can be seen as *like* that of a person with AIDS or cancer, and so one might think that the theme is disease. But Cronenberg has disavowed any such theme. Another possible theme is the dangers of science. See where interfering with nature gets you? But as Cronenberg has remarked, the drama concerns simply an experiment that goes wrong, and who would draw any conclusion from that? Indeed, one might add, all the indications in the film are that Brundle has made a great discovery—he has devised a technique for teleportation. As things start, the machine can transport inanimate things, and after some tinkering (stimulated and accompanied by rambling remarks about the flesh), it can transport animals. The transported baboon supposedly shows no ill effects. When Quaife refuses to be transported (indeed, who can blame her?), knowing that something has gone wrong with Brundle, she is, strictly, making a mistake. There is in fact a genuine unreliability when the process involves two (or more—imagine, indeed, the result of a triple fusion) organisms, but it is not unreliable when only one organism is involved. As far as the film goes, the latter case is perfectly reliable. In fact Brundle probably does deserve a Nobel Prize (or two)!

Cronenberg himself in interviews mentions the theme of aging and death. Although he might have had this parallel in mind, it is, I think, fair to say that the average viewer would not be stimulated by the film to focus on any such theme. This is because, I suggest, although there are parallels between Brundle's fate and growing old—for example, the loss of teeth (at least, that used to be a normal consequence of aging), and also feelings of alienation toward one's body that can develop in aging—there are simply too many differences that overwhelm these similarities. Normally, aging does not involve large parts of one's body falling off, acquiring superhuman strength and the ability to walk on ceilings, and the emergence from one's body of what seems to be a gigantic fly. I suspect that Cronenberg's remarks are a joke or deliberate misdirection.

There are two main elements in the film that I suggest are of central philosophical relevance. The first concerns the precise nature of what is called in the film "teleportation." Brundle's main claim to fame is that he has, as the film starts, discovered how to teleport inanimate objects. Indeed, this is why Veronica initially shows such interest in him. But what is actually going on in so-called teleportation? Why might this be thought to be an issue of interest to philosophers? Well, if one transports an object *O* from place *P1* to place *P2*, it must be the selfsame object that arrives at *P2* as the one that left *P1*. Otherwise it would not be transportation. The notions of transportation (or movement) and identity are linked. So we can ask *why* we should, in the context of Brundle's experiment, count the arriving object as the same thing as the departing object? Quaife puts a stocking in the first pod; it vanishes, and then a stocking appears in the second pod. Is the second stocking the same as the first? This question is important because if it is the *same* stocking, then Brundle has teleported it; if it is not, then he has merely destroyed one stocking and created another one that resembles it. As philosophers, we want to know which verdict is correct. But how do we decide this?

As far as the film's plot is concerned, there is no question but that it is *genuine* teleportation. This is conveyed through Quaife's worry that Brundle is playing a trick on her, and then, once she has dismissed this worry, her simply accepting that it is genuine teleportation. Amazingly, although she is supposedly a probing, liberated, and intelligent reporter, she does not ask *how* the process works. In fact, we are never told what is going on or how things work. And the audience, I think, simply goes with that.

Another question that we might have expected the inquisitive Quaife to have raised is over what distances the process can work. Brundle claims that conventional transportation will be rendered redundant by his discovery. But that is hardly true if it can only transport across thirty feet. Has Brundle any evidence of the range of the process? The issue that *is* raised, and on which they focus, is the problem that Brundle is worried by—namely, that he cannot, as the film starts, successfully teleport animate things, a failure that is illustrated for us by the sad and bloody fate of the first baboon. But to any properly reflective person it cannot be right to grant the status of *genuine teleportation* without much deeper inquiry. And for that, we need to know in more detail what is going on. We need not know in perfect detail, but in general terms, at least.

Here is one possibility. The first pod disassembles the object into tiny material parts and streams them across to the second pod, which reassembles them. If that is what is happening, one might be tempted to view it as like dismantling a bicycle when taking it abroad and then putting it back together once one has arrived. We would count it as the selfsame bicycle.

But another possibility is that the first pod scans the initial object, destroys it, and sends instructions to the second pod to create a new object of precisely the same kind. (How it might assemble the necessary matter we can leave unexplained.) On the face of it, in this second case we do not actually have teleportation. What arrives is not what departs but merely a resembling object. This is, it seems to me, a rather plausible claim, but we can add a little philosophical argument to back it up. If the process I described did actually transport the object, then it is difficult to know what to say about a case where the same process takes place but where there is a malfunction and in a third pod another precise replica simultaneously emerges. This seems possible, but obviously both the replicas cannot be the original object, since there are two of them, and they are separate. So we can say that simply being the replication of an object by such a process is not *in itself* to *be* that object. However, the problem is that in the original case, where there are not two examples of replication, the link between the original and the replicating object seems no closer than it is in the double reduplication case. It seems puzzling how identity can be preserved even in the case where there is only a single object created.

Still, someone might say that this discussion misses a third option. Why cannot we just say that the first pod simply sends the same matter to the second pod? It does not travel in a continuous spatial pathway, but just jumps across a spatial gap. This may be how we are supposed to think of it. In response to this description we can reply, "By what right do you count what is happening as the appearance at the far side of the spatial gap of the original object itself, rather than of another but indistinguishable thing?" To this, we can add a second question: "Suppose that what happens is that we start at time t with object O in the first pod. O then disappears and in two further pods there appear what are replicas of O. Might one be the original and the other not? How could we possibly decide?" Now, these are just questions, and asking them does not amount to a proof that it is impossible for matter to leap across spatial gaps. Indeed, there is as far as I know nothing approaching a proof of this impossibility. There is, also, no proof that it does make sense. What we can say, though, is that this third approach relies on making sense of the idea that the same object is at different places at different times—after all, according to this approach, the matter in question starts out in one pod and then just reappears in the second pod without having traveled through space—where the normal and standard assumptions, and underpinnings, that accompany understanding the idea of the same matter being in different places at different times are absent. We simply lack the surrounding features that normally ground this kind of thought. By the surrounding features I mean the assumption that if an object goes from A to B then it occupied the whole of a route between A and B in the course of its journey. We can say, then, that if the process takes one form where matter is transported, it might count as teleportation; if it takes another, where matter is not transported but resembling matter is created, then it is not; and if it is supposed to be the third case, where matter simply jumps between places, it is to be seriously doubted that it makes any sense at all. It is, then, a considerable problem to make sense of teleportation. So who knows what we should count as happening to the objects involved—including, of course, Brundle.

Personal Identity and Animalism

There is a second, and equally difficult to resolve, philosophical issue that relates to the film. Brundle is what we call a "person," and philosophers have long wondered what persons are and how we should think about them. One issue has been what a person consists of. Is a person a soul or a spirit, or does a person have only physical parts? The former view, popular in religious traditions of thought, has powerful philosophical supporters, but these days a more materialist viewpoint is favored. And certainly, anything spiritual is conspicuous by its absence from Cronenberg's story. So I propose to follow his lead and work within a materialist framework.

It remains a matter of dispute what is essential for each of us to remain in existence over time. This is called (for perhaps confused reasons) the problem of "personal identity." A crucial aspect of this issue is how we can explain what the difference is between those changes that might happen to the person which are consistent with his or her remaining in existence and those that would amount to the person's ceasing to exist. I do not want to give a full account of this issue here, but I will simply assume a certain answer, and relate it to the problem of Brundle.[2] The answer I am assuming is that we should regard Brundle as a (human) animal, so as a thing that remains in existence under the same conditions that the animal he is remains in existence. What, it might be asked, does this mean? Let me mention two apparent implications of this approach. Take a familiar animal such as a pet cat. If a mad scientist did horrible things to its brain and permanently deprived it of consciousness but kept it alive, then we would think that the cat was still in existence, having lost its psychological capacities. For an animal to remain in existence, there need be no psychological states or psychological links to the past. If we are animals, then the same goes for us. Our remaining in existence cannot be analyzed in terms of psychological states. Further, with a cat there is no conceivable way that it, the animal, could be removed from the living cat body. Similarly, if we are animals, then we cannot leave, or separate from, our bodies. Thinking this way, then, has important consequences. As a general approach this is sometimes called "animalism."

Many readers will wonder how saying this can be controversial in the eyes of some philosophers, but the answer is that there are counterarguments that are not obviously absurd and which seem to indicate that the person and the animal are not the selfsame thing. As a general battery of arguments, they will have to remain unexpressed here, but they can be characterized as attempts to conceive of possible cases where the person and the animal come apart, and so cannot be the same thing. A possible example of such a dissociation would be an end-of-life scenario where a human being has suffered a severe trauma and become, as we say, simply a "living vegetable." Some claim about such a case that although the human animal remains, the person—say, your mother—no longer exists, but has "gone" already. If that is the correct verdict, then your mother can hardly be the human animal, since your mother is no longer present, but the human animal undoubtedly is. Of course, this is merely one example of a possible dissociation, and the philosophical literature contains many others. (Indeed, some arguments along similar lines will emerge as we consider the Brundle case.) I am currently assuming that those arguments are not persuasive, and so we can equate Brundle and the animal where Brundle is. So, to know what happens to Brundle, we need to know what happens to the animal that Brundle is.

The first thing to say is that if Brundle is an animal, and the teleportation process does not, in fact, transport the body of the animal, then it can hardly transport the animal itself. Rather, if the body is destroyed, then so is the animal. In which case, so is Brundle. So it may be, then, that Brundle is destroyed as soon as he attempts teleportation, and that Quaife is thereafter dealing with a replica. The pressing question would then be, Who is it that Quaife loves: Brundle or his replica? Fortunately, we can leave that emotional conundrum unanswered.

Leaving that aside, let us assume that the teleporter does transport animals. At this point we hit two deep mysteries. The first is, as one might say, What actually goes on in *The Fly*? What is the biological process involved? But the second mystery, a deep philosophical one, is, What are the conditions under which a particular animal survives? What changes is an animal capable of? And what changes really amount to its destruction?

Metamorphosis or Fusion?

Let us consider the first issue first. Since this is a film, we do not in fact have much to go on. But we are given the following things. First, we learn from the computer that Brundle and the fly *fuse* when they are both in the pod and the process occurs. So what emerges is the fusion of them. In fact we have no real idea what this means, but plainly it means something rather important. Second, we observe what happens. Now, undoubtedly we think of what happens thereafter as something that happens to Brundle. That is clearly the intended interpretation of the narrative of the film. But what does happen to him? Our interpretation is totally guided by the eyes of Quaife. We see the process in the terms she does. And, crucially, she regards it as

Brundle who, having turned into something like a gigantic fly and then something even worse, in the light of his fate, wishes to be shot. Her reluctance to shoot is based on her conviction that the thing begging to be shot *is* Brundle, the person she loves. So her view is that Brundle becomes the large fly-like thing there at the end. In fact Quaife's view is the view of the film and its spectators. She really provides both the emotional core of the film and the narrative that we, the viewers, accept.

But Quaife's own reading of the drama faces two difficulties. One derives from what we observe happening, which is that large chunks of what we feel to be Brundle just drop off, and the fly-like thing *emerges*. This very strongly suggests that if what we have in front of us (after the teleportation) is Brundle, then what is happening is that a large fly-like creature is growing inside him, and Brundle is gradually disintegrating. The evidence of our senses is, I think, not that Brundle himself becomes the fly, but that Brundle disintegrates to be replaced by a fly-like thing.

The second, and more philosophical problem, already hinted at, is that we are told that the thing stepping out of the pod is the *fusion* of Brundle and the fly. What does that mean and imply about what is happening? We need to make as much sense as we can of that notion.

The idea that there has been a fusion means that we are not simply considering what is called "metamorphosis." Since antiquity, there have been many stories in which one animal or thing changes in a dramatic way. When such changes occur, they are called cases of metamorphosis. About such cases the question is whether we should count the original object to be there still in the new form, or whether it is a new object and the original has ceased to exist. In what is called "fusion," by contrast, we start with two objects and then they, in some sense, combine to result in a new thing—their fusion. In such a situation it is hard to regard the resulting single thing as identical to both of the two separate objects. To do so involves holding in an apparently contradictory fashion that there are both objects but also only a single object. In thinking about fusion cases, therefore, we face extra problems.

Certainly, as we think about it we do not suppose that the resulting creature is the *original* fly. Rather, that fly has been fused with and, in some sense, into Brundle. This means that the fly no longer exists. But the fly's nonexistence is not like its nonexistence if Brundle should have happened to swallow it. In that case the fly is destroyed by being eaten and its matter employed by Brundle in and after the process of digestion. (When Brundle sings the song about the man who swallowed the fly, it is quite simply the wrong song.) So although eating and fusing with a fly both involve the fly's ceasing to exist, they are not the same thing. The reason is that the thing resulting from the fusion with the fly is most definitely fly-like. But if the fusion of the fly with Brundle destroys the fly but results in a creature that is deeply fly-like, with its own processes of development and internal structure, we need to ask why it preserves the human animal Brundle. Why is the resulting thing not a new form of life? We can, surely, think of it as a new form of life that begins by resembling Brundle (which does not mean that it is Brundle) but that then develops in ways which are appropriate to its new life-form. So, maybe, when Brundle and the fly fuse, *both* are destroyed and a new monster is created. I am suggesting, then, that it is quite attractive to think that Brundle is not the fly-like thing that emerges from the pod.

There is more to say about this issue. In fact, there are two questions hanging over us. Is the fly-like creature Brundle? And when the fusion occurs, does Brundle, like the original fly, cease to exist? It might be that the Brundle-fly fusion is neither Brundle nor the fly, but that *enough* of Brundle remains so that he is still there, gradually disintegrating, while the fusion is developing inside him.

The Lockean View of Personal Identity

My argument so far about Brundle, then, is that in all probability he ceases to exist when he is first in the teleporter, which has probably been misnamed, because there are serious doubts about what is happening. If, however, the thing is a genuine teleporter, then because there is a fusion of Brundle with the fly, and two things cannot become one, the most likely verdict is that the fusion is neither Brundle nor the fly, but an entirely new creature. We still have the option of thinking that Brundle has not ceased to exist if we think that enough of him remains, but then we need to think of *two* creatures, one inside the other. Brundle then gradually disintegrates, leaving the developing fusion. That is surely how a biologist would view it.

At this point, though, a major intellectual fly in the ointment emerges. I have been assuming that Brundle is a human animal, and so we can think about Brundle's fate by considering what we should say about animals. But as I mentioned earlier, there are philosophers who do not think that persons are animals. Such philosophers would think that there is a human animal where Brundle, the person, is, but hold that the two are not strictly the same thing. Their reason for thinking this, as we have seen, is that they hold the person and the animal can come apart in certain possible circumstances. If that is right, then Brundle, being a person, is not an animal, and we need to trace him through the events in a different way, the way appropriate to persons. But what is that way? Opponents of the conception that I have been assuming so far do not agree on what to put in the place of animalism. But one idea, deriving from John Locke, a seventeenth-century philosopher, has seemed to many people to be on the right track.[3]

The Lockean idea is that a person's history is to be analyzed in terms of the existence of psychological links between things over time. Thus, if person P does X at time t, then someone who later can remember doing X counts as being the person P. Roughly, a person is traced in terms of *psychological* links over time. Now, the crucial point is that the links need not be sustained in any normal way, but can be allowed to be supported by strange causal processes. In normal cases, memory links are preserved by there being traces in the nervous system, but in principle memories might, say, be downloaded onto a disk and then reloaded into another brain. Thus, when Brundle and the fly fuse, since the process seems to preserve Brundle's memories, we should count the result as the person Brundle, despite not knowing really how the link is sustained. Where this Lockean conception makes a significant difference, though, is over how to regard the initial teleportation. I suggested that there was a real chance that Brundle perished at the first hurdle. By contrast, on the Lockean view, since the resulting object does seem to remember Brundle's life, it would qualify as Brundle, whatever one says about the material objects involved. Thus, even if no matter was transported, it remains true that memory links were generated by the process, whatever it was, which accords with the Lockean view of what survival for a person requires. Whether, according to this Lockean idea, Brundle is really there at the end, housed in the fly-like thing begging to be killed, is an open question. We do not know about the mental links that there are between that creature and Brundle's past. But perhaps we are meant to assume that there are such links, in which case Quaife's interpretation of events is vindicated.

Blind Acceptance

I have already criticized Quaife for her total lack of curiosity about what is happening, and I do not propose to heap more criticism on her by arguing against the philosophical approach that might vindicate her general interpretation. Such a task would be impossible here. I want instead to stress three points. The first is that there are indeed philosophical accounts of persons that would agree with Quaife's verdict. Second, I take it that the view that I assumed earlier, that Brundle is a human animal, will have struck you as commonsensical, and as a totally reasonable assumption on which to work. My third point, though, concerns not how we might interpret the fate of Brundle but rather whether the tendency, as we view the film, to go along with Quaife's view in any way *supports* the idea that a philosophical view that would vindicate her approach is correct. The answer to that question, I believe, is no. The reason lies in the combined nature of language understanding and belief. It is obvious that we understand the claim expressed in the words "Brundle is the fly-like thing." We know which objects we are talking about, and we understand that "is" expresses identity. The claim makes sense. In a similar fashion, we understand the plainly false sentence "President Obama is the Statue of Liberty." But, second, when we accept the sentence in reacting to the film, we do so in a manner that discourages us from really thinking about its truth or reasonableness. The audience of *The Fly* is induced to adopt Quaife's view by Cronenberg's skillful direction, and is simply carried along by it. We end up unreflectively accepting a sentence as true. If this is a correct description of the psychology here, then it seems clear that the audience's acceptance of the view cannot indicate that it is somehow true, nor can it support a theory about persons on the basis of its vindicating the view. I believe that this idea of unconsidered acceptance has wide application in human belief formation. Another, and very important, area is that of religion. The way that some cultures raise children induces them to accept certain sentences, expressive of religious belief, without any real consideration as to what they mean. I suggest, then, that our reaction to *The Fly* gives no aid and comfort to nonanimalist approaches to personal identity.

In conclusion, the result of philosophy meeting *The Fly* is a recognition that the idea of teleportation is problematic, and that the most reasonable verdict is that Brundle does not himself become the Brundle-fly fusion. There are the resources in some philosophical views to vindicate Quaife's interpretation, and I have not shown them to be wrong, but I have claimed that it does not count in favor of these philosophical views that they would vindicate the reading of the film to which the viewer naturally inclines.

I will close with two further reflections prompted by *The Fly*. First, the film's plot, as we have seen, raises philosophical questions, but the drama itself does not pause to confront or even articulate them. This is not at all a criticism of the film (far from it, in fact), but it does count against thinking of Cronenberg *as* a philosophical filmmaker. He keeps the lid on philosophy, rather than engaging with it. (This is a verdict that needs to be tested in relation to his other films, of course.) It does not count against this claim that *The Fly* provides much food for philosophical thought. My claim is, rather, that there is no reason to suppose that Cronenberg himself is aiming to stimulate such thought. Second, my essay belongs to a level of activity that is parasitic on the more basic activities of filmmaking and philosophizing. It illustrates, therefore, the ways in which out of two other things there comes a third, not available without them. Sources of pleasure become available through the linking of more basic pleasurable activities. In this way the sources of fun proliferate, and I hope reading this has provided some. Of course, it cannot match the fun that Cronenberg has given us with *The Fly.*

Notes

I thank Simon Riches for the invitation to contribute to this volume on Cronenberg, and also for the help in writing it that he provided to me.

    1. I am grateful to Simon Riches for pressing this question.
    2. For an introduction to this problem, see Paul Snowdon, "The Self and Personal Identity," in *Central Issues in Philosophy,* ed. John Shand (Oxford: Wiley-Blackwell, 2009), 121–36.
    3. The classic exposition of the Lockean view is in John Locke, *An Essay Concerning Human Understanding* (Oxford: Clarendon, 1975), Book 2, chapter 27. Locke's *Essay* was originally published in the seventeenth century. A fascinating modern exposition of a similar view is Derek Parfit, *Reasons and Persons* (Oxford: Oxford University Press, 1986), part 2.

Part 2

Psychology, Skepticism, and the Self

eXistenzial Angst

Duncan Pritchard

One of the key motifs of David Cronenberg's film *eXistenZ* (1999) is the idea that one might not be able to tell the difference between appearance and reality. This is conveyed in the film in terms of the protagonists—Ted Pikul (Jude Law) and Allegra Geller (Jennifer Jason Leigh)—being progressively unable to be sure they aren't inside the game they are playing, rather than in the real world. Although the circumstances in play in the film are of course highly unusual, and very distinct from normal circumstances, there is a general philosophical difficulty at issue here—indeed, it is one of the most fundamental and enduring challenges that philosophers face. This is the problem of *radical skepticism*, a problem that can be traced back to antiquity and that finds expression, in some form, in the work of such diverse figures as Plato, Descartes, Hume, and Kant.

In a nutshell, radical skepticism is the worry that we don't have any adequate basis for distinguishing appearance from reality, and hence that we do not have nearly as much knowledge of reality as we tend to suppose we have. Indeed, in its strongest form it is the claim that all knowledge is impossible. As we will see, this problem is typically thought of in broadly *methodological* terms, where by this I mean as a difficulty that we can use to "test" our theories of knowledge to see whether they can withstand this challenge (this was roughly how Descartes understood the problem, for example). But it can also be thought of as an *existential* problem, a problem that can actually have a bearing on how, at a fundamental level, we think about and live our own lives.

As we will see, one of the interesting aspects of *eXistenZ* is that it makes explicit how the radical skeptical problem might have existential import, by offering a thought-provoking example of how one's own subjective confidence in reality can be threatened by skeptical doubt. We will also note how this film raises some other interesting questions relevant to contemporary epistemology, particularly concerning the possibility of *extended cognition*, where this means a cognitive process that extends beyond the skin of the agent concerned.

The Problem of Radical Skepticism

A standard way of expressing the problem of radical skepticism is via appeal to *radical skeptical hypotheses*. These are hypotheses that, if true, would undermine much of what we currently think we know, but that it seems we are unable to know to be false. A famous example of a radical skeptical hypothesis is the so-called brain-in-a-vat hypothesis. In this scenario, one is to imagine—somewhat along the lines of *The Matrix* (1999), which, interestingly, came out the same year as *eXistenZ*—that one has been abducted and had one's brain removed. It is now placed in a vat of nutrients connected to supercomputers that are "feeding" it experiences so as to give one the impression that one's life is in fact proceeding as normal (i.e., the supercomputers make one think that one is walking around, talking to people, going to work, and so forth, even though all the time one is in fact merely a brain in a vat being given these deceptive experiences). In *The Matrix*, of course, the victim's entire body was suspended in the vat rather than just the brain, but the essential point is the same: those suspended in the vat will think that life is progressing just as normal, when in fact the experiences they are having are entirely fake ones generated by the supercomputers.

The trouble is, if one were a brain in a vat, then one wouldn't know very much about the world around one (one's beliefs about the world around one would be mostly false, for one thing). This is a problem once we realize that we do not have any effective way of knowing that we are not presently deceived in this way. How would we tell? (By seeing whether we had a body? But it would seem as if we had a body even if we were a brain in a vat).

From this point the radical skeptic concludes that we can't possibly have much of the knowledge that we typically credit to ourselves. More generally, the radical skeptic argues that since we can't know the denials of skeptical hypotheses like the brain-in-a-vat hypothesis, we don't know very much (if anything). This conclusion would clearly be intellectually disastrous, so the philosophical challenge posed by radical skepticism is to show how we can evade this problem.[1]

It is often said that radical skepticism is not an existential problem, where this means that it is not a problem that has any *practical* significance for our lives. There is a good reason for this, in that there is a sense in which the very fact that we are unable to distinguish between the radical skeptical scenario and ordinary life makes the possibility that one is in the former scenario an, in a sense at least, existentially idle concern. For example, if we really can't tell the difference between living a normal life and being a brain in a vat that merely thinks it is living a normal life, then why should we care?[2]

Relatedly, it is not as if the problem of radical skepticism gives us a particular reason for thinking that the skeptical scenario is true, since ex hypothesi we could no more have reason for thinking this than for thinking that the skeptical scenario does not obtain. To see this point, think again about the brain-in-a-vat scenario. Could one have a good reason for thinking that one is a brain in a vat? It seems not. For imagine what such a reason would be. Suppose, for example, that someone tells you that you are a brain in a vat. Here is the issue: Why should you give such a reason any credence? After all, if you are a brain in a vat, then that someone is telling you that you are a brain in a vat is itself part of the deceptive stream of "fake" experiences that are being fed to you, and hence should itself be regarded with suspicion. But if you are not a brain in a vat, then you certainly shouldn't place any weight on this "information" that is being offered to you (it's false, for one thing). So, either way, it seems you should ignore "evidence" that seems to suggest you are the victim of this skeptical hypothesis.

So what is the concern posed by radical skepticism, if it is not an existential concern? Well, the standard answer to this question, at least since Descartes's seminal writings on this topic, is that this concern should be understood along methodological lines. On this way of viewing it, we should not be interested in the problem of radical skepticism because it has any practical bearing on our lives, but rather because it poses a standing challenge to our theories of knowledge, such that we need to "test" those theories by seeing whether they can avoid this problem. So construed, radical skepticism is still philosophically important even if it lacks any existential significance.

Radical Skepticism as an eXistenZial Problem

Although the philosophical import of radical skepticism remains even if it is not an existential problem, radical skepticism *can* have existential significance, and the kind of scenario depicted in *eXistenZ* gives us an idea of how we might absorb, and be disturbed by, the skeptical problem. The difference comes in the detectable transition from normality to the skeptical scenario that is vividly described in this film. Normally, radical skeptical scenarios are set up in such a way that there is no detectable transition from normal circumstances to being the victim of a radical skeptical scenario.

One minute you are walking down the street minding your own business, the next minute you are a "harvested" brain in a vat. But skeptical scenarios can be constructed in such a way that they "creep" up on you, and in such cases you *will* directly feel the existential force of the skeptical scenario in question. This is just what *eXistenZ* does.

Consider the fate of the protagonists in this film, Ted and Allegra. To begin with, there is nothing skeptical about the circumstances they are in, but gradually the skeptical force of the situation is built up. By being connected to the game, they are aware that they are, in part, taking on an altered perception of reality, but this in itself does not license any skeptical reflections. After all, having several alcoholic drinks, or taking some mild hallucinogenic drugs, can alter your perception of reality, but no one would try to motivate the radical skeptical problem by appeal to such meager fare. This is because such minor cognitive impairments do not prevent you from being able to tell—at least roughly—that your perception of reality is being altered. With good judgment, you can tell that the elephant that seems to be in the room is not there, but is instead merely the product of the drug that you've ingested.

As the cognitive impairment encountered by Ted and Allegra increases, however, so we move closer to something that resembles a skeptical scenario. Stranger and stranger things happen, and the line between what is real and what is merely part of the game that they are playing starts to blur. Soon our protagonists lack any basis on which to take relatively normal experiences at face value, since they are aware that the course of their experience is liable to change from the normal to the bizarre at the drop of a hat. This psychologically disturbs them, as we would expect. Indeed, as a number of philosophers have noted, to take seriously that one has become, or is becoming, the victim of a radical skeptical hypothesis is to succumb to a particularly dangerous form of *angst*. Such angst is not mere show, like the moody self-aware sulk of a teenager (or the affected pretentious pose of a philosopher). Instead, this way madness ultimately lies.

It is interesting to compare *eXistenZ* and *The Matrix* on this score. In the latter film, when Neo (Keanu Reeves) is told by Morpheus (Laurence Fishburne) that his life is a sham, and that he exists (albeit as more than just a brain) only in the vat, he is prepared, seemingly unaffected by any kind of angst, to simply accept the new reality that is presented to him by Morpheus (via the magic pill that is offered to him). But unless Neo is completely devoid of any nous, it is hard to see why becoming convinced that he has been so radically deceived leaves him in any position thereafter to be confident about *anything* that he (apparently) perceives about the real world around him. To be unable to take anything that one (apparently) perceives at face value, however—to doubt in this way, without restriction—is a recipe for insanity. (It could be, of course, that Neo *is* disturbed in this way, but that the actor playing him was somehow unable to convey this fact; however, let us interpret the film in a way sympathetic to the widely unappreciated acting talents of Keanu Reeves.)

One philosopher who was very sensitive to this essential connection between radical doubt and madness is Wittgenstein. In his final notebooks, published posthumously as *On Certainty,* he writes of how a "doubt that doubted everything would not even be a doubt," and the reason he makes this claim is that radical doubt of this sort inevitably leads to madness, where the madman is not even in a position to doubt or to believe.[3] Doubt, like belief, is something that only the (approximately) sane can have. Wittgenstein argues that the key to understanding why this is so is to realize the priority of belief over doubt. One acquires one's conception of the world by accepting what one is told by those around one. Only once this picture is in place is one in a position to doubt. But the doubt must always be local, because once it is radicalized, it leaves the doubter with no ground on which to stand to present the doubt. Doubt radicalized leaves the doubter all at sea, and as such it undermines the possibility of both doubt and belief. The result is insanity.[4]

Normally, when philosophers talk of skeptical doubt, they have in mind something rather fake. Since the skeptical problem is methodological, the skeptical doubt is merely hypothetical, and hence in this sense unreal (and thus kind of fake). But the way in which the skeptical scenario creeps up on the agents in *eXistenZ* makes vivid how one could over time become subject to a skeptical scenario in such a fashion that one would become aware that something personally momentous was occurring. In such cases one can see the transition from normality to strangeness and be disturbed by it, so that eventually one's doubt extends and one's belief reduces to such a degree that one passes the tipping point, and so loses one's mind.

Ted and Allegra don't in the end lose their minds, of course, but this is because they, apparently seamlessly, pass across to the other side and accept the new presented reality. My own reading of this film—which, it should be noted, is probably not standard—is that the point of the ending is that the deception is now complete, and hence that the protagonists can return to a state of belief. I noted earlier that in virtue of the fact that normal scenarios and radical skeptical scenarios are completely indistinguishable, it follows that they are, arguably at least, existentially neutral: if you can't tell the difference, then there isn't a difference that can make a difference to you. What makes *eXistenZ* philosophically interesting is that it sketches a transition from normality to skepticism in which the agents concerned are aware of the transition, and shows the psychological harm that results. But once the transition is complete, the doubt disappears and a new form of doxastic equilibrium is reached. Sanity requires belief, but it does not require widespread *truth* in one's beliefs.

The way in which one's psyche can unravel in this way is a recurring theme of Cronenberg's films. Think, for example, of his film *Spider* (2002), in which we are unsparingly presented with the complete psychological breakdown of the protagonist.[5] One can only wonder what he would have done with the film *Total Recall* (1990) had he directed it as was originally planned, since this has the potential to explore some very similar themes to *eXistenZ*, themes that are left unexplored in *Total Recall* as it was eventually conceived.

eXistenZ and Extended Cognition

eXistenZ also draws on another recurring theme in Cronenberg's work, which is the way in which technology can dramatically alter our perception of reality. Notice that what gives rise to the skeptical scenario in *eXistenZ* is not something completely disconnected from the agent at issue, as is common to most radical skeptical hypotheses. Compare, on the one hand, the standard brain-in-a-vat scenario where one's brain is unknowably harvested for some sinister purpose by an unknown agent, and on the other hand, the skeptical scenario depicted in *eXistenZ*. For one thing, Allegra is the very designer of the game that leads to their skeptical predicament and initiates the process by which both she and Ted get drawn into the game, with all its skeptical implications.

Indeed, part of what is disquieting about the film is the way in which the line between nature and technology becomes so fuzzy, to the point where the distinction becomes impossible to draw. Cronenberg had explored this theme before *eXistenZ*, of course—think, for example, of his film *Videodrome* (1983). However, *eXistenZ* is arguably the first of his films to explicitly explore how technology could become a genuine part of our natural cognitive processes, and the implications of this.

We tend to think of cognition as a purely internal affair, where this means that it is something that happens in the mind of the subject. Accordingly, at least on a very intuitive picture of the mind, cognition is thus concerned with processes that are entirely under the skin of the agent. One influential thread of thought in contemporary cognitive science, however, is the idea that cognition is often best thought of as being "extended" beyond the skin of the agent. For example, there is a wealth of empirical literature which suggests that cognitive processes are at least sometimes *embodied*, in that the subject's body can itself form part of the cognitive process. There are also good grounds—both philosophical and empirical—for supposing that cognitive processes can take in features of the environment that are completely *outside* the body of the subject.[6]

The "pod" used by Ted and Allegra to access the game provides us with a vivid illustration of how such cognitive extension might occur. Although our natural cognitive processes do not extend beyond the skin, technological development allows us to supplement these processes by artificial means in such a way that we are not merely using these technological supplements as instruments serving our natural cognitive abilities, as might be the case with our use of a calculator. Instead, the technological supplement plausibly becomes an essential part of an extended cognitive process, such that our cognitive processes now extend beyond our skin to take in collaborative technological features of the world. This is just what the pod does in *eXistenZ*, since it is an artificial device that quite literally plugs into our heroes' natural cognitive processes, thereby supplementing them.

But of course, what makes this cognitive extension particularly interesting is that it is not a mere supplementation that takes place here. It is not as if, for example, a calculator has somehow been brought into an extended cognitive process so that the agent's calculating abilities are enhanced by the addition of this new device. Instead, what we have is a technological adaptation of nature that both in a sense enhances and in a sense *subverts* our protagonists' cognitive processes. Technological development is thus shown as not necessarily representing cognitive *progress*. Indeed, since such subversion has the potential to undermine the very agency of our subjects by leading them, via skepticism, to insanity, this narrative theme in *eXistenZ* picks up on a widespread angst regarding our relationship to technology.[7] Although we might flee from nature, red in tooth and claw, we also fear the extent to which the technology that offers us sanctuary from nature has the power to rob us of our autonomy and, thereby, of our very selfhood, particularly when such technology becomes an extension of our agency and so part of our "inner" life.

Notes

I am grateful to Simon Riches for very helpful and extensive comments on an earlier version of this essay.

1. For an overview of the contemporary debate on radical skepticism, see D. H.

Pritchard, "Recent Work on Radical Skepticism," *American Philosophical Quarterly* 39 (2002): 215–57.

2. Underlying this claim is the idea that if a distinction is indiscernible, then it's not a distinction that we should care about. Although many accept such a claim, on closer reflection it is in fact quite controversial. Intuitively, the first book produced on the first-ever printing press is precious in a way that an exact replica is not, but it could well be the case that the two items are indiscernible. Relatedly, one might argue that a "real" life is always better than a corresponding "fake" life in the vat, even if the difference is indiscernible. On this last point, see Robert Nozick's famous discussion of the "experience machine" in *Anarchy, State, and Utopia* (New York: Basic Books, 1974), 42–45. See also D. H. Pritchard, "Absurdity, *Angst* and the Meaning of Life," *Monist* 93 (2010): 3–16.

3. Ludwig Wittgenstein, *On Certainty*, ed. G. E. M. Anscombe and G. H. von Wright, trans. Denis Paul and G. E. M. Anscombe (Oxford: Blackwell, 1969), section 450.

4. Note that this is not to suggest that Wittgenstein was completely unsympathetic to skepticism. Indeed, there are grounds for thinking that he endorsed a certain kind of restricted skepticism. See, for example, D. H. Pritchard, "Wittgensteinian Pyrrhonism," in *Pyrrhonism in Ancient, Modern, and Contemporary Philosophy*, ed. Diego Machuca (Dordrecht, Holland: Springer, 2011), 193–202. For a more general discussion of Wittgenstein's comments on skeptical doubt, see D. H. Pritchard, "Wittgenstein on Skepticism," *The Oxford Handbook of Wittgenstein*, ed. Oskari Kuusela and Marie McGinn (Oxford: Oxford University Press, 2011), 521–47.

5. Think also of Cronenberg's films *Dead Ringers* (1988) and *Naked Lunch* (1991).

6. For some key recent discussions of embodied and extended cognition, see Andy Clark, *Being There: Putting Brain, Body and World Together Again* (Cambridge, Mass.: MIT Press, 1998); Andy Clark and David Chalmers, "The Extended Mind," *Analysis* 58 (1998): 7–19; and Mark Rowlands, *The Body in Mind: Understanding Cognitive Processes* (Cambridge: Cambridge University Press, 1999). For discussion of the specifically epistemological ramifications of embodied and extended cognition, see D. H. Pritchard, "Cognitive Ability and the Extended Cognition Thesis," *Synthese* 175 (2010): 133–51.

7. The idea that our relationship to technology can be problematic in this way also arises in some of Cronenberg's other films, such as *Videodrome*, *The Fly* (1986), and *Crash* (1996).

"Freaks of Nature"
Extrasensory Perception and the Paranormal in the Films of David Cronenberg

Keith Allen

Extrasensory perception (ESP)—the ability to gain knowledge of the world by paranormal (literally, "beyond normal") means—features in a number of David Cronenberg's films. Cronenberg's first feature film, *Stereo* (1969), is a documentary-style art-house film about experiments into telepathic powers conducted by the Canadian Academy for Erotic Enquiry. The film is set in a brutalist concrete building and shot entirely in black and white, without an accompanying soundtrack (just a series of clinical voice-overs). It follows eight subjects who have had the speech-processing centers of their brains surgically removed (two have also had their larynxes removed) to enhance their telepathic abilities: abilities to acquire direct knowledge of other people's thoughts and feelings. Designed to test the theories of the parapsychologist Luther Stringfellow, the experiments take a sinister turn when five of the subjects are brought together in an "enforced community study" to investigate apparently high rates of "telepathic flow" among subjects who nevertheless deny any telepathic contact. These subjects almost immediately retreat into a state of "self-encapsulation," refusing to communicate with others; two subjects commit suicide, and one pierces his skull with an electric drill.

The theme of telepathy is revisited in *Scanners* (1981). This film contains one of the most memorable onscreen deaths, in which Michael Ironside's Darryl Revok, spearhead of an underground movement of telepaths known as "scanners," causes another scanner's head to explode: as the tagline for *Scanners* warns, "Their thoughts can kill!" Dr. Paul Ruth (Patrick McGoohan) describes scanners as "telepathic curiosities" and "freaks of nature." Scanners possess telepathic abilities to hear other people's "inner speech" or "internal monologue": the subvocal speech that accompanies thought. They also possess forms of psychokinetic ability: the ability to directly control physical events with their mind. In particular, they are able to control other people's actions and vital bodily processes. This is because as Cronenberg, speaking through Ruth, conceives of it, "telepathy is not mind reading, it is the direct linking of two nervous systems separated by space." Scanners' curious abilities are the side effect of a tranquilizer, Ephemerol, tested by Ruth on pregnant mothers in 1947. Although the initial trials were abandoned when the side effects were noticed, the use of Ephemerol was reinitiated as part of the "Ripe Project," masterminded by Revok to create an army of scanners to "bring the world of normals to their knees."

The Dead Zone (1983), based on the novel by Stephen King, explores different forms of ESP: *precognition,* the ability to know about events before they happen; *clairvoyance,* the ability to know about contemporaneous events that are hidden; and *retrocognition,* the ability to have direct access to the past. When schoolteacher Johnny Smith (Christopher Walken) wakes from a five-year coma following a terrible car crash, he discovers that he possesses psychic abilities. When he touches other people, he is able to see into their lives. He can see events from their past, such as scenes from a friend's childhood in Nazi Germany. He can see events in their present, as when he sees a nurse's daughter who is trapped in a house fire. And he can see events in the future, such as the vision of a presidential candidate's apocalyptic day of destiny. Johnny not only has the ability to *see* the future, however; he can also change it. This ability to alter the outcome of his premonitions is what Dr. Sam Weizak (Herbert Lom) refers to as his "dead zone."

Extrasensory Perception in Philosophy

Paranormal phenomena of the kind depicted in Cronenberg's films are of considerable philosophical interest. Philosophical interest in paranormal phenomena is sometimes associated with an interest in religion. When we think of paranormal phenomena, it is common to think of ghosts and the claims of mediums and spiritualists to be able to communicate with the dead. Both kinds of paranormal activity require belief in the survival of bodily death, which is a common theme in many religions. Extrasensory perception is also of interest if we think that various kinds of apparently religious experiences can be understood as forms of extrasensory perceptual experiences. After all, if we can be directly aware of God and lesser religious beings like angels, we might wonder whether we could really be aware of them via normal sensory means—the same way that we are aware of ordinary material objects, like tables, chairs, and trees.

Despite Cronenberg's interest in the paranormal, there is perhaps surprisingly little reference to religion in his work. But extrasensory perception is not philosophically important only because of its religious associations; it is of much more general philosophical interest. A number of prominent philosophers have been active members of the Society for Psychical Research—in some respects an actual counterpart of *Stereo*'s Canadian Academy for Erotic Enquiry. Established in 1882, the Society for Psychical Research aimed to investigate in a rigorous scientific manner the increasingly numerous reports of allegedly psychic phenomena in the Victorian period. Famous past presidents include Henry Sidgwick, William James, Arthur Balfour, Henri Bergson, H. H. Price, and C. D. Broad.[1]

Broad and "Basic Limiting Principles"

C. D. Broad became increasingly interested in paranormal phenomena as his career progressed: he published a number of journal articles on the subject, later giving lectures at Cambridge that were published as *Lectures on Psychical Research*.[2] Broad had always believed that there are strict limits to scientific explanation, particularly where consciousness is concerned, and his interest in the paranormal grew out of this broadly antinaturalistic worldview. In "The Experimental Establishment of Telepathic Precognition," Broad argued that the existence of genuinely paranormal phenomena could be established on empirical grounds, referring to experiments conducted by Dr. S. G. Soal in which subjects were asked to predict which of five cards a hidden subject had randomly chosen to focus on.[3] In a later article, Broad went on to argue that the existence of paranormal phenomena forced us to rethink a number of what he called "basic limiting principles": common assumptions about the nature of reality and our relationship to it.[4] These include assumptions about the nature of causation and our knowledge of the world. In addition, paranormal phenomena raise interesting questions about consciousness and moral responsibility. I will consider these in turn.

Causation and Changing the Future

Paranormal phenomena challenge basic assumptions about the nature of causation and causal processes. For instance, telepathy and psychokinesis, the abilities possessed by scanners, challenge the commonly held assumption that there can be no action at a distance. In telepathy, one person can know what another is thinking without the mediation of standard physical processes such as speech and hearing, as when Cameron Vale (Stephen Lack) undergoes the "beautiful and frightening" experience of communal scanning with a group of good scanners led by Kim Obrist (Jennifer O'Neill), in which their "minds begin to flow into each other until they become one mind." In psychokinesis, a person's thoughts can have a direct effect on the world, as when the joint scanning is interrupted by two of Revok's henchmen, who shoot three of the group's members, and Kim Obrist mentally throws the intruders against the wall and sets fire to them. One reason for skepticism about paranormal phenomena is that there are no easily identifiable causal processes by which these phenomena could occur. In contrast, there are familiar causal explanations of standard forms of perception and action: for instance, in terms of light hitting the retina, being processed by the brain, and in turn producing movements in our muscles. Cronenberg's explanation of telepathic abilities as "the direct linking of two nervous systems separated by space" goes some way toward explaining the underlying causal mechanisms: if two nervous systems can be directly linked, then telepathic experiences would seem to be no more mysterious than knowing the contents of our own minds. However, this explanation still requires the possibility of causal action at a distance. Indeed, it is interesting to note that even though Cronenberg imagines worlds in which telepathic action at a distance is possible, he is not entirely immune to the force of the intuition that there can be no action at a distance. In *Stereo,* one of Stringfellow's theories confirmed by the Canadian Academy for Erotic Enquiry's experiments is that telepathic ability decreases as the spatial distance between subjects increases.

Other forms of ESP challenge other widely held assumptions about causation. It is sometimes claimed to be essential to our understanding of the nature of causation that causes occur before their effects; in philosophical terminology, this is supposed to be "analytic," something that we can know simply by virtue of knowing the meaning of the terms ("cause," "effect," "before") involved. However, if precognition is possible, it would seem to require the possibility of backward causation, in which effects come before their causes. In *The Dead Zone,* Johnny Smith sees a boy he is teaching fall through some ice while playing ice hockey on a pond; he warns the boy's father, the boy doesn't take part in the game, and as a result he survives. Johnny's experience of the boy falling through the ice would usually be thought of as an effect of the boy's falling through the ice. But if so, then the cause of the experience would come *after* its effect.

Johnny Smith's ability not only to predict the future but to change it raises particularly interesting philosophical questions. A standard assumption about causation is that effects require the existence of their causes: there can be no fire without a spark, no opposite and equal reaction without an action, and so on. If causes can occur after their effects, then there is already a problem with the assumption that effects require the existence of their causes, because an effect can occur even though the cause does not exist *yet*. But if it is possible to change the future, then it seems that the cause may *never* exist. If the boy's falling through the ice (backwardly) causes Johnny's experience of the boy falling through the ice, then it seems that the event of the boy's falling through the ice must exist; but given that Johnny intervenes to change the future, the event of the boy's falling through the ice not only does *not* exist, but *will never* exist.

There are a number of ways of trying to make sense of the idea of changing the future when the future events have been foreseen. One option would be to deny that precognitive knowledge is properly speaking *knowledge* at all: perhaps it is really just some form of belief, prediction, or hunch. Or we could insist that precognition is a way of knowing, but claim that (unlike standard perceptual experiences) precognitive experiences do not involve causal processes—precognitive experiences are, after all, *para*normal. A different alternative would be to deny that effects need existing causes. The requirement that causes exist might seem too strong anyway, because it threatens to rule out the possibility of remembering past events: for instance, Johnny Smith's friend Sam Weizak can remember being separated from his mother in Nazi Germany even though Nazi Germany no longer exists. Finally, it might be claimed that the future event *did* exist when it caused the precognitive experience, but Johnny's subsequent action changed the future and caused it to stop existing.

Knowledge of the World

Paranormal phenomena challenge not only common assumptions about causation but also widely held beliefs about our ways of finding out about the world. Our knowledge of the world is usually thought to rely on what Broad's contemporary the logical positivist A. J. Ayer called "accredited routes to knowledge."[5] These include the ordinary "physical" senses—sight, touch, hearing, smell, taste, and bodily sensation—along with inference, memory, and testimony. For instance, when Johnny Smith is hiding waiting to assassinate the politician and future megalomaniac Greg Stillson (Martin Sheen), he can know that Stillson has entered the room either by hearing the clapping and cheering and inferring that this is caused by Stillson's arrival, or more directly by seeing Stillson or hearing him speak.

There need not be anything special about *what* is known by extrasensory means. For instance, we often know exactly what other people are thinking and feeling from observing their behavior, or imagining what we would think and feel in their position. We don't need to be telepathic to know that Johnny Smith's extrasensory experiences are painful; we can know this simply from seeing his reactions. Similarly, we don't need to be blessed with the ability of foresight to know that the nurse's daughter will die in the house fire if no one goes to rescue her; we can infer this from our knowledge of the effects of fire and our knowledge of the way in which people behave when they are in danger. Indeed, although he relies on his clairvoyant powers to know that the nurse's daughter is trapped in a fire, Johnny Smith does not himself *foresee* the girl's death: he infers that she will die if she isn't saved from the scene that he foresees.

What is distinctive about ESP is the *way* in which subjects come to know about the world. Ordinary perceptual knowledge is often described as "direct," "immediate," and "noninferential." This means that to know how things are in the world on the basis of experience, you don't need to engage in any kind of thought or reasoning; perception is therefore not just a route to knowledge, but a *basic* route to knowledge. Seeing a fire in the room is enough to know that there is a fire in the room. You don't need to run through anything like the following chain of reasoning: "There are flames on the curtains, flames usually mean fire, therefore the curtains are on fire." Extrasensory perceptual knowledge is like ordinary sensory perceptual knowledge in respect of being direct, immediate, and noninferential. Johnny Smith doesn't need to engage in any kind of thought or reasoning to know that there is a fire in the girl's bedroom: clairvoyantly seeing a fire in the room is enough to know that there is a fire in the room. What is distinctive about ESP is therefore that it gives us direct, immediate, noninferential knowledge about the world that we cannot get by ordinary sensory means.

"What It Is Like"

In the case of normal sensory perception, our perceptual experiences have a distinctive "phenomenological character": there is "something that it is like" to have experiences of that kind, and "what it is like" varies from one experience to another. The phenomenological character of experience in turn appears to be related to the role of experience in prompting us to form beliefs about the world on the basis of experience.

Accounting for the phenomenological character of experience is one of the enduring questions in philosophy and psychology. There is a strong reductivist tendency in much modern philosophy and psychology. On this view, processes in the brain are sufficient to fully explain consciousness—usually because conscious experiences are simply identified with these brain processes. Others, however, are more pessimistic of science's ability to explain consciousness, and think that there is something deeply mysterious about how purely physical processes in a lump of gray matter could give rise to something like conscious experience. For instance, in *The Mind and Its Place in Nature*, C. D. Broad argues that consciousness is not reducible to physical processes in the brain, but "emerges" from them.[6] Interestingly, although Broad was not entirely certain about whether conscious subjects could survive the death of their bodies, unusually the prospect did not particularly appeal to him: "I think I may say that for my part I should be slightly more annoyed than surprised if I should find myself in some sense persisting immediately after the death of my present body. One can only wait and see, or alternatively (which is no less likely) wait and not see."[7] Broad was worried that the afterlife might be too similar to life on Earth: "If death be not the end, then one is confined for all sempiternity in what looks unpleasantly like a prison or a lunatic-asylum, from which there is in principle no escape."[8]

The conscious feel of normal sensory experiences involves what the psychologist and philosopher William James described as their special "tang."[9] James's idea is that "what it is like" to have a sensory experience is, in part, for it to appear to us that the experience is an experience *of* a reality that is independent of us—that experience puts us "into contact" with the world. Perceptual experiences differ in this respect with imagination and belief, modes of thought that lack this distinctive sensational tang. Consider the difference between seeing a tree, imagining seeing a tree ("seeing a tree with the mind's eye"), and merely thinking more abstractly about a tree. Of course, the feeling of "perceptual presence" can be misleading. Hallucinations at least *seem* to present us with an independently existing world, even if they do not—as in the case of Max Renn's (James Woods) vivid hallucinations in *Videodrome* (1983), Bill Lee's (Peter Weller) drug-induced hallucinations in *Naked Lunch* (1991), and Allegra Geller (Jennifer Jason Leigh) and Ted Pikul's (Jude Law) experiences in the virtual reality game in *eXistenZ* (1999).

The peculiar tang of reality that is characteristic of our perceptual experiences is notoriously difficult to describe in detail. The eighteenth-century Scottish philosopher David Hume tried to account for it in terms of the greater "force" and "vivacity" of our perceptual experiences over our imaginings.[10] But as has often been pointed out, perceptual experiences are not always forceful or vivacious (for instance, when you wake up in the morning), and conversely, imaginings can be very forceful and vivacious (as when you have very vivid daydreams). A more complicated account of the differences between perceptual experiences and imaginings will need to appeal to something like differences in determinacy of content (perceptual experiences contain a wealth of information that is normally lacking from imaginings), consistency (perceptual experiences are orderly and coherent in a way that, say, a vivid daydream need not be), and the dependence of imaginings on voluntary control (imagining is normally something that we decide to do, whereas perception is something that happens to us).[11]

But whatever exactly the differences between perception and imagination are, if ESP is to count as genuine *perception*, then it should have a phenomenological character that is more like normal sensory perception than imagination or thought. As it happens, many alleged cases of ESP turn out to lack distinctively perceptual phenomenology—the peculiar tang of reality—and for this reason it has sometimes been suggested that it is misleading to call ESP extrasensory *perception* at all. In many cases, the best candidates for having psychic abilities do not realize at the time that they are having extrasensory experiences; only afterward, in light of the way that events pan out, do they take what they initially thought of as idle thoughts, guesses, or hunches to be premonitions. In this respect, subjects who are claimed to have extrasensory perception are similar to patients with an actual clinical condition called blindsight, which results from damage to certain regions of the brain associated with visual perception. Blindsighted subjects claim to have no visual awareness of objects in parts of the visual field, but when prompted to make guesses about the properties of presented stimuli (for example, whether a shape is an *X* or an *O*) perform significantly above chance.

The extrasensory experiences of many of Cronenberg's characters lead them to form beliefs about spatially distant events, the past, the future, and the mental states of others—for instance, when Johnny Smith uses his experience of events at the scene of a murder to identify policeman Frank Dodd (Nicholas Campbell) as "the Castle Rock killer." As such, these experiences often appear to have a similar phenomenological character to genuine perceptual experiences. Indeed if anything, the extrasensory experiences Cronenberg depicts often appear to have a kind of "hyperreality"; they appear almost more real than real. As Cronenberg scholar William Beard points out, in Johnny Smith's vision of the burning house in the *Dead Zone*, "the images are extraordinarily colorful and violent, especially compared to the drabness of the surrounding 'real-life' scenes."[12]

Power and Responsibility

Perceptual experience is a source of knowledge about the world, and knowledge about the world is valuable because of what it allows us to do. Perceptual experience allows us to successfully navigate the world: from relevantly mundane tasks, like walking across a room without bumping into any of the furniture, to more complicated tasks, like finding the leader of the Ripe Project or assassinating a future Hitler. Clearly, extrasensory perceptual abilities would be incredibly useful abilities to possess: ordinary perceptual abilities might enable someone to save a boy when he has actually fallen through the ice, so long as the person is on hand and able to swim in the freezing water, but Johnny Smith's precognitive abilities enable him to stop the boy from falling through the ice before it happens, without the injuries Johnny sustained in the car crash making any difference to his ability to influence the outcome.

Yet one of the recurring themes in Cronenberg's work is also the darker side of paranormal abilities. Extrasensory perception is often called "the gift," but as Johnny Smith complains, it can also be a curse.

Telepathic experiences can obviously be disturbing for the people whose minds are read—and not only when their heads are made to explode. Telepathic experiences can be a way of communicating, as they are between the subjects in Stringfellow's experiments in *Stereo*, and among the benign group of scanners led by Kim Obrist. But reading someone else's mind can also be a form of violation, or "mental rape."[13] The contents of our own minds are often thought to be private. We enjoy "privileged access" to them, and can let other people know what we are thinking if we choose to tell them—but if we do not choose to tell anyone, then no one else need know. Telepathy, however, breaks down the boundaries between individual subjects. The belief that others can know your thoughts is one of the most profoundly terrifying symptoms of paranoid schizophrenia.[14] Schizophrenics' beliefs that others can read their minds are delusional; but if telepathy is possible, then people could know exactly what you are thinking without your telling them. The prospect of others knowing all the thoughts that pass through your mind minute by minute is a horrifying one. For this reason, one of the subjects in *Stereo* develops an "intrusion avoidance device," creating a "false self" that she projects telepathically through her thoughts. The danger of this, of course, is that the subject becomes schizophrenic, and eventually her true self "begins to suffocate."

With Cronenberg, the master of "body horror," extrasensory experiences are often also painful and disturbing for the subjects who have them. In

Stereo, the telepathic experience is described as "likely to be an overwhelming, and extremely exhausting one, verging on pain and hallucination." This is why two of the subjects commit suicide and another self-harms in a peculiarly disturbing fashion (with an electric drill). In *Scanners*, when Dr. Ruth finds Cameron Vale—the person who will eventually kill Revok and stop the Ripe Project—Vale is thirty-five years old, "a derelict . . . a piece of human junk" who is unable to lead a normal life because of the psychic abilities that he is unable to control. But even when he is able to control his abilities, the scanning process is "usually a painful one, sometimes resulting in nosebleeds, earaches, stomach cramps, nausea." Similarly, in *The Dead Zone*, Johnny's experiences are also physically draining and painful, making him feel as though he is "dying inside."

Paranormal powers are not only painful and disturbing but also place great responsibilities on the people who have them. Cameron Vale is the only person who is able to stop his brother Darryl Revok. But it is ultimately at the expense of his own body, which is destroyed in the final showdown with Revok when Vale transfers himself into Revok's body—raising interesting questions about personal identity that Cronenberg later explored in more detail in *The Fly* (1986). Johnny Smith also feels the heavy weight of responsibility that his gift places on him. Early on, the usually sweet, caring, dutiful teacher vindictively lashes out at a journalist harassing him after saving the nurse's daughter from the house fire: "What do you want to know? You want to know the future? You want to know if you're going to die, is that it? You're going to die, I'm going to die. You want to know if you're going to die tomorrow—is that right? You want to know why your sister killed herself?"

But later, Johnny becomes more considered in the use of his powers. Seeing into the future of presidential candidate Greg Stillson presents Johnny with an acute ethical dilemma. Should he kill Stillson to avert nuclear Armageddon? As he asks Dr. Weizak: "If you could go back in time to Germany, before Hitler came to power, knowing what you know now, would you kill him?" The question is a classic ethical dilemma: are actions right in virtue of their consequences, or are there some actions that are morally wrong whatever their outcome? Smith decides to kill Stillson, and also at the expense of his own body—although for Smith, unlike for Vale, there is no life after his body's destruction.

Skepticism about the Paranormal

Belief in paranormal activity among the general public is still relatively widespread. For instance, a poll of Americans in 1991 found that around 25 percent reported having had telepathic experiences, about the same again claimed to believe in the existence of ghosts, and around 10 percent reported having been in the presence of a ghost.[15] (And this is to say nothing about the prevalence of religious beliefs and reports of religious experiences, which might be thought of as being no less paranormal.)

However, reports of paranormal phenomena are typically greeted with skepticism by the scientific community. The evidence for the existence of paranormal occurrences is strongly disputed. For instance, the results of S. G. Soal's studies cited by Broad were never particularly convincing—the two subjects (Mr. Shackleton and Mrs. Stewart) who were reported to have performed above chance on the card-guessing experiments hadn't correctly guessed the card they were trying to identify, but only its immediate predecessor or immediate successor. These studies were fatally undermined, however, when they were subsequently shown to be fraudulent.[16]

An interesting debunking explanation of seemingly paranormal experiences suggested by psychologist Susan Blackmore is that many allegedly extrasensory experiences are actually just illusory experiences, of the kind that perfectly normal subjects have when their cognitive apparatus misfires because of the context in which it is used—as when we look at the famous Müller-Lyer illusion, in which horizontal lines of equal length are made to appear different in length by adding arrows to the end.

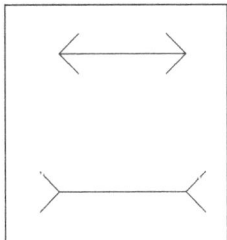

Blackmore's suggestion is that ostensibly psychic experiences are also illusory experiences, but specifically illusory experiences in which subjects represent the existence of causal links where in fact there are none: for instance, a causal link between a dream of someone's death and the event of their dying.[17]

Despite the interest that the paranormal provoked in the latter part of the nineteenth century and first half of the twentieth century, and although the issue of consciousness remains highly controversial and widely discussed, there is currently little philosophical interest in the paranormal. This is perhaps because many contemporary philosophers are naturalists, who believe that the world is, at least roughly, as it is described by our best scientific theories.

The Paranormal in Philosophical Thought Experiments

However, even if philosophers do not believe in the *actual* existence of paranormal phenomena, they often appeal to the *possibility* of paranormal phenomena in thought experiments designed to investigate key concepts. Reflection on how the world would have to be if ESP existed can be a useful way of thinking about how the world actually is.

In one famous example, philosopher Laurence BonJour uses the hypothetical case of a reliable clairvoyant, Norman, to investigate our concept of "epistemic justification": the justification that we have for believing certain things and disbelieving others, which is closely connected to the concept of "knowledge."[18] Although Norman is a perfectly reliable clairvoyant, he has absolutely no reason to believe that he possesses any clairvoyant powers. Beliefs occasionally "pop into" his head as if from nowhere, but Norman does not know why and has never himself checked whether any of these beliefs are in fact true. Although Norman forms *true* beliefs about the world on the basis of his clairvoyant powers, many people have the intuition that Norman's beliefs are not *justified*—that he does not have good reasons to hold these beliefs. BonJour uses this to argue for an "internalist" theory of justification, according to which beliefs are not justified simply by virtue of being produced by reliable means: there also needs to be a subjectively available reason to believe that the belief is justified. In Norman's case, his beliefs would be justified only if he possessed good reasons for trusting his psychic abilities.

The concept of justification plays a key role in philosophical theories of knowledge. According to the traditional philosophical account of knowledge, knowledge is justified true belief: in order to know that something is the case, you must believe it, your belief must be true, and your belief must be justified. Famous examples from philosopher Edmund Gettier show that justified true belief is not sufficient for something to count as knowledge.[19] In one of Gettier's examples, Smith and Jones are at an interview. Smith is justified in believing that Jones will get the job, because he has it on good authority that he will. He is also justified in believing that Jones has ten coins in his pocket, because he has seen Jones count the coins in his pocket. He is therefore justified, by performing a simple inference, in believing that the man who will get the job has ten coins in his pocket. But suppose, now, that Jones does not get the job, but Smith does: the person who told Smith that Jones would get the job was in a good position to know (perhaps he was on the hiring committee), but he got it wrong. Moreover, suppose that Smith in fact also has ten coins in his pocket. Then Smith's belief that the man who will get the job has ten coins in his pocket is a justified, true belief—but, intuitively at least, it is not knowledge.

Although Gettier's examples show that justification is not *sufficient* for knowledge, it is often thought that justification is at least *necessary:* something *more* than justified true belief might be required, but for a belief to count as knowledge it must at least be justified and true. If this is right, then the internalist theory of justification that BonJour uses the Norman example to support will entail an internalist theory of knowledge: there will have to be some reason that is available to the subject to think that his or her belief *is* knowledge. Internalist views of justification and knowledge have a lot of intuitive appeal, but as critics point out, they appear to set the standards for justification and knowledge very high. For instance, does Johnny Smith need to have good reasons to believe that his otherwise seemingly mysterious abilities are reliable? Does he need to understand how precognition is possible before he is justified in believing that his visions of the future represent events that will really happen? Indeed, do any of us need to have good reasons to believe that beliefs formed on the basis of ordinary sensory perception, inference, testimony, or memory are justified? After all, what reason do we have for thinking that our experiences of the world present the world as it really is? Couldn't our experiences of the world be exactly as they are, and yet the world not exist at all? These are enduring philosophical questions and remain widely debated. So even if the kind of parapsychological phenomena depicted in Cronenberg's films do not actually occur, imagining a world in which they do is nevertheless of considerable philosophical importance.

Notes

1. Henry Sidgwick, the society's first president, was Knightbridge Professor of Moral Philosophy at Cambridge from 1883 to 1900 and is well known for his writings on moral philosophy. William James, brother of the novelist Henry James, was professor of philosophy and psychology at Harvard. Arthur Balfour was the British prime minister from 1902 to 1905, and a philosopher and theologian. Henri Bergson, one of the most influential French philosophers of the late nineteenth and early twentieth centuries, won the Nobel Prize for Literature in 1927. H. H. Price was Wykeham Professor of Logic at Oxford from 1935 to 1959 and is well known for his work on perception. C. D. Broad was one of Sidgwick's successors as Knightbridge Professor of Moral Philosophy at Cambridge, from 1933 to 1953. For details, see the Society for Psychical Research's website, http://www.spr.ac.uk/expcms/.

2. C. D. Broad, *Lectures on Psychical Research* (London: Routledge, Kegan and Paul, 1962).

3. C. D. Broad, "The Experimental Establishment of Telepathic Precognition," *Philosophy* 19 (1944): 261–75.

4. C. D. Broad, "The Relevance of Psychical Research to Philosophy," *Philosophy* 24 (1949): 291–309.

5. A. J. Ayer, *The Problem of Knowledge* (Harmondsworth: Penguin, 1956).

6. C. D. Broad, *The Mind and Its Place in Nature* (London: Routledge, Kegan and Paul, 1925).

7. Broad, *Lectures on Psychical Research*, 430.

8. Broad, *Lectures on Psychical Research*, x.

9. William James, *The Principles of Psychology* (New York: Dover, 1950), ii, 7.

10. David Hume, *A Treatise Concerning Human Understanding*, ed. D. F. Norton and M. Norton (Oxford: Oxford University Press, 2000).

11. See, for example, Colin McGinn, *Mindsight: Image, Dream, Meaning* (Cambridge, Mass.: Harvard University Press, 2004).

12. William Beard, *The Artist as Monster: The Cinema of David Cronenberg* (Toronto: University of Toronto Press, 2006), 177.

13. Beard, *The Artist as Monster*, 101.

14. For an excellent introduction, see Richard P. Bentall, *Madness Explained: Psychosis and Human Nature* (London: Penguin, 2004).

15. G. H. Gallup and F. Newport, "Belief in Paranormal Phenomena among Adult Americans," *Skeptical Inquirer* 15 (1991): 137–46.

16. James E. Alcock, *Parapsychology: Science or Magic?* (Oxford: Pergamon, 1981).

17. Susan Blackmore, "Psychic Experiences: Psychic Illusions," *Skeptical Inquirer* 16 (1992): 367–76.

18. Laurence BonJour, "Externalist Theories of Empirical Knowledge," *Midwest Studies in Philosophy* 5 (1980): 53–74.

19. Edmund Gettier, "Is Justified True Belief Knowledge?" *Analysis* 23 (1963): 121–23.

Deception and Disorder
Unraveling Cronenberg's Divided Minds

Simon Riches

Amid a growing sense of paranoia and fear, Tom Stall (Viggo Mortensen) sprints back from work to save his wife and children from the horror that might ensue when ruthless gangster Carl Fogarty (Ed Harris) and his henchmen arrive at his home. On his arrival, he realizes his panic is a false alarm triggered by the events from a day earlier when he apprehended two mobsters at his diner, and he remarks, with plausible exasperation, "I think I'm losing my mind." By this point in the story, viewers of *A History of Violence* (2005) can already see that a strange tale of double identity is unfolding. Seemingly unbeknownst to Tom himself, at least initially (and insofar as we can refer to "himself," given the double identity), he is actually a man named Joey Cusack, a violent gangster apparently quite unlike family man Tom Stall. Tom's return home leads in to a pivotal scene in which he seems to switch between his two identities. When his son Jack (Ashton Holmes) asks what he means by "losing his mind," Tom rationalizes his apparent paranoia: "Some mob guys showed up at the diner," he explains. "They saw me on TV ... and they came by to take a look at me. ... They thought they knew me. They thought I was somebody else," he says, laughing. Through this sequence Tom appears authentic, and his son smiles. "That's weird," Jack says, and Tom agrees; but then Tom's voice goes flat and his demeanor changes. Something is occurring to him: the Joey Cusack in him begins to emerge. But then it quickly recedes when Jack suggests that perhaps "they don't like this guy they think you are." Tom looks resigned, leaning back in his chair. "Apparently not," he replies. For Tom, the confusion of being targeted by gangsters rankles: "That's ... that's the losing my mind part," he tells Jack. "I mean ... I was down at work, and, y'know, suddenly I thought maybe ... maybe ... they'd come looking around. Y'know?" Self-deprecatingly, Tom then observes the apparent clichéd absurdity of a so-called hero returning to save the family. But when Jack asks his father, "*What if you're right?*" this triggers Joey Cusack's full emergence. From the viewers' perspective, we have been watching Tom, looking down, deep in thought, but we are now faced with Joey, who looks up and says without hesitation and with a cold, flat conviction, "Then we deal with it." Joey cocks his gun; Jack gulps and looks intimidated, clearly shocked by his father.

Tom Stall's phrase "losing my mind" can evoke stereotypical and caricatured ideas of madness. But Tom does not resemble the manic and crazed high-rise occupants in *Shivers* (1975), and he has not lost his grip on reality like *Dead Ringers*' (1988) Mantle twins (Jeremy Irons) and *Videodrome*'s (1983) Max Renn (James Woods). His identity crisis is subtle by comparison and occurs in a context of foreboding that recalls *High Noon* (1952). On the surface he appears to be the all-American family man, but this mask of convention allows Cronenberg to exploit two prevalent themes that occur throughout much of his work: first, the idea that the way things appear can be deceptive; and second, the idea that the conventions and categories we use in our everyday lives may be highly dubious or ill defined. If we think about Tom Stall's predicament in the wider context of Cronenberg's work as a whole, it is clear that Cronenberg's depiction of rationality and irrationality has evolved. His later work in particular highlights how unclear the boundary between rationality and irrationality may be in certain cases, and gives us great cause to reflect on what this means.

In this chapter I look at Cronenberg's changing approach to these issues and suggest that central to the development of his ideas is a shift in perspective, from madness initially being tied to an individual's *physical* or *bodily* identity and its gory manifestations, to a later focus on the psychological unraveling of his characters' *inner* worlds. This latter concern has enabled Cronenberg to engage with philosophical questions about the boundary between mental disorder and mental order in more sophisticated ways, and allowed him to develop the idea that the distinction between losing one's mind and keeping it—between mental disorder and mental order—can be highly unclear. This is especially so in the context of Cronenberg's perennial concern that our perception and understanding of everything from ourselves to the objects in the world around us may be subject to various forces of deception.

From Body Horror to Psychological Horror

With his shocking imagery and grotesque mutations, Cronenberg has come to be practically synonymous with the term "body horror." However, two driving forces underlying Cronenberg's brand of body horror have gradually subsided. First, early Cronenberg flaunted the familiar idea that the scientist—that paradigm of rationality—is actually masking some underlying mental instability, *Dead Ringers'* Mantle twins being a prime example. Second, early Cronenberg's idea of "madness" was depicted stereotypically; often sensationalist and overblown, drawn from Victorian asylum horror stories, it was the stigmatizing depiction of madness that contemporary mental health practitioners wish to resist.[1] We see this kind of depiction in the decline of Seth Brundle (Jeff Goldblum) in *The Fly* (1986) and in the raving lunacy of the zombielike high-rise inhabitants of *Shivers*.[2] Of course, these two themes combine in highly entertaining ways. Characteristically, freak accidents or the mad scientist's antics cause mayhem. In certain cases, such as *The Fly* and *Rabid* (1977), changes in bodily identity lead immediately to changes in behavior, and we see this represented to horrifying effect. The body horror films were about physical identity, and because of this, a certain depiction of madness was generated. Perhaps consideration of the stereotypical idea of madness naturally leads us to think of the physical: to behavioral and observable manifestations, where madness is defined by the "mad" acts of the individual. But as a depiction of insanity, this was extreme and caricatured.[3]

The shift toward focusing on psychological, rather than bodily, phenomena came gradually. Early films, like *Stereo* (1969), *Scanners* (1981), and *The Dead Zone* (1983), deal with individuals experiencing psychological abnormalities. Highlighting extrasensory perceptual capacities, these films represent an idiosyncratic element of Cronenberg's interest in the mental: although such capacities are depicted as emotionally challenging for the bearers, viewers' empathy for these characters suffers in part because without possessing extrasensory perception ourselves we do not identify with them. The "realist" development embodied in more character-based studies like *M. Butterfly* (1993), *Spider* (2002), *A History of Violence*, and *Eastern Promises* (2007) signaled a pause in the phase of mad scientists and crazed monsters while depicting a more subtle kind of mental unraveling. Without wholly rejecting his distinctive body horror (given certain scenes in *A History of Violence* and *Eastern Promises*), these films are more unsettling because this time we can identify with the emotional turmoil. We can understand the characters' crises because they appear to resemble the crises of ordinary people. However, they are also more unsettling because of the way that Cronenberg shows how notions of deception can be tied in with our own identity. With various forces of deception continually undercutting the apparent newfound realism, Cronenberg makes us question the deepest ideas we have about who we are.

Minds, Machines, and Forces of Deception

The idea that things might not be as they appear has featured prominently in the history of philosophy. Subjecting himself to intense skeptical doubt, seventeenth-century French philosopher René Descartes considered how we know that the objects of our experience are genuine. This philosophical question is especially important given our susceptibility to visual illusions and reasoning fallacies, and—as Descartes observed—the apparent reality of our dreams.[4] Perhaps it is possible, as Descartes thought, that we are being deceived in some way. For instance, how do we know we are not dreaming? If we can be the victims of deception from an external force or even from our own fallible minds, then this is going to have an important bearing on how we conceive of our beliefs and of ourselves.

Spider's (Ralph Fiennes) hallucinatory and delusional experiences are characteristically pathologized as symptoms of psychosis.[5] Hallucinations carry philosophical interest by involving perception of objects that supposedly are not present or events that are not actually occurring. This philosophical interest involves consideration of the nature of our perceived reality. Strange occurrences might make us ask whether an event is really happening or whether our brain (or even something external to ourselves) is deceiving us. Cronenberg's interest in psychoanalytic thought might lead one to speculate that certain psychic forces—coupled with cognitive malfunctioning—are shaping Spider's perception of reality.

If these kinds of mistrusted mental capacities are to count as a case of deception, then it is clear that they are far removed from straightforward cases of interpersonal deception (like Nikolai's [Viggo Mortensen] deception as an undercover FSB agent in *Eastern Promises*). However, the role of deception is complicated even further if it appears that "reality" itself is being distorted by some external agent.

In *Videodrome* and *eXistenZ* (1999), Cronenberg presents a disorienting occurrence that may be phenomenally indistinguishable from hallucinatory experience, although arguably the prime agent of deception is no longer his characters' minds in any straightforward sense, but machines that are implementing programs and potentially taking over their minds. (Note that this is not necessarily the case, given the way Cronenberg retains the uncertainty over the distinction between minds and machines.) Although game designer Allegra Geller (Jennifer Jason Leigh) and accomplice Ted Pikul (Jude Law) appear to be willingly drawn into the dangerous virtual reality of the eXistenZ video game trial, by the final scene they—like the viewers—appear unsure whether the game is over. This uncertain scenario makes them—and the viewers—wonder where virtual reality ends and genuine reality begins; such is the deep psychological confusion created by the multilayered game-within-a-game deception. In a moment of frank honesty at the Trout Farm, Pikul expresses their traumatizing predicament aptly: "I don't like it here. I don't know what's going on. We're both stumbling around together in this unformed world, whose rules and objectives are largely unknown, seemingly indecipherable, or even possibly nonexistent, always on the verge of being killed by forces we don't understand." In a very similar way, Max Renn's shattering discovery that Videodrome is more than a TV show appears to bring about the disintegration of his inner world. But the important point is that to understand how much of his experience is brought about by distortions of reality, and how much is brought about by deceptive forces controlling his mind, we really need to know how much of what he perceives around him is genuine and how much is generated by the mysterious, apparently reality-distorting force of Videodrome. Has Renn lost his mind and started to hallucinate, perhaps caused by the potentially mind-altering videocassette playing in his stomach feeding him otherworldly perceptual experiences of events that are not actually occurring in reality? Or is the videocassette controlling events in reality? If the distinction between ordinary perceptual experiences and hallucination is unclear—as it inevitably will be in the world of Videodrome—one cannot make reliable assessments of Renn's mental state. The only thing we can be sure of is that Cronenberg wants to blur the distinction between fiction and reality, and show how the various forces of deception may cause us to question our experience.[6]

In these films, Cronenberg gives us reason to doubt even the most basic forms of perceptual experience. The result is that in these cases, we have problems even characterizing and evaluating hallucinations because we are so unclear on what is "real." However, it might be possible to make some progress with this issue by considering the underlying causes of hallucination for cases that do not raise such difficult questions about the nature of reality. Establishing clear causal links for hallucinations can be difficult, but studies have shown them to be strongly related to trauma.[7] To take some examples from Cronenberg: after unintentionally killing his wife, Bill Lee (Peter Weller) in *Naked Lunch* (1991) enters the seemingly imaginary world of Interzone. However, the key question here is: Is Interzone real, or a hallucination brought on by a combination of drugs and the traumatic death of his wife? And the problem is, we do not know. With Spider, the traumatic causes of his hallucinations are more straightforward. With no indication of virtual realities or substance use, we are more certain that his hallucinations are caused by a trauma, which has resulted in symptoms of psychosis. Spider's memories and perceptions are deeply shaped by traumatic experience, so while the radical skepticism in *eXistenZ* and *Videodrome* blurs the line between the external forces of deception and the deceptive force of our own minds, Spider shows us the possibility that the hallucinatory experience may be a perception of reality framed by previous experiences. In Spider's case, Cronenberg wants to show that hallucinations are not necessarily meaningless. As clinical psychologist Richard Bentall writes, "The unusual beliefs and experiences of psychiatric patients all seem to reflect preoccupations about the position of the self in the social universe."[8] We see this as Spider's story unfolds. Combining the inner world of the self with the social universe is key to Cronenberg's work.

The theme of "deception" constantly makes us question what is real and what is genuine. Cronenberg's sympathetic depiction of Spider reveals that pathologizing anomalous experience, including hallucination, must be grounded in certain assumptions about our reality; about what we count as real and about what we count as unreal, and about what that distinction consists in. Cronenberg's work raises issues over the contingency of the category of mental disorder by blurring the boundaries between apparent distinctions like minds and machines, and appearance and reality, and suggests that thinking of hallucinations as "disorders" is not as straightforward as it first seems. In this context it is interesting to observe that one of the most powerful themes in his work is the idea that the ultimate agents of deception can be ourselves.

From Deception to Self-Deception

The general theme of straightforward deception pervades the early part of *A History of Violence*. Tom Stall, proprietor of a small-town diner, deceives his family and local townspeople about his life history. This deception is first indicated early on when the tranquil, idyllic small-town atmosphere is shattered by the arrival of two threatening gangsters from out of town. The clinical fashion by which Tom Stall dispatches these gangsters is our first indication of his questionable identity. But we subsequently learn that his deception runs much deeper. It seems that Tom Stall deceives himself.

Superficial deceptions similarly mask deeper ones in *M. Butterfly*. Chinese opera singer Song Liling (John Lone) deceives French diplomat René Gallimard (Jeremy Irons) into believing that Song is a woman during their twenty-year affair; Song convinces him that their love affair is genuine, when in fact Song is a spy for the Chinese government and is using Gallimard to solicit information.[9] The wave of deception continues as Song fakes pregnancy, maintaining her dishonesty by claiming that it is traditional for women to go away during pregnancy and childbirth, and returns with a child she claims is Gallimard's son. Despite Gallimard's cultural arrogance, Song's deception relies—rather ironically—on exploiting Gallimard's cultural ignorance. But the real deception here relates directly to Gallimard. It is staggering to think that Song could actually deceive his lover about his biological sex. It is more plausible to think that, like Stall, Gallimard deceives himself. Evidently, Gallimard walks a fine line between fantasy and reality. He is deeply charmed by Song, even transfixed by her. He adopts Chinese customs and decor even after leaving China, and he has an idolized conception of the Oriental woman. But his willingness to accept Song's reasons for remaining clothed when they sleep together ("Modesty is so important to the Chinese," she explains, unconvincingly) is at odds with other aspects of his character. Clearly Gallimard likes being in control. While picnicking, Song inquires, "René, there is a mystery you must clarify for me. . . . With your pick of Western women, why did you pick a poor Chinese with a chest like a boy?" Smiling, Gallimard replies, "Not like a boy, like a girl . . . like a young, innocent schoolgirl . . . waiting for her lessons." Observing this scene, we feel that in some sense Gallimard must know that Song is male, and yet he seems so wrapped up in denial. The conflict suggests a case of self-deception.

Self-deception generates a philosophical puzzle, partly because it is hard to understand what is occurring in such cases. Contemporary philosopher Jonathan Glover writes that in self-deception, "we adopt a conscious strategy of concealing certain things from ourselves."[10] More formally construed, philosophers claim that in self-deception a person holds one belief but also concurrently holds another belief that contradicts that first belief. One might argue that Stall and Gallimard are doing something along these lines. But if self-deception is possible in this sense, then it is philosophically puzzling because it appears paradoxical. After all, how can we withhold information from, or even lie to, ourselves? Intuitively, it just does not seem possible. Philosophers have tried to unravel the paradox in various ways: Oxford philosopher David Pears takes this idea of concealment or forgetting very literally;[11] American philosopher Alfred Mele denies that the two traditional conditions are necessary for self-deception, and claims that self-deceivers just believe what they want to believe;[12] but a further (and not uncontroversial) way of understanding self-deception avoids the paradox by relinquishing the conventional idea that there is unity to human consciousness. Instead, this theory argues that we should regard minds as "divided." Just as Cronenberg wishes to threaten the categories of appearances and reality, this is another disunity that a certain reading of his work suggests he might endorse.

Divided Minds

There have been numerous findings that seem to support the broad conclusion that given the right circumstances, "ordinary" people can be driven to evils.[13] How might we explain this phenomenon? Various thinkers have composed theories that attempt to divide or compartmentalize the mind. Notably, ancient Greek philosopher Plato conceived of a tripartite self, according to which reason drives personality and controls desires, giving us a fundamental basis in rationality.[14] Viennese founder of psychoanalysis Sigmund Freud inverted Plato's tripartite structure. For Freud, reason is the weakest part of the self. Instead, we are an energy system driven by unconscious instincts. These fundamentally irrational psychic energies are characterized as "the id." The id is an impulsive, behavior-shaping bundle of instincts directed at gaining pleasure and avoiding pain. Freud called the id "a cauldron of seething excitations."[15]

American philosopher Donald Davidson uses a weaker notion of divided minds (without definite parts or faculties) specifically to explain self-deception. He writes, "People can and do sometimes keep closely related but opposing beliefs apart. To this extent we must accept the idea that there can be boundaries between parts of the mind."[16] Elsewhere he argues, "Only by partitioning the mind does it seem possible to explain how a thought or impulse can cause another to which it bears no rational relation."[17] There is some controversy over this idea, as Davidson himself acknowledges: "The idea that the mind can be partitioned at all has often been held to be unintelligible, since it seems to require that thoughts and desires and even actions be attributed to something less than, and therefore distinct from, the whole person."[18] Contemporary thinkers in the psychoanalytic tradition are careful as to how such mental structures should be understood. According to psychotherapists Anthony Bateman and Jeremy Holmes, Freud's structural model of the id, ego, and superego is nowadays best understood in terms of "*functions*, rather than structural entities, as metaphors for psychological configuration."[19] They also write: "Contemporary psychoanalysis still uses topographical concepts but has divested itself of their anatomical overtones, just as Freud did, by talking about each part of the mind as a 'system'—the 'system unconscious,' the 'system preconscious,' etc. This enables a smooth transition to the 'structural model' . . . which is primarily concerned with the functions of the different parts of the mind."[20]

In terms of self-deception, the broad idea here is that by positing mental partitioning, we can gain paradox-free understanding of how it is possible to intentionally and concurrently hold a belief and its contrary. In this respect, Glover writes that "one way of eliminating the paradoxical element of self-deception would be to treat the self-deceiver as really being two people, one consciously deceiving the other."[21] As a lighthearted example, we might get a more vivid sense of Glover's metaphorical description by thinking of the unsettling way the Mantle twins are depicted in *Dead Ringers,* which gives us a rather odd sense of one mind divided between two bodies. The Mantle twins appear mutually dependent, inseparable, and parasitic on each other. Even the "conjoined twins" story appears to parallel their own case. However, a more realistic example of mental division occurs in *Spider.* Powerful metaphors like the puzzle that so frustrates Spider, the fractured pieces of glass of the smashed window in the psychiatric hospital, and the spider's web in his mother's story serve to highlight the fragmentation of Spider's psychotic episodes. As a metaphor of protection, deception, and mental breakdown, the spider's web that so fascinates Spider enables him to conceal his crimes with false memories and represents his fragmentary cognitive functioning. The fragmentation carries an Oedipal attachment to his mother and antipathy for his authoritarian father;[22] and it is disorienting for viewers because it is hard to know what is real and what is an invention of Spider's mind. And this is precisely Cronenberg's aim: to disorient us from within the perspective of a delusional person. Unlike for *Videodrome*'s Max Renn and *eXistenZ*'s Allegra Geller and Ted Pikul, there is no agent of deception other than Spider's fragmentary and disordered cognitive functioning. And yet—when viewed in the broader context of Cronenberg's work—we can see that Cronenberg still wants to blur the possible agents of deception, and to blur the distinction between ordered and disordered cognitive functioning.

This fragmentation also pervades *A History of Violence.* When Cronenberg removes Tom Stall's mask of conventionality, we see a Spider in Cronenberg's archetypal everyman; because if Tom Stall's self-deception is to be explained in terms of a divided mind, then this appears to blur the distinction between his own apparent sanity and Spider's fragmentation. As a consequence, it no longer seems so clear how to draw the line between mental order and mental disorder. Removing this mask of convention raises one of the most fundamental issues in human psychology: the way social factors impinge on our understanding of psychological phenomena.

Psychology and the Social Universe

The fact that Cronenberg wants to bring context and meaning to a phenomenon like hallucination is illuminating in terms of the way he sees the mental and the social coming together. In doing so, his work highlights a tension at the heart of the discipline of psychology. Key to this tension is the distinction between objective facts and human values. Social constructionist or "critical" psychologists aim to question the basic assumptions of experimental psychology for understanding human nature. Early experimental psychology advanced from physiology, Franz Joseph Gall's craniology, and biological advancements, and aspired to a "positivistic" methodology based on the hard sciences. The logical positivists of the Vienna Circle, who denied German philosopher Immanuel Kant's transcendental idealism as unverifiable, endorsed a realism about facts (and our knowledge of those facts) that was supposedly untainted by human values.[23] However, American historian and philosopher of science Thomas Kuhn influentially disputed value-free observation of facts and highlighted the social and historical contingencies of scientific methodology. For Kuhn, "observation is theory laden."[24] The period he classified as "normal science" may be a productive time, but, throughout, scientists are constrained by the prevailing value-laden paradigm. Capitalizing on Kuhn's destabilization of the facts/values distinction, social constructionists reveal the sociocultural relativism in mainstream psychological methodology. Influenced by the European phenomenologists, they argue that participants in psychology experiments discursively construct (rather than discover) their experience. Social constructionists like Kenneth J. Gergen and Vivien Burr argue that all psychological knowledge is socioculturally specific.[25] For Burr, such value-laden observation means *our* ways of understanding are no nearer the truth than other ways. Similarly, psychologist Kurt Danziger argues that Western psychology is just one psychology among many, and further, he claims that other cultures employ psychological concepts that are untranslatable into our own.[26]

Against this theoretical background, some thinkers have argued that societal values infiltrate conceptualizations of mental disorder. French philosopher Michel Foucault claims psychological facts are morally and politically laden: mental illness replaced leprosy insofar as it allowed governments to create outcasts to institutionalize and control.[27] He argues that even the idea of madness is historically relative. Following medieval collectivism, where the church was the sole arbiter of truth, post-Enlightenment individualism "constructed" madness by conceptualizing it as the absence of reason. In the nineteenth century, influential thinkers reconceptualized (and medicalized) the same phenomena as mental "illnesses" or "disorders." In this regard, Canadian philosopher Ian Hacking argues that conceptualizations of mental illness involve a "looping effect": schizophrenia is a "moving target" (an "interactive," rather than a "natural," kind);[28] and clinical psychologist Mary Boyle has questioned the conceptualization and biological evidence of schizophrenia, highlighting differing diagnostic content throughout history.[29] Contemporary critics of the American Psychological Association's *Diagnostic and Statistical Manual of Mental Disorders,* like psychiatrist Jerome Wakefield, develop similar positions insofar as they question and analyze what underlies our *concept* of mental disorder.[30]

One broad conclusion from this literature would be to see the category of mental disorder as fluctuating in accordance with historically and socially contingent factors. Against this background it is illuminating to think about how Cronenberg is blurring the distinction between Stall and Gallimard, on the one hand, and Spider, on the other. Evidently, Spider is overtly thought-disordered, living in a halfway house in a poverty-stricken area of East London, whereas Gallimard and Stall are, in their own very different ways, successful and conventional: Gallimard is a diplomat, and Stall is the archetypical happily married family man.[31] But Cronenberg's approach here is to use these contingent social conventions to create the appearance of a clear categorical distinction, before exposing it to be just a rather superficial difference in kind.

One way he exposes this fact is with his use of irony. Like American pragmatist Richard Rorty, Cronenberg seems to endorse the idea that acknowledging this sociocultural relativism leads to an "ironist" position.[32] At times Cronenberg makes his characters' conventional lives appear almost inauthentic. In a schmaltzy early scene of *A History of Violence,* Tom is awoken by the piercing scream of his young daughter Sarah (Heidi Hayes). Walking bleary eyed into her bedroom, he asks, "Sarah, honey, what's wrong? Huh? What is it sweetie?" followed up with a soothing "Daddy's here. Daddy's here." When Sarah explains that "there were monsters," Tom reassures her: "No sweetie. There's no such thing as monsters. You were just having a bad dream." Then, highly reminiscent of Tom's entrance only moments earlier, older brother Jack enters his sister's bedroom and asks, "What's wrong, Dad?" Embodying the fatherly figure, Tom replies, "Hi kiddo, Sarah's just having a bad dream," to which Jack is very sympathetic. Jack's approach changes from just woken into a kind of protective and yet playful big-brother role. With an intake of breath and sudden playful change of facial expression he asks, "Monsters? What kind?" Sarah replies, "I don't know. They came out my closet and then they were in the shadows." Playing along, Jack responds,

"Mmm, shadow monsters. Well, they look pretty scary, but they really can't do anything, especially when the lights are on." He whispers in Sarah's ear, "They're scared of the light." Then mother Edie (Maria Bello) enters in a similar manner to the previous two, the similarity of these entrances seeming somehow to emphasize their family unity. "What happened, baby? You okay?" Edie says, and she hugs Sarah. "Sarah had a bad dream about monsters," Tom tells Edie; "I was telling her that there's no such thing as monsters." Sarah says, "I'm going to turn on my nightlight just in case," and Edie replies, "That sounds like a brilliant solution." She hugs and kisses Sarah, and the "crisis" is averted. This scene is overtly sentimental and family oriented. Young Sarah is "sweetie" and "baby" throughout; Tom Stall's bedside manner almost recalls James Stewart with Zuzu's petals in *It's a Wonderful Life* (1946). But of course, the irony is that Tom is no George Bailey. Shortly afterward, a love scene between Tom and Edie compounds the family unity, as well as the underlying dishonesty; as they lie in bed holding each other, Tom says, "I remember the moment I knew you were in love with me. I saw it in your eyes. I can still see it." Edie replies, "Of course you can. I still love you.... You are the best man I've ever known." Yet ironically she does not really know her husband at all. Their family life is a lie.

Cronenberg continually depicts Stall as the everyman while, concurrently, toying with the idea that he is much more odd than he appears; even making the viewer doubt the authenticity of Tom Stall before he becomes aware of his own unraveling. For instance, after the diner shootout, Tom wears the exhausted facial expression we might expect of a family man in such circumstances. However, his handgun proficiency and his clinical dispatching of the mobsters gives away the fact that things are not as they appear. Later, as Tom sits in the hospital watching local news reports of his bravery, including interviews with colleagues, descriptions of Tom's character traits abound: "hero," "family man," "long-standing ties to the community," "hard working" "small business owner." Edie then arrives with a newspaper. The front page reads: "Tom Stall: Local Hero." By the time he arrives home, he has been elevated to "American hero" by a television news reporter. When interviewed, Tom is noticeably disoriented: "What I did was . . . I mean, anyone would've done that. It was just . . . it was a terrible thing. I think we'll all be better off when we get past it." The news reporter, persisting in this progression of social elevation, replies, "Yeah, but you really went beyond what the average . . ." But Tom replies, "I . . . I need to . . . I really need to be with my family." Interestingly, although the news reporter tries to identify Tom as someone who goes beyond the average, Tom straightaway reaffirms his everyman status: he denies any heroics and instead just wants to be with his family. Once inside, Tom adds, "Man it's good to be home. Hope there won't be too much of that." This whole early phase of the film is steeped in irony, from the ongoing identification of Tom Stall as a hero to Tom's moralistic reprimanding of his son for hospitalizing the school bully ("In this family we do not solve our problems by hitting people"). But shortly after the reporters have gone, Tom sees a mystery car over the road, and viewers are treated to a revealing facial expression. Perhaps the pressure to elevate him out of his everyman status, coupled with the sighting of this car, is what causes this first instance of Tom's mask slipping and of Joey's emergence.

Despite its wholly different setting, *M. Butterfly* employs irony to achieve similar ends. This is no more so than when Gallimard says to Song, quite earnestly, "I want honesty. No falseness between us." And yet deceit clearly permeates their entire relationship. In this regard, it is notable that rather than explicitly acknowledging Gallimard's homosexuality, *M. Butterfly* depicts Gallimard as believing that Song is female. Yet their sexual relationship, among other things, renders Gallimard's belief highly dubious. As viewers, we find the whole story so unbelievable, and we have good reasons to doubt Gallimard's authenticity. Can he *really* believe that Song is a woman? And yet, swept away in a fantasy of love for his "butterfly," Gallimard seems so committed to the idea.

Cronenberg presents Stall and Gallimard as outwardly upstanding members of the community, while using irony to undermine this presentation. As viewers, we feel conflicted with the outward normality and underlying uncertainty, knowing that we can be prone to fooling ourselves in similar (although perhaps less extreme) ways. Compare this to the presentation of Spider, who is banished to the psychiatric hospital and eventually returns there because his delusional episodes are uncontrollable. Inherent confusion eventually leads full circle in the tragic scenes of Spider's childhood with the matronly head of the halfway house. But if we look beyond the exterior presentation, Gallimard and Stall also hold a very odd set of beliefs, which are masked only by the socially contingent appearance of conventionality. The contents of their contradictory beliefs might be said to border on the delusional. Indeed, philosopher Robert Audi claims that Alfred Mele blurs the distinction between self-deception and delusion in his attempt to explain self-deception.[33] Tom Stall's situation leaves him somewhere between self-deception and delusion: the boundary is unclear, thus posing the question of what counts as disorder and what counts as just a normal variant of human behavior. This distinction is grounded in our sociocultural notions of what count as normal or rational beliefs and behavior, and what count as abnormal beliefs and behavior, and is a key philosophical issue underpinning the practice of psychiatry and clinical psychology.

So what are the boundaries of this concept, and how do we draw them? What is mentally disordered, and by the same token, what is mentally ordered? What kinds of beliefs count as delusional? There may be many borderline cases. For instance, sociologist Allan V. Horwitz and psychiatrist Jerome C. Wakefield argue that psychiatrists are misdiagnosing sadness as clinical depression, and biologist and new-atheist author Richard Dawkins claims that belief in God is delusional.[34] However, given our societal norms, considering religious belief as akin to delusion is not the conventional perspective, highlighting the fact that what counts as delusional may be partly a matter of our cultural conventions. As Richard Bentall writes, "The standard psychiatric response . . . is to rule the beliefs of other cultures non-delusional by definition."[35] Such social and cultural contingencies underpinned the 1960s antipsychiatry movement. American psychiatrist Thomas Szasz revealed how closely mental disorder can resemble nonpathologized religious belief. He wrote: "If you talk to God, you are praying; If God talks to you, you have schizophrenia. If the dead talk to you, you are a spiritualist; If you talk to the dead, you are a schizophrenic."[36] Under the influence of the existentialist movement, Scottish psychiatrist R. D. Laing located mental illness in social (and existential) dynamics; and American psychologist David Rosenhan blurred the sanity/insanity boundary by showing that the sane could satisfy diagnostic criteria and be institutionalized.[37] It is clear that Cronenberg is deeply interested in the way these kinds of social factors impact on our understanding of people. He shows how once the deceptive mask of convention is removed, delusions and hallucinations can closely border nonpathologies, like self-deception.

Multiple Selves and Coping Strategies

If Tom Stall's self-deception can be said to border with delusion, we might view him as exhibiting symptoms of multiple personality disorder (also known as dissociative identity disorder). However, for American philosopher Daniel C. Dennett, our understanding of multiple personality disorder is predicated on what he takes to be the mistaken notion that we have a unified "self" in the first place. Dennett claims that we are not born with "selves," but rather we construct them, much like a spider spins a web (and to similar evolutionary ends). Dennett writes:

Our fundamental tactic of self-protection, self-control, and self-definition is not spinning webs or building dams, but telling stories, and more particularly concocting and controlling the story we tell others—and ourselves—about who we are. And just as spiders don't have to think, consciously and deliberately, about how to spin their webs, and just as beavers, unlike professional human engineers, do not consciously and deliberately plan the structures they build, we (unlike *professional* human storytellers) do not consciously and deliberately figure out what narratives to tell and how to tell them. Our tales are spun, but for the most part we don't spin them; they spin us. Our human consciousness, and our narrative selfhood, is their product, not their source.[38]

Acknowledging that multiple personality disorder "almost invariably owes its existence to prolonged childhood abuse, usually sexual, and of sickening severity," Dennett explains that what those with multiple personality disorder do, "when confronted with overwhelming conflict and pain, is this: They 'leave.' They create a boundary so that the horror doesn't happen to *them*; it either happens to no one, or to some other self, better able to sustain its organization under such an onslaught."[39] So, for Dennett, much like for Davidson with his idea of divided minds, commitment to the disunity and narrative construction of selves means that there is no great psychological mystery to multiple personality disorder; rather it is a way of coping with traumatic experience that directly employs the disunity of our consciousness.

If Dennett is correct, then just as these mental boundaries can be put up, it is theoretically possible for them to come down and, of course, for further "selves" to be created. Now, it is unclear exactly where Tom Stall should be situated in terms of the differences between self-deception and multiple personality disorder, but one thing that is clear is that he is partially forced out of his identity crisis by the events that expose his lies and by subsequent family distrust. Despite his emergence as a local celebrity and town hero after the initial shootout in the diner, his wife soon becomes suspicious about his identity. In the shopping mall, gangster Carl Fogarty informs her that Tom is not who he says he is, and this creates conflict and suspicion in both Edie and Jack. Tom's confrontation with Fogarty outside his home is the final straw. Although Tom denies that he is Joey, Carl's assessment is damning: "You almost believe your own crap, don't you? You know, you're trying so hard to be this other guy. It's painful to watch." It transpires that Fogarty has taken Jack hostage, and as Edie panics and Tom comforts her,

Joey starts to emerge in Tom. Tom's expression noticeably shifts, and the tone of his voice changes; a menacing quality emerges in him as he faces up to a standoff with Fogarty and his men. As the fight ensues, and with Fogarty standing over him threatening to blow his brains out, we get the first confirmation of Tom's true identity. It is Joey who says, "I should've killed you back in Philly." Once this scene is over, the secret of Tom's true identity is out. We can see this on Jack's face. Later Edie says, "I saw Joey. I saw you turn into Joey right before my eyes. I saw a killer—the one Fogarty warned me about."

Tom Stall's sense of identity, as well as his accent, gradually shifts. The "Tom Stall" character appears to unravel, and "Joey Cusack" is acknowledged. Cronenberg depicts the partitioning of the self as consciously motivated. Tom Stall initially seems to believe his fabrication completely, but in the hospital for the second time, Tom explains to Edie how Joey formed a new identity. When questioned about having killed men, Tom explains, "Joey did . . . I didn't. Tom Stall didn't." Edie is violently sick: "Oh God. Oh my God. . . . Oh God it's really happening. What are you, like some multiple personality schizoid? It's like flipping a switch back and forth for you?" "I never expected to see Joey again," Tom explains; "I thought I killed Joey Cusack. I went out to the desert and I killed him. I spent three years becoming Tom Stall."

After Tom returns from the hospital, one or two setbacks aside, family life appears to resume: we see Tom fixing the car and, crucially, Edie covers for her husband when Sheriff Sam (Peter MacNeill) asks Tom again for the truth about his connection to the mobsters. As Sam makes his excuses and leaves, Cronenberg lingers on a family photograph lying flat on the counter. We now have a very different view of this family from the one created by the early "bad dream" scene involving the young daughter Sarah. Then, despite providing cover for Tom in front of Sam—perhaps in order to protect her family in public—Edie's anger at Tom emerges. Tom tries to console her, but she retorts angrily and sarcastically: "Fuck you, *Joey.*" They physically fight on the staircase, and Tom seemingly attempts to rape her; she initially fends him off, but when he recoils, she overtly consents to sex—which seems at times to be both intimate and violent—before, finally, Edie looks at Tom with disdain, casts him off her, and walks off upstairs leaving Tom lying alone on the staircase. This is evidently no return to the intimate happiness of the earlier love scene: afterward Tom is banished to the sofa for the night. But what is interesting here is that even during sex, Tom acted on Edie's command: he backed away. So although "violent" Joey started to reemerge, Tom was never lost. Certainly the transition between these selves appears fairly fluid throughout this part of the story.

Gallimard seems similarly situated in between self-deception and delusion. In the prison van, he asks Song, "Are you my butterfly?" Song's response is initially harshly rejecting, to which Gallimard replies with disdain, "You're nothing like my butterfly." But this is all a sham. When Song removes her clothes, René cannot face reality. "Look at me!" Song demands, but suddenly René is laughing, and replies, "I just think it is ridiculously funny that I wasted all this time on just a man." But the deception of Song then triggers the self-deception of Gallimard: "I'm not just a man," Song tells him, bringing back the intimacy between them. René touches Song's face. "The curve of that cheek," he says longingly. "I am your butterfly," Song replies. But thoughts of the betrayal emerge again in Gallimard's mind, and, tellingly, he bemoans the destruction of "the perfect lie" that he loved. As Gallimard puts it, so aptly: "I'm a man who loved a woman created by a man. Anything else simply falls short." The multilayered deception of this thought is then expounded in Gallimard's closing speech in the prison:

> I, René Gallimard, have known and been loved by the perfect woman. There is a vision of the Orient that I have. Slender women, in jiamsangs and kimonos, who die for the love of unworthy foreign devils. Who are born, and raised, to be perfect women, and take whatever punishment we give them, and spring back, strengthened by love, unconditionally. It is a vision which has become my life. My mistake was simple, and absolute. The man I loved was not worthy. He didn't deserve even a second glance. Instead, I gave him my love . . . all of my love. Love warped my judgment. Blinded my eyes. So that now, when I look into the mirror, I see nothing but . . . I have a vision of the Orient, that deep within her almond eyes, there are still women. Women willing to sacrifice themselves for the love of a man. Even a man whose love is completely without worth. Death with honor is better than life with dishonor. And so, at last, in a prison, far from China, I have found her. My name is René Gallimard. Also known as Madame Butterfly.

Gallimard then slits his throat, thus completing the Madame Butterfly fantasy. Despite his espousing precisely the imperialist conception of Oriental women for which Song mocked him on their first meeting, we now ask: Is he still the fantasist whose judgment is warped by love? At almost all times he seems to waver between recognizing and not recognizing reality.

In terms of various concepts, like self-deception and delusion, Cronenberg presents something of a spectrum of transition: Tom Stall begins deluded, but as Joey-thoughts reemerge, he passes into self-deception, and finally, he admits his true identity and relinquishes his false beliefs. The sequence of change here interestingly parallels but inverts that of *Eastern Promises:* as the undercover cop who infiltrates the London wing of the Russian Mafia, Nikolai immerses himself in this lifestyle, convincing those around him, the viewers, and seemingly himself. In his gangster "role," Nikolai likes to get his hands dirty; he revels in removing fingers and teeth from victims and seems genuinely honored by the prospect of stars. At the end, when Nikolai's identity is revealed and his mission appears to be over, he wishes to remain undercover to take over the entire organization. Nikolai's necessary initial subterfuge seems to have transitioned into a genuine identity change that inverts Tom Stall's transition. Whereas we watch Tom pushed into facing his real self, Nikolai's real identity gets absorbed in the creation of his cover character—just as Joey must have become Tom. There is even a point where Cronenberg almost playfully challenges Nikolai's mask to slip and hints at a clichéd Hollywood ending, in which romantic leads Nikolai and Anna (Naomi Watts) appear to come together around a baby in need of parents. This gateway to escaping gangster life is rejected by Nikolai. By contrast, we know that Joey Cusack stripped away his entire identity for the opportunity of family life.

The exact nature of the strategies employed by these characters suggests that there is a more practical (rather than pathologizing) stance to be considered here. It seems possible that self-deceptive strategies can sometimes constitute a natural and healthy (and perhaps even a necessary) adjustment to certain new life situations. After all, one might argue that given the complexities of modern lives, to be psychologically healthy or happy requires at least a certain amount of self-deception. If one were below average or deficient in certain ways, one may be more psychologically healthy if one were self-deceived into believing that this is not the case. These kinds of self-deceptions are things that, arguably, we all do. As Donald Davidson remarks, self-deception is often benign.[40] Contemporary philosopher Amélie Oksenberg Rorty argues that self-deception is a fact of life and that it has practical utility.[41] Evolutionary biologists have even argued that our self-deceptive strategies are adaptive insofar as they help us to deceive others.[42] So even if we consider self-deception to be epistemically irrational, there might be ways in which it has a practical utility. Perhaps it is not simply a matter of categorizing something as irrational or as a disorder. Perhaps some things that we might classify as such, like cases of self-deception, are not best captured in this way. Of course, if the distinction between self-deception and delusional thinking is no longer clear, then we might also consider the practical utility of delusions. And this reopens the issue of where we draw the line in cases where we cannot trust our perception of reality. Allegra Geller is the creator of the videogame that she enters and thus the instigator of her own deception. She then appears to be deceived by it; but how is this so? Is this a sophisticated way of conducting a "project" of self-deception? Did she create eXistenZ as a vehicle of deception and then enter it? We might think that people arrange their world in certain ways and that this is a futuristic metaphor for self-deception of this kind. This question is further complicated by whether she created the game-within-a-game transCendenZ, as a self-deception within a self-deception. We cannot be sure. Consciously motivated self-deceptive strategies may have some practical utility, but where does this leave our desire for honesty—both in ourselves and in our relationships? Freud once said that "being entirely honest with oneself is a good exercise."[43] This might be true in an ideal world. The Tom Stall mask clearly creates a better world for Joey Cusack for a while, but the problem is that his previous identity eventually catches up with him. Freud's view raises the question of whether such honesty is realistic: after all, as the tagline for *A History of Violence* says, "Everyone's Got Something to Hide."

Notes

Thanks to Sophie Archer, Fern Day, Liam Ennis, Anna Ferguson, Craig French, Poly Pantelides, Terry Rhodes, Jill Riches, Suzanne Riches, and Jasmine Synnott for comments and suggestions on earlier drafts.

1. For a good introduction to the history of asylums, see Roy Porter, *Madness: A Brief History* (Oxford: Oxford University Press, 2003). For further analysis, see Michel Foucault, *A History of Madness* (Oxon: Routledge, 2006), and Erving Goffman, *Asylums: Essays on the Social Situation of Mental Patients and Other Inmates* (London: Penguin, 1997).

2. Unlike the inhabitants of *Shivers* (who are not Hollywood zombies of the "living dead" type anyway), distinctively *"philosophical* zombies" (as they are known), which are supposedly physical replicas of humans but lacking phenomenal consciousness, have been much debated in philosophy of mind thought experiments because they raise important questions for understanding human consciousness. See Robert Kirk, "Zombies," *Stanford Encyclopedia of Philosophy,* http://plato.stanford.edu/entries/zombies.

3. On another level, it is clearly possible to argue that Cronenberg is satirizing a certain kind of genre cinema, and deliberately caricaturing insanity in an attempt to subvert the stereotype. Even with this level acknowledged, it is the general depiction of insanity that I will focus on in this chapter.

4. René Descartes, *Philosophical Writings,* trans. and ed. Elizabeth Anscombe and Peter Thomas Geach (London: Nelson's, 1975).

5. I adopt the convention of italicizing for film titles such as *Spider, eXistenZ,* and *Videodrome,* but not italicizing for Spider the character, eXistenZ the game, and Videodrome the TV show.

6. As Cronenberg's first original screenplay after *Videodrome, eXistenZ* resumed the earlier film's theme of the distinction between appearance and reality. For more on this development, see Cronenberg scholar William Beard's *The Artist as Monster: The Cinema of David Cronenberg,* rev. and expanded ed. (Toronto: University of Toronto Press, 2006), 424. Interestingly, 1999 was Hollywood's year of radical skepticism. Beard compares *eXistenZ* to a spate of films released in 1999 that deal with the skeptical scenario: *Dark City, The Matrix,* and *The Thirteenth Floor.* He makes the interesting point given the present discussion that "those films, together with a couple of other contemporary artificial-reality movies such as *Pleasantville* and *The Truman Show* (both 1998), are a striking reflection of the anxieties felt by American culture at the end of the twentieth century about the loss of authenticity and the omnipresence of simulations" (424).

7. Richard Bentall, *Madness Explained: Psychosis and Human Nature* (London: Penguin, 2004), 481–83.

8. Bentall, *Madness Explained,* 204.

9. In what follows, I interchange between "he" and "she," as and when appropriate.

10. Jonathan Glover, *I: The Philosophy and Psychology of Personal Identity* (London: Penguin, 1991), 28.

11. David Pears, "Motivated Irrationality, Freudian Theory and Cognitive Dissonance," in *Philosophical Essays on Freud,* ed. R. A. Wollheim and J. Hopkins (Cambridge: Cambridge University Press, 1982), 264–88.

12. See Alfred R. Mele, "Self-Deception," *Philosophical Quarterly* 33 (1983): 365–77, and *Irrationality: An Essay on Akrasia, Self-Deception and Self-Control* (Oxford: Oxford University Press, 1987).

13. For instance, at the Adolf Eichmann trial, which began in 1961, political theorist Hannah Arendt famously observed what she regarded as "the banality of evil." See Hannah Arendt, *Eichmann in Jerusalem: A Report on the Banality of Evil* (London: Penguin, 2006). As it appeared to Arendt, Eichmann's Nazi crimes were somehow at odds with his ordinariness, his banality. With the Nazi crimes in mind, Yale psychologist Stanley Milgram's experiments, which also began in 1961, showed how obedient ordinary people could be in the face of authority, even if this meant that they were asked to perform awful acts like severely harming others. See Stanley Milgram, *Obedience to Authority: An Experimental View* (New York: HarperPerennial, 1974).

14. Plato, *The Republic,* trans. H. D. P. Lee (London: Penguin, 1955), and *Phaedrus,* trans. R. Hackforth (Cambridge: Cambridge University Press, 1997).

15. Sigmund Freud, *New Introductory Lectures on Psychoanalysis* (New York: Norton, 1964), 73.

16. Donald Davidson, "Deception and Division," in *Problems of Rationality* (Oxford: Clarendon, 2004), 211.

17. Donald Davidson, "Paradoxes of Irrationality," in *Problems of Rationality,* 185.

18. Davidson, "Paradoxes of Irrationality," 171.

Deception and Disorder   111

19. Anthony Bateman and Jeremy Holmes, *Introduction to Psychoanalysis: Theory and Practice* (London: Routledge, 1995), 35.

20. Bateman and Holmes, *Introduction to Psychoanalysis*, 32.

21. Glover, *I: The Philosophy and Psychology of Personal Identity*, 28.

22. There is also the suggestion of Capgras syndrome, the neurological disorder in which patients hold the delusional belief that a loved one has been replaced with an imposter.

23. See Immanuel Kant, *Critique of Pure Reason*, trans. Norman Kemp Smith (London: Macmillan, 1923). For an overview of the Vienna Circle position, see A. J. Ayer, *Language, Truth and Logic* (London: Penguin, 2001).

24. Thomas Kuhn, *The Structure of Scientific Revolutions*, 3rd ed. (Chicago: University of Chicago Press, 1996). For background, see Thomas Nickles, ed., *Thomas Kuhn* (Cambridge: Cambridge University Press, 2003).

25. See Kenneth J. Gergen, "The Social Constructionist Movement in Modern Psychology," *American Psychologist* 40 (1985): 266–75; "Psychological Science in a Postmodern Context," *American Psychologist* 56 (2001): 803–13; and Vivien Burr, *Social Constructionism*, 2nd ed. (London: Routledge, 2008). For further background, see Graham Richards, *Putting Psychology in Its Place: Critical Historical Perspectives*, 3rd ed. (London: Routledge, 2010).

26. Kurt Danziger, *Constructing the Subject: Historical Origins of Psychological Research* (Cambridge: Cambridge University Press, 1998). Following Davidson ("On the Very Idea of a Conceptual Scheme," in his *Inquiries into Truth and Interpretation*, 2nd ed. [Oxford: Clarendon, 2001]), we might consider how Danziger could recognize these as "alternative" psychological concepts at all. Contemporary analytic philosophers, with their positivistic heritage, have been resistant to this development in the social sciences. See, for example, John R. Searle, *The Construction of Social Reality* (London: Penguin, 1995); and Paul Boghossian, *Fear of Knowledge: Against Relativism and Constructivism* (Oxford: Clarendon Press, 2007).

27. Michel Foucault, *Madness and Civilization: A History of Insanity in the Age of Reason* (London: Routledge, 2005).

28. Ian Hacking, "Making Up People," *London Review of Books* 28, no. 16 (2006): http://www.lrb.co.uk/v28/n16/ian-hacking/making-up-people; *The Social Construction of What?* (Cambridge, Mass.: Harvard University Press, 1999); and *Mad Travelers: Reflections on the Reality of Transient Mental Illness* (Cambridge, Mass.: Harvard University Press, 2002).

29. Mary Boyle, *Schizophrenia: A Scientific Delusion?*, 2nd ed. (London: Routledge, 2002).

30. Jerome Wakefield, "Disorder as Harmful Dysfunction: A Conceptual Critique of *DSM-III-R*'s Definition of Mental Disorder," *Psychological Review* 99 (1992): 232–47.

31. The changing way social factors impinge on our understanding of mental disorder also runs in parallel with related issues like stigma. See Charles Barber, *Comfortably Numb: How Psychiatry Is Medicating a Nation* (New York: Pantheon Books, 2008), chapter 1, for an interesting discussion, quantified in terms of Academy Award nominations, of

how, in the 1990s and later, mental illness became more accepted—and destigmatized—in Hollywood cinema. Nevertheless, Ralph Fiennes was not Oscar nominated for *Spider*.

32. Richard Rorty, *Contingency, Irony, and Solidarity* (Cambridge: Cambridge University Press, 1989).

33. Robert Audi, "Self-Deception and Self-Caused Deception: A Comment on Professor Mele," *Behavioral and Brain Sciences* 20 (1997): 104. See also Alfred Mele, "Approaching Self-Deception: How Robert Audi and I Part Company," *Consciousness and Cognition* 19 (2010): 745–50.

34. See Allan V. Horwitz and Jerome C. Wakefield, *The Loss of Sadness: How Psychiatry Transformed Normal Sorrow into Depressive Disorder* (Oxford: Oxford University Press, 2007), and Richard Dawkins, *The God Delusion* (London: Black Swan, 2007).

35. Bentall, *Madness Explained*, 133.

36. Thomas Szasz, *The Second Sin* (London: Routledge, 1974), 101.

37. See R. D. Laing, *The Divided Self: An Existential Study in Sanity and Madness* (London: Penguin, 1969), and David Rosenhan, "On Being Sane in Insane Places," *Science* 179 (1973): 250–58.

38. Daniel C. Dennett, *Consciousness Explained* (London: Penguin, 1993), 418.

39. Dennett, *Consciousness Explained*, 420.

40. Davidson, "Deception and Division," 206.

41. Amélie Oksenberg Rorty, "User-Friendly Self-Deception," *Philosophy* 69 (2009): 211–28. See also Sebastian Gardner, *Irrationality and the Philosophy of Psychoanalysis* (Cambridge: Cambridge University Press, 1993).

42. See Robert Wright, *The Moral Animal: Why We Are the Way We Are* (London: Abacus, 2009).

43. Letter to Wilhelm Fliess, October 15, 1897, in Sigmund Freud, *Origins of Psychoanalysis: Letters, Drafts and Notes to Wilhelm Fliess, 1887–1902* (Garden City, N.Y.: Doubleday, 1957).

Psychological Determinism in the Films of David Cronenberg

Daniel Shaw

One of the most fruitful ways to interpret a film philosophically is to explore what it has to say about a fundamental issue in the discipline. My intent here is to survey the films of David Cronenberg with two questions in mind: (1) Do his films reflect a deterministic view of human nature, or is he an advocate of human freedom? and (2) Does his oeuvre embody a consistent position on this issue, or does his position vary from film to film?

I begin by offering an in-depth analysis of what, to my mind, is Cronenberg's masterpiece, *Dead Ringers* (1988). Taking this as a paradigm, I then discuss several of his other films, trying to get a sense of both his overall worldview and his position on the issue of human freedom, which I believe (despite his protestations to the contrary) to be unmistakably deterministic.

Psychological determinism, in its most famous formulation by B. F. Skinner, claims that all of our actions have causal antecedents that necessitate their occurrence. This implies that humans cannot choose between real alternatives based on reasons, hence Skinner's demand that we go "beyond freedom and dignity" and recognize that we cannot be held morally responsible for our actions.[1] I will show how Cronenberg embraces determinism in most of his films, in striking contrast to one of his most recent films, *Eastern Promises* (2007), which abandons the pattern.

Psychological Determinism in *Dead Ringers*

David Cronenberg created his most subtle and haunting vision of depravity in *Dead Ringers*.[2] After his mainstream success with *The Fly* (1986), a relatively conventional exercise in sci-fi that exhibited Cronenberg's continued fascination with fantastic horror, complete with gruesome special effects, he largely abandoned such effects to explore the psychological complexities of a relationship between twin brothers who specialize in problems with female fertility. Based on a notorious case of two New York gynecologists who were found dead of drug overdoses in their (completely trashed) Upper East Side apartment, *Dead Ringers* is a stunningly realistic film that gives Hitchcock a run for his money in its relentless and terrifying depiction of characters on the brink of mental collapse.

The Mantle brothers, Elliot and Beverly (both brilliantly played by Jeremy Irons), have a thriving private practice in which they play fertility gods, working virtual miracles in enabling previously infertile women to conceive. Cronenberg chose their names carefully: the second definition of "mantle" in the American Heritage Dictionary—"anything that covers, envelops, or conceals"—suggests the deep tensions that exist underneath the brothers' competent facade. As their first names (and an old drawing in the title sequence) indicate, the two respectively embody the masculine and feminine sides of the human personality, with Elliot being a socially adept Casanova who does the public presentations and writes the scholarly articles, while his retiring brother Beverly grinds out the difficult research and deals with the personal anxieties of their most problematic patients. They enjoy an apparently satisfying symbiotic relationship, in which they share both professional and sexual triumphs, posing as each other when convenient.

This delicate balance is upset by the entrance into their lives of film actress Claire Niveau (Genevieve Bujold), who has a trifurcate uterus (with three cervixes) that fascinates them both. Elliot successfully propositions her while she is in the gynecological stirrups, then passes her on to Beverly, forcing him to be the one to inform her that she can never have a child. After refusing to respond to her initial advances (as they involved her being spanked), Beverly later carries out a bondage fantasy of Elliot's with her. Surgical clamps and rubber arterial ties have never been put to better use in a consensual sexual act, and soon Beverly becomes romantically hooked. He refuses, for the first time, to share his experience with Elliot, who yells disparagingly, "You haven't fucked Claire Niveau until you tell me about it!" Claire soon discovers their charade and rejects them both. Elliot is unmoved, but Beverly is crushed and pursues a reconciliation with her that will drive a wedge between him and his brother.

Beverly meets up with her again in a showroom of Italian furniture. As is usual in Cronenberg's films, the mise-en-scène contains essential cues to understanding the meaning of the work. The Mantle apartment is furnished in contemporary Italian style, with shades of blue predominating. These visual elements create an atmosphere of cool detachment, suggesting the repression that dominates the brothers' lives. Hence, it is quite significant that, just before seeing Claire, Beverly remarks on the austere geometry of that type of furniture, observing that it "seems so cold and empty." This indicates that he is beginning to gravitate away from his previous lifestyle. Reuniting with Claire, Beverly quickly becomes addicted to the tranquilizers and speed that are "an occupational hazard" of Claire's profession. His descent into madness has begun, as has his alienation from his brother.

Beverly's uncontrollable drug abuse is the first clearly neurotic symptom that he is seen to exhibit in the film. He quickly descends into psychosis, which results in a growing antipathy for his patients. Calling them "mutants," he begins his assault by utilizing a surgical retractor on a patient's vagina during an examination. Unsatisfied with the efficacy of his tools, Beverly approaches an artist to produce "gynecological instruments for operating on mutant women" according to his strict specifications. In one of the most riveting scenes of the film, he tries to use one of these tools on a patient, while garbed in a scarlet surgical gown that makes him look like the Grand Inquisitor in a Spanish auto-da-fe. The tools are positively prehistoric, with this particular one resembling the claw of a pterodactyl. Needing to "slow things down" (as he puts it), he rips the anesthesia mask from the patient and greedily inhales the gas himself. His attendants tear him away from the operating table at this point, and both brothers are banned from working at the hospital.

Beverly's motivation here is perplexing. It is not enough to say that he is simply drug crazed, because the question then becomes why he consumes such vast quantities of drugs to begin with. It is revealing to note that Beverly first uses strong drugs as a way of escaping from a terrifying dream that he has while staying with Claire. After a particularly passionate session with her, he dreams that he and his brother are Siamese twins, joined at the chest in the manner of Chang and Eng (whose story becomes a recurring theme in the film). They are in bed with Claire, who bends down and starts tearing at the area where they are joined with her teeth. In an image echoing the process of birth, she extracts bloody innards from its interior. Beverly awakens in an absolute panic, and Claire gives him a Seconal (a barbiturate) to ensure that he will not dream this again. As he was already doing speed, an endless cycle of uppers and downers commences.

The dream is an obvious embodiment of Beverly's fears of being separated from Elliot. If one accepts the Freudian theory of dreams as wish fulfillments, the dream also suggests that Beverly *desires* such a separation. Ambivalence is pervasive in Beverly's responses throughout the rest of the film, and I believe that it is this ambivalence that gives rise to his psychotic assaults on his patients, as well as to his eventual murder of Elliot.

Beverly's ambivalence about women is brought out in the film's first sequence, when the two brothers, as children, are shown discussing sex and asking a girl in the neighborhood to have intercourse with them in a bathtub. Elliot observes that fish can reproduce without having to come into physical contact, and Beverly says that he would prefer it that way. This ambivalence about physical contact continues throughout his life. His repressed hostility toward his brother surfaces because of his relationship with Claire, which makes him acutely conscious of his desire to be an independent individual.

Sigmund Freud considers conflicts of ambivalence in several places within his writings, but nowhere more clearly than in his discussion of the case of Little Hans (a young patient with a puzzling phobia for horses) in "Inhibitions, Symptoms and Anxiety." His generalized characterization is illuminating: "Here, then, we have a conflict due to ambivalence: a firmly rooted love and a no less well grounded hatred directed against one and the same person."[3] Little Hans felt a deep ambivalence about his father, due to the usual Oedipal struggles. He substituted a phobia for horses, and a related inhibition that led him to refuse to go out into the street, for his (particularly strong) repressed instinctual impulse to kill his father. Freud notes, "In the case of little Hans, the ascertained fact that his father used to play at horses with him doubtless determined his choice of a horse as his anxiety-animal."[4]

Adapting this model to the case at hand, my analysis of Beverly's psychosis is that he substituted his abhorrence of his infertile female patients for his strong desire to kill his brother. The catalyst for this can be easily traced: it was Claire, herself an infertile "mutant," who brought his conflict to the fore. He first uses the term "mutant" to describe her to her gay male secretary, who answers the phone in her hotel suite, misleading Beverly into believing she is having an affair. When he finally kills his brother, he uses the grotesque surgical instruments mentioned earlier, now described by Beverly as being designed "for separating Siamese twins."

Beverly is also seriously ambivalent about Claire, but loves her enough to refrain from injuring her. This is quite significant in a film that is otherwise striking in its persistent misogyny. Claire Niveau is granted a fundamentally sympathetic portrayal, one of the few women in Cronenberg's films to be so treated. She is a self-sufficient businesswoman who is not reluctant to take control of her own career, in spite of disagreements with her agent. Her anguish at being unable to bear a child is poignantly portrayed. It is true that she has kinky sexual desires and consumes a fair amount of drugs, but this is presented as not uncommon in the entertainment industry. Although she appears, at the beginning of the film, to be a simple hedonist, she develops a true affection for Beverly. She abandons her self-described promiscuous lifestyle and remains adamant in her rejection of the callous Elliot.

She will not, however, sacrifice her career goals to become Beverly's caretaker. This is part of what attracts him to her, for he is too weak to extricate himself from Elliot without the strong emotional support she could provide. Yet it is her departure for another movie shoot that precipitates Beverly's rapid disintegration. She, like Elliot, is more "masculine" in this regard, a fact that is telegraphed by the padded shoulders of the coat she is wearing as she leaves Beverly to film her location scenes.

Elliot, immediately realizing that Beverly is in love with Claire, is insanely jealous of her. He suggests that she is pursuing them only in order to support her drug habit, and he mocks her sexual prowess. Elliot finally makes an unsuccessful attempt to seduce Claire again and "restore the balance." When Claire leaves to go on location, Beverly is frantic and ends up in Elliot's office bemoaning her (imagined) infidelity. Because of Elliot's emotional stake in the situation, Elliot naturally attributes Beverly's degeneration exclusively to his brother's relationship with Claire. When Beverly collapses and almost dies in their apartment (after an abortive attempt at a threesome with their receptionist), Elliot resolves to see him through the painful process of withdrawal. Elliot shows genuine solicitude for his brother, but primarily because of his narcissistic concern that he will die if Beverly does.

All of Elliot's efforts are in vain, however, as Beverly destroys their private practice as well, injecting himself with drugs in the office rather than treating their patients. Elliot finally resorts to locking Beverly in, but Beverly escapes and reunites with a recently returned Claire. At this point a satisfying closure seems possible, with Beverly and Claire making a life together apart from Elliot. But the bonding of the brothers is too strong, and Beverly returns with tools in hand, ready to put them to the use for which they were always (unconsciously) intended.

After the brothers share several days of drug-induced regression to childhood, Beverly kills a willing Elliot, using the clawlike instrument he had planned to use in his last disastrous "operation." He cleans himself up and, in the only exterior daylight shot since the opening sequence, emerges from the clinic to call Claire. Beverly's final chance at escape is made all the more attractive by this break in the claustrophobic atmosphere that dominates the film. His love for Claire, and her loving recognition of him, has made it possible for him to take decisive action.

Yet his only hope seemed to lie in the unjust and psychotic murder of his brother, an act so horrific that his own conscience will not let him walk away from it. As in many great works of art, there is a growing sense of inevitability about the inexorable fate that the brothers face. In an interview with Anne Billson for the *Monthly Film Bulletin,* Cronenberg noted the similarity to tragedy himself: "*Dead Ringers,* to me, is as close to classical tragedy as I've come, in that it is inevitable right from the opening what the twins' destiny will be."[5] Yet unlike most classical tragedies, this fate does not come about as the result of conscious choices they have made.

Cronenberg's fascination with twins derives, in part, from contemporary research that showed how remarkably similar twins who are raised in separate environments turn out to be. "It's very mysterious, but the implication of all this is that a huge amount of what we are is biologically predetermined," concludes Cronenberg.[6] The actions of both brothers are depicted as resulting from biological and/or psychological predestination, and not from deliberately chosen acts that they could have avoided.

Cronenberg's explorations of determinism predate *Dead Ringers.* In an interview conducted by William Beard and Piers Handling in May 1983, the director stated: "I actually think that is the way the world works, that we are in fact fumbling around in the dark. Nobody's in control. There is only the appearance of control, or on the part of individual people the illusion of control."[7] In spite of this, he claims not to be fatalistic, unconvincingly urging us to "continue to wrest control from the world, from the universe, from reality, even though it might be hopeless."[8]

There is little in *Dead Ringers* to suggest anything but hopelessness. Neither Beverly nor Elliot can do anything about their self-destructive paths, and all of Claire's efforts are in vain (one is hard pressed to think of anything she could have done to avert the catastrophe, except maybe to refrain from offering Beverly drugs in the first place). *Dead Ringers* is a profoundly pessimistic work that mocks all efforts of the human will to wrest control of its future from deterministic forces. As the successor concept to the notion of tragic fate in the modern age, psychological determinism is ill suited to generate tragic pathos but is fine grist for the horror mill.

Dead Ringers is Cronenberg's most dramatic exploration of psychosis, if not his only one (*Spider* [2002] is perhaps more generally illuminating psychologically). His approach here is comparatively less sensationalistic (there are no exploding heads, or penile projections coming out of women's armpits, or vaginal slits in men's stomachs, or alien parasites, or human flies), and as a result, it is his most terrifying film. *Dead Ringers* is the work of a master who had come into his own, a mature creation that is profound in its depth of characterization and psychological insight. We must now turn to the rest of his films to see whether this picture of the human psyche is an aberrant anomaly or characteristic of his oeuvre.

Monsters and Clairvoyants

Cronenberg has been the subject of much auteur-style criticism, in part because of his obsessionally neurotic treatments of sexuality, violence, and repression. His interest in psychology has been made explicit in several places, as, for example, when Ernest Jones's book *The Life and Work of Sigmund Freud* turns up in *Rabid* (1977), or when he terrifies us with the work of a psychotherapist in *The Brood* (1979). He frequently refers to Freud in public interviews, especially to the Freudian theses that civilization is based on repression, that dreams are the "royal road" to the unconscious, and that art can be a safe vicarious outlet for repressed instinctual desires. *Dead Ringers* is his most penetrating and insightful exploration of these themes, but it is by no means the only one. As I will attempt to show, Freudian determinism colors and shapes almost his entire oeuvre. The obsessive themes with which his films typically deal are directly relevant to the issue of free will versus psychological determinism.

His first two mainstream horror films, *Shivers* (1975) and *Rabid*, depict a complete loss of control, which in the former is caused by alien parasites, and in the latter by a disease (or genetic mutation) that turns Rose (Marilyn Chambers) into a rabid vampire who attacks with a penile appendage that protrudes from her armpit. *The Brood* is the tale of a disturbed patient of Dr. Raglan (Oliver Reed), a psychotherapist who encourages people to externalize their rage in grotesque (and vengeful) physical manifestations. Her husband, concerned for her despite their ongoing divorce, eventually is called upon to kill her with his own hands to save their daughter. All of the central characters (you can't call them protagonists in any traditional sense) in these early films are pictured as being at the mercy of the parasite, disease, or psychological abnormality that causes their actions.

Scanners (1981), *The Dead Zone* (1983), and *The Fly* deal with notions of telepathic power, future sight, and genetic transformation, respectively, and depict protagonists who are overwhelmed by their supernatural powers. *Videodrome* (also 1983) raises the nightmarish specter of a media empire that can cause physical alterations in the brains of its unsuspecting viewers, and ends in the helpless suicide of cable channel executive Max Renn (James Woods). *Naked Lunch* (1991) focuses on a hopeless drug addict who shoots his wife in the head at the behest of his hallucinations. The Ballards in

Crash (1996) become uncontrollably obsessed with sex and auto accidents, to a degree that seems certain to end in their demise. The title character in *Spider* is in the grips of an overwhelmingly debilitating mental illness caused by childhood abuse. Even the apparently humane Tom Stall (Viggo Mortensen) irresistibly reverts to his former ruthless ways in *A History of Violence* (2005). Despite triumphing over the associates from his criminal past (and killing his brother), his desperate stare at his family in the last shot of the film speaks volumes about his horrified recognition that life with them will never be the same again.

In short, and with some exceptions (especially his more recent, and most redemptive, work, *Eastern Promises*), the vast majority of Cronenberg's films deal with human beings who are totally in the grips of external or internal forces beyond their control. Furthermore, as William Beard points out in *The Artist as Monster*, half a dozen of Cronenberg's central characters commit suicide (if you count Brundlefly successfully pleading with Ronnie to euthanize him in *The Fly*).[9] One of our deepest fears is such loss of control, and this is part of why his films are so disturbing. Consider some of the aforementioned examples in more detail.

The occupants of the condominium infected with parasites in *Shivers* are reduced to violent sexual zombies, acting on their basest instincts without guilt, regret, or remorse. One of the many mad scientists that populate Cronenberg's films released the parasite in Starlight Towers for this very purpose, to put people back in touch with their instinctual lives. Cronenberg himself, in an interview with Xavier Mendik, protested that *Shivers* was an ambivalent portrayal of sexual repression, not a reactionary condemnation of unbridled sex as Robin Wood had contended.[10] But it certainly reflected the director's fascination with Freud, especially *Civilization and Its Discontents*, where Freud claims that the displeasure that results from the repression of our instinctual drives (which is required for us to live in civilized societies) explains why so many of us are unhappy.[11]

The Brood is a film where the director was working out his own rage over his (particularly messy) divorce and lengthy custody battle for his young daughter.[12] This time the mad scientist has developed a radical new approach to psychotherapy. Dr. Raglan induces his patients (in some mysterious fashion) to externalize their rage, at first in the eruption of boils and cancerous growths, and eventually in giving birth to demon seed who act out that rage in the real world.

Nola Carveth (Samantha Eggar) is the only patient to exhibit such a powerful and apt externalization. Abused by her mother (either physically or mentally), and angry at her father for letting the abuse continue, she has bottled up her anger to the point of insanity. Raglan's treatment allows her to hatch a brood of murderous parthenogenic creatures, who act out her Oedipal fantasies in killing first her mother, then her father, and finally the school teacher she fancies is her rival. To save their daughter Candice from the clutches of this demonic brood, Frank Carveth (another of Cronenberg's unremarkable male protagonists, played by Art Hingle) must choke his estranged wife to death. It is a scene that smacks of wish fulfillment on the writer/director's part, a catharsis of his own deep-seated resentments.

The film ends with a close-up of eruptions on Candice's arm, suggesting that the mother's psychosis has somehow "infected" the daughter and that she has not survived unscathed. This is indeed a depressing, and deterministic, conclusion. Beard is spot on in observing that *The Brood* is "a narrative that covers only a few days but crams into them events indicating a chain of obscure necessity stretching backwards and forwards and determining the lives of those caught in its web."[13] The remarks with which he concludes his discussion of the film concur with my thesis explicitly: "There is a bleak determinism in *The Brood* that is visually manifested in its cold settings and which is hard for even the most self-preserving viewer to dodge—and that determinism ... return[s] to take up the seat of control through Cronenberg's work for the next fifteen years [i.e., through *Crash*]."[14]

The Fly returns to the theme of the excessive repression of our instincts, which civilization requires for its continued existence. As Seth Brundle (Jeff Goldblum) physically transforms, he slowly throws off all vestiges of human civilization as well. His desire for sex (and sweets) is insatiable, he breaks a man's arm just for the fun of it (and for the feeling of power that it gives him), and rejects his girlfriend, Ronnie (Geena Davis), for not going through the (obviously dangerous) teleporter herself. Eventually he warns Ronnie to stay away and then proceeds to execute a plot to assimilate her in order to minimize the fly DNA that has been fused with his.

Dead Ringers and *The Fly* are two of the saddest of Cronenberg's creations. One of the major reasons for this is that both Beverly Mantle and Seth Brundle are sympathetic characters in the grips of forces totally beyond their control (the ending of *Crash* is just as shattering, but we don't care for the main characters nearly as much there). Beverly cannot extricate himself from the symbiotic relationship with his twin brother, while Seth cannot reverse the transformation that increasingly robs him of his humanity. *The Fly* is the last monster movie Cronenberg made before turning his attention to more realistic themes and protagonists in recent years.

Realistic Horror

The epitome of many of the bleak tendencies on which I have been focusing thus far can be found in *Crash*, Cronenberg's most controversial film. It is a literal adaptation of a J. G. Ballard novel that was itself a scandalous publication. *Crash* is one of the most potent examples in the history of cinema (along with *Last Tango in Paris* [1972] and *The Night Porter* [1974]) of the possible union of the Freudian instincts Eros and Thanatos—respectively, the erotic drive for sexuality and community, and the death instinct, a self-destructive tendency that, when turned outward, leads to violence against others. It is also one of the most nihilistic movies ever made, despite late romantic *liebestod* undertones that are reminiscent of such operatic classics as Richard Wagner's *Tristan and Isolde*.

James Ballard (James Spader) and his wife Catherine (Deborah Kara Unger) are a jaded and childless couple who are bored with their open marriage. They rehearse empty affairs with little enthusiasm and stare off into space, as though facing oblivion. James is revitalized by a head-on collision with Helen Remington (Holly Hunter) and her husband; the latter is killed by being thrown through two windshields and into Ballard's front seat. While in the hospital, James meets Helen, and they commence an affair that will lead him into a cult that celebrates car crashes.

The leader of the cult is a virulent figure named Vaughan (Elias Koteas), who is obsessed with restaging car crashes of the rich and famous (James Dean, Albert Camus, Jayne Mansfield), and having sex in cars (mostly with prostitutes). He introduces James and Catherine to an underground world of excess and carnality, and dies in a spectacular accident of his own design. But before his demise, he infects the couple with a passion for his unique amalgam of sex and death.

About halfway through the film, Vaughan plays bumper tag with Catherine, his huge Lincoln threatening to force her little Miata convertible off the road. In the film's final sequence, James has put the crashed Lincoln in drivable shape, and he uses it to push Catherine's sports car into a ditch. When the accident fails to kill her, he reassures her that maybe it will next time. We are left with the distinct impression that they will follow their mentor in pursuing this obsession to the point of death.

As author J. G. Ballard acknowledged on an appendix to the laserdisc version of the film, *Crash* was a cautionary tale.[15] Cronenberg, with his characteristic recalcitrance, refuses to see it as such. Indeed, in his commentary on that laserdisc, he calls it an "existential romance" between two people for whom "all the old forms have lost their meaning."[16] In his view, they are seeking to redefine the meanings of sex, death, and love in a way that is liberating (because we tend to think of these concepts as "immutable"). I prefer the author's interpretation over the director's, in part because it is hard for me to see an obsession with self-destruction as liberating (even Camus argued that suicide is not the proper response to recognizing the absurdity of existence).

Generally speaking, the plots of films that wish to champion the human spirit turn on the choices of their protagonists, choices that are usually celebrated as the right ones. By contrast, Cronenberg's films largely highlight the unavoidable fates of persons who are acting on their natures and seem to have little choice in the matter. As I have noted, the exception that proves the rule is *Eastern Promises*. Many of Cronenberg's typical narrative patterns are altered in this film. Male protagonist Nikolai (Viggo Mortensen, in the performance of his career) is an undercover cop who has penetrated a Russian Mafia family in London. He helps Anna (Naomi Watts) save the orphaned baby that mob boss Semyon (Armin Mueller-Stahl) conceived by raping a fourteen-year-old girl (who died in childbirth in the hospital where Anna works). By dint of his own herculean efforts, Nikolai succeeds, while managing not to blow his cover. Proof that Semyon is the father of the baby also provides the evidence that will bring the bad guy to justice for his child prostitution ring, putting Nikolai's best buddy (and willing pawn) Kirill in charge of the mob family.

As in *A History of Violence*, Viggo plays a true tough guy. But unlike Tom Stall in that (much more disturbing) film, Nikolai is in control of his violent tendencies here. He is a soft-spoken man of action, who gets things done, and the sequence where he takes apart two goons who are trying to kill him in a steam bath is one of the most riveting fight scenes in the history of cinema. In short, Nikolai is a traditional, laconic, Hollywood-style hero who remains in control of his world throughout, and who survives his ordeals and saves the baby from being drowned.

The contrast with the rest of Cronenberg's male protagonists is striking, and only serves to highlight the impotence and lack of control of the vast majority of them. Whether *Eastern Promises* represents a gestalt shift in the director's oeuvre, or simply an experiment in doing a mainstream film, remains to be seen. But it cannot alter the fact that the body of Cronenberg's work embodies a deterministic, and profoundly pessimistic, worldview.

Notes

1. B. F. Skinner, *Beyond Freedom and Dignity* (New York: Knopf, 1971).

2. An earlier version of this section of the essay appeared as "Determinism and Dead Ringers," *Film and Philosophy* 3 (1996).
3. Sigmund Freud, "Inhibitions, Symptoms and Anxiety," in *Great Books of the Western World*, vol. 54 (Chicago: Encyclopaedia Britannica, 1952), 724.
4. Freud, "Inhibitions, Symptoms and Anxiety," 725.
5. Anne Billson, "Cronenberg on Cronenberg: A Career in Stereo," *Monthly Film Bulletin* 56 (January 1989): 6.
6. Karen Jaehne, "Double Trouble," *Film Comment* 24 (1988): 22.
7. William Beard and Piers Handling, "The Interview," in *The Shape of Rage: The Films of David Cronenberg*, ed. Piers Handling (Toronto: General Pub. Co., 1983), 187.
8. Beard and Handling, "The Interview," 188.
9. William Beard, *The Artist as Monster: The Cinema of David Cronenberg* (Toronto: University of Toronto Press, 2001), 271.
10. Xavier Mendik, "Logic, Creativity and (Critical) Misinterpretations: An Interview with David Cronenberg," in *The Modern Fantastic: The Films of David Cronenberg*, ed. Michael Grant (Westport, Conn.: Praeger Paperbacks, 2000), 168–86; Robin Wood, *Hollywood from Vietnam to Reagan* (New York: Columbia University Press, 1986), 178.
11. Sigmund Freud, *Civilization and Its Discontents* (New York: Norton, 1989).
12. Chris Rodley, ed., *Cronenberg on Cronenberg* (Toronto: Knopf, 1992), 72.
13. Beard, *The Artist as Monster*, 74.
14. Beard, *The Artist as Monster*, 95.
15. J. G. Ballard, interview, *Crash* (Criterion Collection, 1996), laserdisk.
16. Quoted in Beard, *The Artist as Monster*, 411.

Self-Creation, Identity, and Authenticity
A Study of *A History of Violence* and *Eastern Promises*

Daniel Moseley

David Cronenberg's early work in science fiction and horror may seem to bear only a faint similarity to *A History of Violence* (2005) and *Eastern Promises* (2007). These later films broaden Cronenberg's repertoire into the genres of action and gangster movies. However, there are important thematic continuities between these films and his earlier films. Cronenberg's work continuously explores questions about the nature of the self and the relation of the self to the human body: *Shivers* (1975), *The Brood* (1979), *Scanners* (1981), *Videodrome* (1983), and *The Fly* (1986) all raise challenging philosophical questions about personal identity. It is helpful to distinguish two main groups of problems that are usually classified as philosophical questions of personal identity: *metaphysical* problems of personal identity, and *practical* problems of personal identity. The metaphysical problems of personal identity are a main point of concern in Cronenberg's earlier work in horror and science fiction. By directly addressing the practical problems of personal identity, *A History of Violence* and *Eastern Promises* expand the range of philosophical reflections on the self that are explored in Cronenberg's films.

Metaphysical Problems

The central metaphysical problems of personal identity are concerned with determining both the criteria for being a person and the criteria for persons to persist over time. The genre of science fiction is an excellent medium for exploring these metaphysical puzzles. In *The Fly*, Seth Brundle (Jeff Goldblum) is an ordinary scientist who is conducting research on teleportation. Brundle uses himself as a guinea pig to test whether his transporter pods can successfully transport a human. When he steps into the transporter pod he does not realize that a fly is in the pod with him. Their bodies are disintegrated, and Brundle appears to emerge from another pod. However, the post-transportation Brundle soon learns that the pretransportation Brundle and the fly have been genetically fused. The hybrid body sheds its human appearance and eventually transforms into a human-size fly. Since the hybrid creature that results from the transportation process is not human, the philosophical question is: Did Seth survive the transportation process? Suppose that two people step into a transporter pod and the transportation process fused them into one living creature that appeared to be a normal human being. Would the resulting person be strictly identical with either of the original persons whose bodies were fused? In addition to stories involving the fusion of persons, or the fusion of insects and persons, there are science fiction cases involving the *fission* of persons. Suppose that Seth steps in one transporter pod, the original body is destroyed, and two people are created by the process. Would the pretransportation Seth survive the process? The resulting persons would think that they were Seth, and they would have all of Seth's memories and dispositions. Would they be duplicates of Seth, or would Seth now have two bodies? These philosophical questions that emerge from cases involving the fission and fusion of persons are some of the central metaphysical problems of personal identity.

Practical Problems

Practical problems of personal identity, in contrast with the metaphysical problems, are not primarily concerned with *what* it is to be a person. The practical problems of personal identity focus on the question of *who* a person is. They often emerge from the first-person perspective and commonly arise when one seriously asks, "Who am I? Am I really who I think I am?" Seriously reflecting on these questions is often not an exercise in philosophy, and this kind of reflection may also serve as an ordinary attempt to understand one's own character and commitments. The results of this kind of reflection are often central decisions and choices that are involved in the processes of *self-discovery* and *self-creation*.

The form of self-discovery involved in having a practical identity is a matter of discovering, from the first-person perspective, who one really is. This form of self-discovery neither requires one to formulate a comprehensive metaphysical theory about personhood and persistence nor requires one to discover the best causal/scientific explanation of one's behavior. Metaphysical theorizing and scientific explanations of the world are concerned with providing an accurate representation of the world from a third-person perspective (from the point of view that an all-knowing being would have on the world).[1] This form of self-discovery is also a form of self-creation. It is a creative process that is an endless task of experimenting with various projects, roles, and relationships.[2] The concept of self-creation may seem paradoxical or incoherent if it is understood as a metaphysical description of one's relation to oneself. How could a person create (or author or constitute) oneself unless there is already a self there to do the creating?[3] However, if we understand the "self" in these concepts to refer to one's *practical identity,* the air of paradox is dispelled. The concept of the self (practical identity) and the concept of personhood are not identical. A practical identity could be the result of the free choices of an immaterial soul, or it could result from the completely determined activity of the human brain. Practical identities are *created* and *discovered* by individuals. The apparently paradoxical concepts of *self-authorship, self-articulation,* and *self-creation* are neither genuinely paradoxical nor metaphysically problematic.

Authentic and Inauthentic Persons

The practical problems of personal identity often occur in contexts in which one is unclear about one's most fundamental desires, projects, commitments, and responsibilities. They usually occur when one does not have a clear understanding of who one really is. For instance, Cronenberg reports that when he was directing his first feature-length film, *Shivers,* he had no idea what he was doing and he was trying not to convey this to his cast. He was acting as director of the film, but he found himself asking, "Am I really a director?"[4] Cronenberg certainly knew that he was the director of the film, and he knew that he wanted to be a director. His question can plausibly be understood to reveal that he had some uncertainty about who he really was at the time: it raises doubts about his practical identity and his authenticity.

A person's practical identity is a salient aspect of his or her self-conception: a person's practical identity is a conception, from the first-person perspective, of the nature and value of one's own life and actions.[5] Authenticity is intuitively understood to be a matter of being true to oneself. What is the nature of the *self* that authentic people are true toward? What is involved in being *true* to it? Arguably, authentic people are true toward their *practical identities:* questions about authenticity are practical problems of personal identity. So, in what sense are authentic individuals true to their practical identities? To address this question, it is helpful to consider people who are *in*authentic: such persons are often guilty of a form of betrayal—they betray themselves in an important sense. Inauthentic persons are normally characterized by unreflective role-playing in society, having an unreflective obsession with fitting in, and failing to deliberate about their commitments or becoming inundated with pointless or trivial commitments.[6] Authentic persons tend to avoid these traits because they remain true to themselves by examining themselves. Authentic persons reflect upon their practical identities and their relations to others and to the world that they inhabit.

Cavell on Movie Stardom

Just as science fiction is an excellent genre for exploring metaphysical problems about personal identity, gangster films, or films that examine the psychology and culture of gangsters, are excellent venues for exploring practical problems of personal identity. The main, or most interesting, characters in these films usually struggle with conflicting loyalties and commitments.[7] The ethical conflicts that these characters face often lead them to a deeper understanding of themselves and provide them with an opportunity to live more authentically. *A History of Violence* examines a family man (Viggo Mortensen) in a small town who is terrorized by a group of gangsters who believe that he is a former gang member against whom they have a vendetta. *Eastern Promises* shows how the life of a midwife (Naomi Watts) in London is transformed when her search for the family of an orphaned baby creates ties with a group of dangerous Russian mobsters. Both of these films provide genuine insights into what it is to live authentically.

It is striking that in each of these films, Viggo Mortensen stars as a character who is involved with an organized crime family. To identify what is striking about Mortensen starring in these specific roles, it is helpful to consider some of Stanley Cavell's thoughts about movie stardom.[8] Cavell maintains that movie stars are human subjects that fulfill the film medium's need for *individualities*. According to Cavell, individualities are individuals who have become *film types*. Just as there are genres of film (prison films, Civil War movies, science fiction, etc.), within these genres there are certain recurring types of figures, which Cavell describes as film types: for example, the Villain, the Family Man, and the Dandy. Cavell contends that one important feature of films is their capacity to create individualities—individual people who achieve the status of a film type: for example, Buster Keaton, Marilyn Monroe, Marlon Brando, Sigourney Weaver, and Arnold Schwarzenegger. Movie stars achieve the status of being individualities: their recurrence in Hollywood films has resulted in their becoming film types that are on a par with traditional film types such as the Sheriff, the Priest, the Reporter, and the Other Woman. Individualities can inhabit various social roles, but they do so in a unique way. Cavell contends that the individualities captured on film have priority over the social roles that they also inhabit. Movie stars, the individualities who usually capture our full attention in films that feature them, are figures whom we have met in previous circumstances and will meet again.

With these Cavellian thoughts in mind, it is striking that David Cronenberg selected Viggo Mortensen to play the central character in both *A History of Violence* and *Eastern Promises*. These films appeared a short time after Mortensen achieved stardom with his performance as Aragorn in the *Lord of the Rings* trilogy (2001, 2002, 2003). Mortensen's stardom brings a certain philosophical depth to the specific characters that he plays in his films with Cronenberg.

Authenticity in *A History of Violence*

In the role of Aragorn, Mortensen plays a man who is a Warrior at the beginning of the story and becomes a King at the end of the tale. Aragorn is the son of a former king, and his destiny is to restore nobility and honor to his royal bloodline. Mortensen's role in *A History of Violence* breaks away from the unambiguous Hero that we remember from *Lord of the Rings*. Tom Stall is a small-town family man who becomes a local hero by killing two men who attempt to murder him and the patrons of his diner. Tom's heroic deeds spark national attention, and soon he is visited by gangsters from Philadelphia who believe that Tom is really a mobster named Joey Cusack. This is not a case of mistaken identity. Tom/Joey must resort to extreme acts of violence when he faces his old enemies Carl Fogarty (Ed Harris) and his brother Richie Cusack (William Hurt) in order to protect himself and his family from the vendettas that these men have against him. Tom must also break away from his past as Joey in order to resume and maintain his role as a Family Man. Tom's history as Joey also raises questions about whether the violent response to the men who attempted to rob his business was genuinely heroic or merely the instinctive reaction of a violent man. A warrior who returns home after war may no longer be fit to live as a husband: the desirable qualities of a man of war may be antithetical to the qualities of a nurturing parent and husband.[9]

In the final scene of the film, Mortensen's character returns to his rural family home. He has killed all his enemies and enters the kitchen while his family is eating dinner. They are angry at him. They feel betrayed by the fact that he never told them about his identity as Joey Cusack. They are also frightened of him because they witnessed him kill two of Fogarty's thugs and since they are now aware of his violent history as a mobster. When he enters the kitchen, they shun him initially, not speaking to him or looking at him, but eventually his children serve him food and his wife looks at him, in tears, with an expression of acceptance. The scene fades to black. The film leaves it an open question whether the man who enters the kitchen in the final scene is really Tom Stall, Joey Cusack, or someone else entirely. That question is also one in need of clarification. Not only are the audience and the family onscreen wondering, "Who is this man?" but Tom/Joey is also in the process of exploring that question.

One can view *A History of Violence* as raising metaphysical questions about personal identity. Someone might reasonably wonder whether Tom Stall and Joey Cusack are distinct persons sharing a single body. The scenes I will describe explicitly raise those questions. However, there is much to be gained by viewing the film as primarily exploring practical questions about personal identity. The question of whether Mortensen's character is *really* Tom or Joey can be understood as an ethical question about which practical identity he ought to adopt: the commitments and values of a family man or those of a gangster. It is a question of who he really is and which practical identity is more authentic. The man who enters the kitchen in the final scene is Viggo Mortensen, and we know that he has been a hero in previous roles. However, we might also remember some of his darker roles (e.g., the cannibal Tex in *Leatherface: The Texas Chainsaw Massacre III* [1990]) and the potential his character has for villainy. The character's practical identity as Tom involves a range of values and commitments that reinforce his role as a Family Man. His practical identity as Joey involves a range of family commitments and past transactions that wed his life to organized crime. There are three scenes from the film that vividly describe the nature and depth of these conflicts. I will call these scenes "Standoff," "The Truth," and "Questions and Answers."

"STANDOFF"

There is a scene in the front yard of the Stall residence where Tom has his last encounter with Fogarty and Fogarty's thugs. After Tom kills Fogarty's goons, Fogarty shoots Tom in the shoulder. Tom hits the ground and drops his pistol. Fogarty kicks the gun away and asks him if he has any last words. Tom replies, "I should have killed you back in Philly." Fogarty responds, "Yeah, Joey. You should have." Fogarty's chest then explodes as Tom's son, Jack (Ashton Holmes), shoots him from behind with a shotgun. (There is an interesting parallel between Jack's growing disposition to violent solutions to problems and his growing knowledge of his father's past. Jack changes from being mild mannered to having the will to savagely beat up a school bully and then becoming willing to shoot people who are a threat to his family.) Mortensen's character rises, and with Fogarty's blood splashed all over his face and upper body, he snatches the gun away from Jack and they look at each other in a new way. Jack did not know anything about his father's history with Fogarty or his life in Philly. He looks afraid of his father, and his father seems wild from the violent frenzy, and slightly proud of his son. Joey then embraces his son, as the knowledge sets in that Jack heard the confession to Fogarty.

"THE TRUTH"

In the next scene, Mortensen's character is in the hospital recovering from his gunshot wound, and his wife, Edie (Maria Bello), enters the room. Edie has been in the dark about her husband's past as Joey Cusack. They are alone in the room, and she asks him to tell her the truth. Edie tells him: "I saw Joey. I saw you turn into Joey right before my eyes." She continues, "I saw a killer—the one Fogarty warned me about. You did kill men back in Philly, didn't you? Did you do it for money, or did you do it because you enjoyed it?" He replies, "Joey did, both. I didn't. Tom Stall didn't." Edie physically responds by running into the bathroom to vomit. When she returns she asks, "What are you, like some multiple personality schizoid? It's like flipping a switch back and forth for you?" He replies, "I never expected to see Joey again." She asks, "What, was he in hiding? Was he dead?" As he responds, his Philadelphia accent gets much thicker: "I thought he was. I thought I killed Joey Cusack. I went out to the desert and I killed him. I spent three years becoming Tom Stall. Edie, you have to know this. I wasn't really born again until I met you. I was nothing." She replies, "I don't believe you. I can't believe this is happening." She points out that he lied about having adopted parents, growing up in Portland. She also says, "And our name . . . Jesus Christ, my name . . . Jack's name . . . Sarah's name . . . Stall? Tom Stall? Did you just make that up? Where did that name come from?" He replies, "I mean, it was available." She says, "Yeah. I guess I was available too." Edie leaves the room, crying.

The medical setting in this scene and the fact that Mortensen's character is wearing a hospital gown make it natural to think that he has a psychological condition that is some form of medically treatable pathology: multiple personality syndrome or some form of schizophrenia.[10] Edie initially worries that he suffers from some type of psychopathology. Is he delusional? Does he have distinct centers of consciousness that inhabit a single body? However, she quickly forms the opinion that he has just been lying to everyone about his past. Lying is more blameworthy than being mentally ill. The fact that he describes the process of becoming Tom Stall as being "born again" suggests that the adoption of his identity was a deliberate choice. If he is a former criminal who made a rational decision to break away from his life of crime, then he seems more like a double agent than a psychiatric patient. His circumstances suggest that his life was in danger and he no longer enjoyed being part of an organized crime syndicate. So, he changed his name and took steps to make a new life for himself as a family man in the Midwest. Joey Cusack saw another possible future for himself and decided to adopt another practical identity and discard his old one. It is plausible that the roles of Tom and Joey involve different orientations to the world and different patterns of response to it, but these roles are just different aspects of this character's practical identity. He has compartmentalized himself into these two different orientations to the world. Interpreting this compartmentalization with psychiatric categories alienates this person from his choices and character.[11] Mortensen's individuality also inhabits these roles with a passionate demeanor, which suggests that his authentic character is more robust than the identities of Tom the Family Man and Crazy Joey. This character's practical identity as Joey is constricting because he has a strong desire for wholesome goodness that the life of Joey cannot provide him. His practical identity as Tom is suffocating because of his strong desire for a life of action. This is not only a problem for Tom, but it is a general form of conflict that is often experienced by individuals who take up family life.

"QUESTIONS AND ANSWERS"

In the next scene, Mortensen's character arrives home from the hospital and sees his son. He says, "Hey, Jack." His son responds by asking an important question, "What am I supposed to call you now?" His father replies, "You're supposed to call me dad. That's what I am, your dad." Jack responds, "Are you really? So, you're some kind of closet mobster dad?" Jack then turns and rushes away. Jack's questions reveal that he doubts his father is really Tom Stall. Jack now sees that his father's life as Tom Stall is inauthentic, that his father is betraying himself by living as a mild-mannered family man in the American Midwest. Later in the film, Richie Cusack also accuses his brother of living an inauthentic existence. Richie regards his brother's life as Tom Stall as a joke. Richie asks him, "When you dream, are you still Joey?" Mortensen's character replies, "Joey's been dead a long time." Richie responds, "But here you sit, big as life." Richie and Fogarty refuse to acknowledge that Mortensen's character is really Tom Stall. When Jack discovers his father's history, he does not know what to call him. Richie, Fogarty, and Jack know that the man named Tom Stall is numerically identical with the man named Joey Cusack. Their denial that Joey Cusack is *really* Tom Stall is a rejection of Mortensen's practical identity as Tom Stall. They think his practical identity as Tom Stall is inauthentic and that his true identity, or his authentic practical identity, is that of Joey Cusack. When Mortensen's character denies that he is Joey Cusack, he is not merely trying to maintain his cover as Tom Stall. He is also reaffirming his practical identity as Tom Stall and rejecting his practical identity as Joey Cusack. His struggle with Fogarty and Richie is not only over his bodily survival but also over his practical identity and over his authenticity as Tom Stall. Although Mortensen's character physically survives the battles with Fogarty and Richie, it is unclear whether the practical identity of Tom Stall survives. We do not know whether the man who returns home in the final scene of the film is Tom Stall, Joey Cusack, or some new character. He may be in the process of rejecting his identities as Tom and Joey, and embarking on the project of forging a new practical identity.

In the DVD special feature "Acts of Violence," a documentary on the making of *A History of Violence*, Cronenberg says that the whole movie is about the question of identity that is raised by the final scene.[12] One important conclusion that is suggested by the ending of the film is that practical identities are usually not fixed, determined, or complete: we are often groping around in this world trying out different practical identities that work for us with varying degrees of success. Practical identities may be discarded or updated to accommodate shifting social worlds. This process of self-creation and self-discovery rarely, if ever, achieves an ending point other than our death.

Authenticity in *Eastern Promises*

While Mortensen's character in *A History of Violence* is trying to exit his relationship with a crime family, his character in *Eastern Promises* is trying to forge a stronger association with the Russian crime family that employs him. The various types of family bonds that exist in both of these films raise important questions about the nature of one's commitments and whether one's family relationships usually undermine or support one's authenticity. In *A History of Violence*, Joey and Richie are brothers, and their sibling rivalry is one of the main sources of tension between them. Shortly before Richie attempts to kill Joey, Richie says, "You always were a problem for me, Joey. When Mom brought you home from the hospital, I tried to strangle you in your crib. I guess all kids try to do that. She caught me and whacked the daylights out of me." The parallels with the story of Cain and Abel are clear.[13] Richie does not succeed in playing the role of Cain, but he does try.

The family relations of the various characters in *Eastern Promises* are important to the film's plot. Anna (Naomi Watts) is a midwife who begins to care for an orphaned baby whose mother, Tatiana (Sarah-Jeanne Labrosse), died in childbirth. Tatiana leaves behind a diary written in Russian, and it contains a card for the Trans-Siberian Restaurant. Anna visits the restaurant, on Christmas Day, with the aim of finding contact information for the baby's family. During her first visit to the Trans-Siberian, she meets the proprietor, Semyon (Armin Mueller-Stahl), his dangerous-looking son Kirill (Vincent Cassel), and his son's even more dangerous-looking associate Nikolai (Mortensen). Anna soon learns that Tatiana was kidnapped by an organization of Russian mobsters called the *Vory v Zakone* ("Thieves in Law," Russian mobsters) and was forced into slavery in a brothel in London. It also turns out that the Trans-Siberian Restaurant is a front for London's branch of the *Vory*. Semyon is the top boss of this crime syndicate, the King of this realm of Russian mob culture. He is also the main patriarch of the film: his subordinates in the *Vory* call him "Papa," he is Kirill's father, and he is the father of Tatiana's orphaned daughter.

Nikolai, Mortensen's character, is attempting to unseat Semyon from his throne. Nikolai occupies many roles in the film. Throughout the film he says, "I'm just a driver." During a scene in which he is removing all the identifying features of the corpse of an assassinated gangster, he is described as an undertaker. Later in the film, he is initiated as a full-fledged member of the *Vory v Zakone* and has their symbolic stars tattooed on his knees and above his heart. However, Mortensen's character does not authentically inhabit any of those roles, because he is really a Russian secret service agent who is working undercover with Scotland Yard to break apart Semyon's crime ring. Eventually, Scotland Yard confirms that Semyon is the father of Tatiana's daughter, and he is arrested for raping Tatiana (and possibly charged for her kidnapping and murder). Nikolai never blows his cover, and at the end of the film, he and Kirill are the new Kings.

Kirill may be the least authentic of the main characters in *Eastern Promises*. I do not intend to suggest that Vincent Cassel's performance is not authentic; I mean that Kirill, the character, is the least authentic of the main characters in the film. The criminal world of the *Vory v Zakone* has its own structure, codes, and conventions. The world of the *Vory v Zakone* is ordinary for Kirill: he grew up in it. He claims that the stars are a birthmark for him. Kirill's own life is overly conventional: it is governed by the strict rules of the *Vory*, and he does not seem to reflectively endorse the code and way of life. Kirill seems to simply assume that his life is the life of a *Vor* and there is nothing else to be said. Kirill is not a completely inauthentic person, because he betrays his father, who is also his senior in the *Vory v Zakone*, when he is convinced by Nikolai that his father's order to kill his baby half sister is illegitimate. As Kirill is about to throw the baby into the river, Nikolai arrives and says, "We do not kill babies. This would be bad for us. Your papa has gone too far. You're either with him or with me." He tells Kirill that his father is going away and the business is now going to be in Kirill's hands. Nikolai takes the baby and gives her to Anna. (By becoming a new mob boss and passing the baby to Anna, Nikolai symbolically takes up the new role of papa.) Anna asks Nikolai why he helped her and baby Christine. Nikolai replies, "How can you be king if the king is still in place?" Kirill's decision to give the baby over to Nikolai and Anna may be a result of some moral misgivings, but it is also clearly motivated by his intense attraction to Nikolai. Even in Kirill's best moments he appears to be primarily motivated by a desire to be accepted by others, which is an indication of his inauthenticity.

Semyon probably exemplifies more authenticity than any other character in *Eastern Promises*. To back up this claim, it is helpful to consider some general characteristics of authenticity. Authentic persons are true to themselves: their projects are truly their *own* and not the products of blind allegiance to social conventions. Authentic persons are not alienated from their own projects. Anna's first impression of Semyon is that he loves good food and music, and he takes pride in his Russian heritage, cuisine, and culture. This impression is correct: it seems that he would be a successful restaurant owner even if he were not involved with the Russian Mafia. Moreover, he is a prominent member of the *Vory v Zakone* who reflectively deals with problems facing his organization and his family. He abides by the code of the *Vory*, and he adheres to it with a seriousness that reveals a reflective affirmation of his practical identity. Semyon is also loyal to his son and deploys a great deal of cunning to protect Kirill from Chechen assassins who are trying to kill him. He may have the vices of being a morally wicked person and being involved in a vast amount of violent crime, but he seems to be true to himself and true to his convictions.

Individualist Authenticity

Authenticity is commonly considered to be an aesthetic ideal that sharply contrasts with the moral ideal of sincerity.[14] (Philosophers commonly distinguish *moral* evaluation, which is concerned with judging the moral permissibility of actions, from *aesthetic* evaluation, which is focused on the judgment of whether something is beautiful.) Since a morally wicked person such as Semyon can be authentic, there is reason to believe that authenticity is not a moral virtue or ideal. Before examining the issue of whether Semyon really does exemplify authenticity, I will consider some of the philosophical debates surrounding the topic of authenticity.

The ideal of authenticity is closely related to the contemporary aesthetic ideals of originality, creativity, and distinctiveness: authentic persons are original, creative, and distinctive in the way that they exemplify their processes of self-discovery and self-articulation. Various existentialist philosophers condemn the *inauthenticity* that they perceive in conventional role-playing by persons such as waiters who take their jobs too seriously, and they denounce those types of inauthentic performances of one's social roles as symptomatic of "bad faith." The classic discussion of bad faith is found in Jean-Paul Sartre's *Being and Nothingness*.[15] This conception of authenticity is strongly *individualist*. Individualist conceptions of authenticity stress the importance of individuals' being true to themselves, and this form of self-understanding is often contrasted with conformity to the demands of society.

Individualist conceptions of authenticity are often criticized on the grounds that they promote self-indulgence and a "culture of narcissism." One salient example of this line of criticism is presented by Charles Taylor in *The Ethics of Authenticity*.[16] Taylor contends that individualist conceptions of authenticity may involve an overly obsessive concern with the self that leads one to shut out or ignore issues that are greater than or transcend the self: issues about religion, politics, or human history.[17] Although Taylor is ultimately critical of strongly individualist conceptions of authenticity, he maintains that many critics of these conceptions fail to acknowledge the genuine value of self-discovery and self-articulation. He also argues that any plausible theory of authenticity must describe its importance to the individuals that possess it, but one must also recognize that there are moral constraints on the *content* of the projects that can be pursued by authentic persons. Taylor claims that individualist conceptions of authenticity fail to distinguish the *manner* of being authentic (i.e., the manner of pursuing one's ends or projects) from the *matter* (i.e., content) of the ends of authentic persons.[18] Thus, Taylor contends, the emphasis that individualist conceptions of authenticity place on authentic persons' pursuing ends that are their *own*, as opposed to the ends of society or another person, fails to recognize that the projects of many authentic persons connect their practical identities to a social order. In sum, Taylor argues that authentic persons must be reasonable, and being reasonable requires that one respond to moral demands that fall outside the gamut of mere economic (instrumental) rationality. So,

Taylor's theory of authenticity goes against the commonly held view that authenticity is an aesthetic ideal and not a moral ideal.

One serious problem facing Taylor's conception of authenticity is that morally wicked persons like Semyon can exemplify a great deal of authenticity. Taylor maintains that there are moral constraints placed on the content of the projects of authentic persons, because authentic persons may deeply identify with projects or ends that transcend the self. However, Semyon reasonably identifies with his commitment to the *Vory v Zakone:* this is a commitment to a social order that is greater than him. He is committed to the "moral code" of the *Vory,* but their social conventions are morally illegitimate. The moral code of the *Vory* requires a subordinate member to obey a superior's command to kill an innocent person or to rape a woman. However, the boss of a criminal organization does not have the genuine moral authority to make it morally legitimate for a thug to either kill an innocent person or to rape someone. So, Taylor's theory of authenticity does not make a strong case for the view that authentic persons cannot be morally wicked. Perhaps there are strong reasons for believing that authentic persons cannot be morally wicked, but Taylor's argument does not provide them. Considerations of a person's authenticity do raise important questions about a person's practical identity, but those questions do not straightforwardly settle the issue of which practical identities or commitments it is morally legitimate for a person to identify with or adopt. Nikolai's double life as a mobster and as a government agent may diminish his authenticity, but the moral value and decency of his attempt to end the criminal activity of the *Vory v Zakone* provide him with strong reasons to live a less-than-fully-authentic life.

A History of Violence and *Eastern Promises* together provide a compelling and important meditation on the topics of practical identity and authenticity. Although Cronenberg does not provide any decisive resolutions to the puzzles and problems surrounding these topics, these films move us toward a deeper understanding of them.

Notes

I thank C. D. C. Reeve, Simon Riches, and Benjamin Bagley for helpful feedback on an earlier draft of this essay.

1. For more on the distinction between the first-person and third-person perspectives, see Thomas Nagel, *The View from Nowhere* (Oxford: Oxford University Press, 1986).

2. Iris Murdoch describes the "endless task" of shaping one's moral vision in the chapter "The Idea of Perfection" in *Existentialists and Mystics*, ed. Peter Conradi (Harmondsworth: Penguin Books, 1998), 317–18. I understand the task of shaping one's moral vision to be a central element of the process of self-creation. C. D. C. Reeve's chapter "Seeing, Improvising and Self-Love" in *Love's Confusions* (Cambridge, Mass.: Harvard University Press, 2007), 15–35, is rich with insights into the nature of this process of self-creation.

3. The apparent paradox that emerges from the concept of self-constitution is carefully discussed by Christine Korsgaard in *Self-Constitution: Agency, Identity and Integrity* (Oxford: Oxford University Press, 2009), 41–44.

4. Cronenberg expresses these self-doubts in an interview that is available on the 1998 DVD release of the director's cut of *Shivers* (Image Entertainment).

5. I use the term "practical identity" in roughly the same way it is used in Christine Korsgaard, *The Sources of Normativity* (Cambridge: Cambridge University Press, 2000). Korsgaard formulates her conception of practical identities in the following passage: "The conception of one's identity in question here is . . . understood as a description under which you value yourself, a description under which you find your life to be worth living and your actions to be worth undertaking. So I will call this a conception of your practical identity" (101).

6. C. D. C. Reeve's reflections on the relation of sentimentality to inauthenticity in the chapter "Sentimentality and the Gift of the Self" in *Love's Confusions* (92–104) helpfully illustrate how a society's fantasies can foster inauthenticity.

7. For a philosophically sophisticated discussion of the types of conflicting obligations that a mafioso might experience, see Korsgaard, *The Sources of Normativity*, 254–58.

8. Stanley Cavell, *The World Viewed: Reflections on the Ontology of Film* (New York: Viking, 1971), 33–35.

9. Reeve's *Love's Confusions* contains enlightening reflections on this issue.

10. Cronenberg's latest film, *A Dangerous Method* (2011), is about the relationship between Sigmund Freud and Carl Jung. Viggo Mortensen is cast as Sigmund Freud!

11. One of the central topics in the philosophy of psychiatry is whether individuals who are categorized with mental disorders are mad or bad. For a discussion of this issue, see Mike W. Martin, *From Morality to Mental Health: Virtue and Vice in a Therapeutic Culture* (Oxford: Oxford University Press, 2006).

12. "Acts of Violence," *A History of Violence* (New Line, 2006), DVD.

13. The documentary "Acts of Violence" reports that in the original screenplay, Joey and Richie were old friends. Cronenberg changed the script to make them brothers. This change was intended to intensify the dramatic tension between them.

14. For the classic discussion of the relation of authenticity and sincerity, see Lionel Trilling, *Sincerity and Authenticity* (Cambridge, Mass.: Harvard University Press, 1971). For another outstanding, and more recent, discussion of philosophical perspectives on authenticity, see Charles Guignon, *On Being Authentic* (London: Routledge, 2006).

15. Jean-Paul Sartre, *Being and Nothingness* (New York: Philosophical Library, 1956),

and Martin Heidegger, *Being and Time* (New York: Harper and Row, 1962), argue that authentic persons are not guided by the conventional norms of "the they." Heidegger's perspective on the topic had an enormous influence on the version of existentialism formulated by Jean-Paul Sartre in *Being and Nothingness*.

16. Charles Taylor, *The Ethics of Authenticity* (Cambridge, Mass.: Harvard University Press, 2002).

17. Taylor, *The Ethics of Authenticity*, 14.

18. Taylor, *The Ethics of Authenticity*, 82.

Part 3

Words and Worldviews

The Fiction of Truth in Fiction
Some Reflections on Semantics and *eXistenZ*

Graham Stevens

It is a fact that Jennifer Jason Leigh plays the part of a character called Allegra Geller in David Cronenberg's film *eXistenZ* (1999). It is a fact that Jude Law plays a character called Ted Pikul in the same film. *Within* the fiction *eXistenZ*, however, neither Geller nor Pikul is played by anyone, for according to the fiction, these characters are real, existing people, not fictional characters portrayed by actors. What is the case in fiction is not generally the case in fact. But a fiction presents things as fact *within* that fiction. That Allegra Geller exists is not a fact. But it is assumed to be a fact by the fiction *eXistenZ*. A fiction assumes the truth of what is actually false. To follow the narrative of the fiction, we must in some sense entertain these assumptions. It does not strike us as puzzling that, in the fiction *eXistenZ*, Ted Pikul enters into conversation with Allegra Geller. We do not think it is inappropriate for him to do so, though we would think it inappropriate for David Cronenberg to try to enter into dialogue with Allegra Geller in the actual world. This is because Allegra Geller does not exist in the actual world. But she does exist according to the fiction, as does Ted Pikul.

By what process do we interpret fiction so as to distinguish it from reality and gain entertainment from it? A natural suggestion is that we *entertain* the fiction; we enter into it imaginatively in some way. In other words, we imagine the "world" portrayed in the fiction as being real. This natural idea has been exploited by philosophers of language who, for reasons I will explain, often take a special interest in our use of language in the context of discourse concerning the fictional. In this essay, however, I suggest that *eXistenZ* provides us with a compelling reason for thinking that this natural way of thinking about fiction is wrong. We cannot make sense of *eXistenZ* by imagining the world portrayed by the film to be real. We should not, in fact, imagine that there is a "world," even a fictional one, in which the events of *eXistenZ* occur at all.

eXistenZ and the Philosophy of Fiction

In the opening scene of *eXistenZ*, a group of game players assembles in a church to play the prototype of a new game (eXistenZ) designed by one of the lead characters, Allegra Geller.[1] These game players are members of the public who have been invited by the company that markets the game to test out the prototype. A small selection of volunteers is invited onto a stage at the front of the church to take the first turn at playing eXistenZ. To play the game, the players must connect to a somewhat grotesque, apparently organic, console (the game pod), which is, in turn, networked to Geller's own console. (We learn later in the film that connection between player and pod is achieved by plugging the pod into the player's central nervous system via a surgically inserted "bioport" in the player's spine.) Once the game begins, we see the players lapse into a trancelike state, their only movements being to manipulate the game pods on their laps. However, shortly after this, a would-be assassin steps forward from the audience of people waiting their turn to test out the game and attempts to kill Geller. He shoots her, wounding her, before being shot himself. A security guard, Ted Pikul, carries the wounded Geller away, and the two of them flee in a car. They then go into hiding, suspecting that more assassins are hunting Geller.

As the story develops, Geller and Pikul decide to start playing eXistenZ from the safety of the motel room where they are staying. The remainder of the film follows Geller and Pikul through a series of "virtual reality" scenarios, which are apparently part of the game written by Geller.

eXistenZ is rich with material that lends itself to philosophical reflection. The fact that the bioport in players' spines through which they access the virtual reality of the game allows the game pod to override their perceptions of the external world, replacing them with the virtual perceptions of the game (which are qualitatively indistinguishable from real perceptions), brings classic philosophical problems to mind: most notably, of course, the problem of skepticism about the external world. Descartes, as every first-year philosophy student quickly discovers, exploited a similar scenario to pose the skeptical challenge, How do we know that we are not currently under the spell of a malevolent demon who distorts our sensory perceptions to lead us to believe in an external world that does not really exist?[2] Updated for the twenty-first century: How can we know for sure that we are not disembodied brains in vats, our apparent "perceptions" of external things resulting from the prods and pokes of an evil scientist? We are pretty sure that we are not, but, of course, if we allow that such a scenario is (at least in theory) possible, then we must surely concede that the subject whose brain was located in the vat would have absolutely no way of knowing of his or her predicament. Their perception of reality would be just like ours. So, although we might be *pretty* sure that we are not brains in vats, we ought to concede (so the skeptical argument goes) that we cannot be *absolutely* sure: it is not impossible that it is the case. But, in that case, we ought to say the same thing about the possibility that we are currently plugged into a virtual reality game that is qualitatively indistinguishable from actual reality (or so the skeptical argument goes).

My concern in this chapter, however, is not directly with this problem, although it does bear a substantial relation to it. I will use *eXistenZ* to shed light on a problem in the philosophy of language. Philosophers of language are concerned with how language functions. How, for example, are sentences able to represent things truly or falsely? The problem I am interested in is a problem concerning how language functions when we use it to create or describe a fiction. In particular, what does it mean for something to be true in, or of, a fiction? This is really a problem in the philosophy of language, but it has very wide repercussions for other areas of philosophy, including aesthetics (philosophy of art) and metaphysics (the philosophical inquiry into the nature of reality). It is no surprise, of course, that aestheticians should be interested in the nature of fiction. In metaphysics it has become a pressing problem as a result of the rise of *fictionalism* as a proposed explanation of our talk of objects whose existence many philosophers are wary of countenancing. For example, in the philosophy of mathematics, unwillingness to accept that abstract objects like numbers and sets are as real as the everyday things of the physical world has made mathematical fictionalism—the view that mathematical objects are fictional items, and that mathematical truth is merely truth in a fiction—increasingly popular. According to fictionalism, our talk of a given class of objects is best understood as talk about a fiction in which such objects are real, rather than talk about really existing objects. But, obviously, we need to know what it is to "talk about a fiction" in this sense if the theory is to succeed in making our talk of the class of objects any less mysterious.

It is at this point that we turn to the philosophy of language for help, for what we really want an explanation of is the meanings of statements like "According to the fiction f, p," where "f" stands for some fiction, and "p" is some statement; for example, "According to the fiction *eXistenZ*, Allegra Geller is female." The need to turn our attention to statements of the form just provided is evident if we compare the following two examples:

(1) Allegra Geller is female.
(2) According to the fiction *eXistenZ*, Allegra Geller is female.

Example (1) is false because Allegra Geller is not anything. Therefore she is not female. Nor is she male, or human, or happy, or sad, or whatever. Only things that exist can have those kinds of properties, and fictional characters don't exist. Example (2) is quite different, however, because according to the fiction *eXistenZ*, Allegra Geller does exist. And in that fiction, the existing Allegra Geller is female. So, unlike what is said by (1), what is said by (2) is indeed the case. So (2) is true.

We can, arguably, say *some* true things about Allegra Geller, without the "According to the fiction *eXistenZ*" prefix. For example:

(3) Allegra Geller does not exist.
(4) Allegra Geller is played by Jennifer Jason Leigh.

Notice that both (3) and (4) will be false if prefixed by "According to the fiction *eXistenZ*." Examples (3) and (4) are true, but not true in the fiction *eXistenZ*.[3]

It is the meanings of statements prefixed by locutions of the form "According to the fiction f" that I will be concerned with in what follows. To make life a little easier, I will just call the locution and its synonyms the *fictional operator*. I now turn to a brief explanation of the most influential accounts of what the fictional operator means.

Possible World Semantics for Fiction

When philosophers of language and linguists want to investigate what an expression means, a common method they employ is to look at the conditions under which the expression, or a larger expression containing it, is true. Such conditions are called, for obvious reasons, *truth conditions,* and the systematic theory of the meanings of expressions in a language that draws on these truth conditions is known as *truth-conditional semantics.* For many sentences of a language, it is a simple enough matter to specify their truth conditions. For example, the sentence "David Cronenberg is American" is true if and only if David Cronenberg, the person, has a certain property, namely the property of being American. Likewise, the sentence "David Cronenberg is Canadian" is true if and only if David Cronenberg, the person, has a certain property, namely the property of being Canadian. One sentence happens to be true, one happens to be false. Whether they are true or not, we can state the conditions under which they *would* be true. We can also specify the truth conditions of expressions that connect together sentences like these: "David Cronenberg is Canadian, and David Cronenberg is a movie director" is true if and only if *both* David Cronenberg has the property of being Canadian *and* David Cronenberg has the property of being a movie director. We can even abstract away from the particular sentences joined by the word "and" here to get the *truth-conditional content* of the expression "and": if *A* and *B* are *any* declarative sentences, then *A* and *B* is true if and only if both *A* and *B* are true.

Words like these, sentence connectives whose meanings can be characterized by such abstract truth conditions, are of particular interest to logicians and form the basis of the languages of formal logic that were developed in the beginning of the twentieth century. As these languages developed, it was natural for logicians to try to import other natural language expressions into their formal languages. This led to the development of modal logic. The languages of modal logic contain expressions that prefix sentences to allow the expression of truths about what is possible and/or necessary (or impossible). So, for example, we can now consider sentences like "David Cronenberg directed *Videodrome* (1983), but he *could* have directed *Star Wars* (1977)." Here the word "could" expresses a modal property, modifying the claim that Cronenberg directed *Star Wars* so as to yield the claim that it is in some sense possible for Cronenberg to direct (or have directed) *Star Wars*.

What are the truth conditions of sentences containing modal expressions like "could" or "possibly"? If the truth conditions of a sentence are to be enlightening about the meaning of the sentence, then it won't do to say that, for example, the sentence "David Cronenberg could have directed *Star Wars*" is true if and only if David Cronenberg could have directed *Star Wars*. This does nothing to tell us what the modal expression "could" means. The now standard way to interpret modal expressions (and to provide interpretations for modal logics) is by a theory known as *possible world semantics*. What this involves is relativizing the truth conditions of sentences to various possible situations (known as "worlds"), which may or may not be actual. So, for example, we can interpret "David Cronenberg could have directed *Star Wars*" as, roughly, a claim that there is a possible situation in which David Cronenberg directed *Star Wars*. Had the world been different in this respect—that David Cronenberg directed *Star Wars*—then the sentence "David Cronenberg directed *Star Wars*" would be true. The word "could," added to this sentence, is therefore understood as an expression that performs an operation on the sentence "David Cronenberg directed *Star Wars*"—namely, the operation of saying that the situation the sentence describes is *possible*. We thereby arrive at a paraphrase of the original sentence as something akin to "There is a possible world in which David Cronenberg directed *Star Wars*," which is true if and only if there is a possible world (situation) in which "David Cronenberg directed *Star Wars*" is true. These possible worlds or situations appealed to in the theory are just the possible ways the world could have been.

The world could, presumably, have turned out to be such that Cronenberg directed *Star Wars*. But it could not have turned out such that 2 + 2 was not 4. There is a possible world in which Cronenberg directed *Star Wars*, but no world in which it is not the case that 2 + 2 = 4. So it is *necessarily* true that 2 + 2 = 4, and *this* modal claim just means that, *in all possible worlds*, 2 + 2 = 4.

In David Lewis's influential 1978 paper "Truth in Fiction," he argues that the semantic theory briefly sketched in the previous paragraph is ideally suited to resolve the problem of how to explain the sense in which fictional sentences have truth-values.[4] His suggestion is that the fictional operator acts as a modal operator on sentences, relativizing their truth conditions to possible worlds. Very roughly, the idea is that a sentence like "In the fiction *f*, David Cronenberg directed *Star Wars*" is to be understood as stating that the sentence "David Cronenberg directed *Star Wars*" is true *in the world of the fiction f*. A first approximation at specifying which possible world exactly this might be is that it is the world in which the events of the fiction actually occur. This basic claim needs some revision. One problem with the basic claim, first pointed out by contemporary philosopher Saul Kripke, is the following: it is entirely possible that authors may compose what they intend to be a fiction and, by pure chance, write something that turns out to be true.[5] But in that case, should we say that the fiction is really *about* the actual world? Surely not—if there really was someone actually called Allegra Geller who, unbeknownst to Cronenberg, had all of the properties and engaged in all of the acts attributed to Geller in the movie, then it wouldn't therefore be this individual whom the movie was about.

To overcome problems of this sort, Lewis opts to treat fictions not as just sets of sentences but as stories told by a storyteller. This leads to the following account of which worlds are to be invoked in explaining the semantics of fiction: "The worlds we should consider . . . are the worlds where the fiction is told, but as known fact rather than fiction. The act of storytelling occurs, just as it does here at our world; but there it is what here it falsely purports to be: truth-telling about matters whereof the teller has knowledge."⁶ This initial analysis (Lewis calls it "analysis 0") is deemed ultimately inadequate by Lewis. The main reason for this is that Lewis takes there to be many varied worlds that would have an equal claim to being the worlds of a particular fiction on this analysis. To modify one of Lewis's examples a little, a world in which the events of *The Fly* (1986) are reported as known fact and in which Brundle has a third nostril, and one otherwise identical to that world except in the respect that Brundle does *not* have a third nostril, are equally good candidate *Fly* worlds on analysis 0. For this reason, Lewis introduces "analysis 1," which, roughly, adds to analysis 0 the condition that the worlds in question should be the closest akin to ours in all respects apart from what is explicitly stated in the story. Thus we get the apparently desirable result that the world of *The Fly* fiction is one in which Brundle has only two nostrils.

There may, however, be facts regarding our world that, intuitively, should not be facts of the fictional worlds. The following example is a slight modification of one given recently by contemporary philosopher Mark Sainsbury: if we suppose that precisely 1,756 arrows were fired at the Battle of Hastings, then the world of *eXistenZ* should also contain this fact. That is to say, it ought to be true *in our world* that, according to *eXistenZ*, exactly 1,756 arrows were fired at the Battle of Hastings.⁷ But this is clearly not something that most would agree with. In response to similar concerns, Lewis also offers "analysis 2," according to which the relevant worlds should be those in which things are not just how the fiction states, but also (where not stated) in accordance with the overt beliefs of the narrator and the intended audience.

I will not pursue the details of Lewis's semantic proposals further, as in the next section I will argue that *eXistenZ* provides a counterexample to Lewis's proposal. This counterexample is sufficient to provide a refutation of Lewis's theory, as it demonstrates that the modal interpretation of the fictional operator he proposes is unable to capture the literal meaning of the simple phrase "According to the fiction *f*, . . ."

eXistenZ as a Counterexample to Lewis's Analysis

Let us return to the narrative of *eXistenZ*. The lead protagonists, it will be recalled, on the run from would-be assassins, have fled to the security of a remote motel room, where they have plugged themselves into their game pods and begun playing eXistenZ. The plot thickens as Geller and Pikul (or, perhaps, the characters they are playing in the game) become embroiled in a (virtual) world of double-crossing employees of companies competing in a multibillion-dollar virtual reality games market. Along the way, they find themselves in some unusual situations, including one where Pikul shoots a waiter in a restaurant in which mutated amphibians are served as a delicacy. At this point in the movie, Lewis's account of fiction would seem to work well enough. The world of the fiction—the world in which the events of the fiction are reported as known fact—is the world of the opening scene of the movie. In this world it is true that Geller and Pikul are on the run from assassins (or, at least, are on the run because they believe they are being hunted by assassins); it is true that they are playing a virtual reality game called eXistenZ, in which Pikul plays the role of a character who shoots a waiter in a restaurant where mutated amphibians are served as a delicacy. It is not true in the world of the fiction that Pikul has actually shot a waiter.

As things progress, however, it becomes less clear whether this world really is the world of the fiction. At first, we the audience watch as Pikul and, later, Geller begin to doubt whether the apparently real world is what it appears to be or whether it is just another layer within the game. Sometime after the scene in which Pikul shoots the waiter, Geller and Pikul find themselves back in the motel room of what we have so far taken to be the world of the fiction, only to be confronted in that world by characters from the game they thought they were playing. Within this world, Geller eventually kills Pikul, declaring herself the winner of the game. At this point, there occurs a twist in the narrative that is particularly important for our current concerns. The film cuts to a new scene in which many of the central characters of preceding scenes in the film are now seated on a stage, wearing futuristic headsets and wristbands. It quickly becomes apparent that the situation we are now observing is one in which the entire film thus far has been part of a game. The earlier scenes in which the characters sat on a stage playing the game eXistenZ turns out to have been just an episode in a virtual reality game called transCendenZ that the participants of this scene have been playing via the headsets and wristbands. This game was not designed by Geller but by a character called Yevgeny Nourish (Don McKellar), who previously appeared as a different character in the restaurant scene, and who has also been on the stage playing the game. Finally, at the end of this scene (which is the final scene of the movie), Geller and Pikul confront Nourish and assassinate *him*. As they turn to flee, the character who played the role of the waiter murdered by Pikul in eXistenZ blocks their path. They point their guns at him, and he pleads with them not to kill him. Then, visibly confused, he asks: "Hey, tell me the truth; are we still in the game?" The movie ends at this point.

What is the world of *eXistenZ* (the movie, not the game)? The question cannot be answered with certainty. Furthermore, it is surely a crucial part of the story that we cannot answer this question. The ending of the film works because we do not know the answer to the question asked in its last line of speech. And if we do not know the answer to that question, then we do not know what world is the real world according to *eXistenZ*. We do not know what world is the world in which the events of the film could be reported as known fact. It might be replied that our failure to answer this question is just a consequence of our limited knowledge—there is a real world of the fiction, but we do not know what that world is. Perhaps there is a world in which Cronenberg intended the fiction to be set, the identity of which he chose not to reveal to his audience. This is possible; only Cronenberg knows if it is true. But even if it is true, it is certainly possible that he had no such world in mind at all—that he deliberately set out to create a fiction that is not set in any particular world and that he did so in order to create a fiction according to which the division between fact and fiction is indeterminate. As this is possible, it is therefore possible that a fiction may lack a world in which its events could be reported as known fact. Thus we have a clear counterexample to Lewis's analysis of truth in fiction, for there are many true things we can say about the events of *eXistenZ*, not least that the characters of the fiction often have reason to doubt whether their experiences are genuinely of reality. The truth of these claims shows that the fictional operator does not have the meaning that Lewis ascribes to it, for the claims cannot be assessed relative to a particular world. We have no reason to believe there is any world that is the real world of *eXistenZ*.

Some Consequences and Conclusions

What exactly does this counterexample show? Note that it does not merely challenge a local aspect of Lewis's theory in a way that shows the theory to be incomplete. Rather, it challenges the fundamental idea of the theory— namely, that the truth conditions of statements containing the fictional operator relate to a world, or set of worlds, in which the fiction is nonfiction. Therefore, it challenges the intuitions that motivated Lewis's project in the first place. Those intuitions are intuitions that there is more to a fiction than what is explicitly stated by the fiction. For example, Lewis's analysis takes it as obvious that it is true of *The Fly* that Brundle did not have a third nostril. This intuition is right only if there is a determinate fictional world that the story told in *The Fly* is true of.[8] But the case of *eXistenZ* should make us suspicious that this is so.

Let us test similar intuitions against *eXistenZ*. Is it obviously true that Allegra Geller does not have a third nostril? Certainly not. It is quite coherent to imagine a further development of the plot such that the players of transCendenZ are in fact players of yet another virtual reality game, meta-RealitY. Players of metaRealitY enter the game by plugging their game pods directly into their surgically created third nostrils. It is far from obvious that the sincere assertion that Allegra Geller does not have a third nostril is warranted. (It is, of course, far from obvious that the sincere assertion that Allegra Geller *does* have a third nostril is warranted. Rather, it is surely that the fiction simply does not determine the answer to this question.) If this seems too far-fetched, then let us test our intuitions with a less exotic example. At the beginning of *eXistenZ*, when Geller and Pikul meet, it appears to be the case that they are meeting for the first time. Yet, when we arrive at the scene in which they are players of transCendenZ, they announce that they are in a romantic relationship with each other. Is it true in the fiction *eXistenZ* that Allegra Geller and Ted Pikul are in a romantic relationship that began before the narrative of the fiction did? Again, neither this claim nor the claim that Allegra Geller and Ted Pikul are not in a romantic relationship that began before the narrative of the fiction did is warranted by the fiction.

The intuition that questions about a fiction that are not explicitly answered by the fiction must nonetheless have determinate answers relies on the assumption that a fiction presents a fictional world that has something like the completeness and determinateness of the real world (or, for that matter, of a possible world). The intuition is therefore sound only if fictions are true of such complete and determinate worlds. But *eXistenZ* shows that this is not the case. Therefore, we have good reason to doubt the intuition that led to positing such worlds in the first place. I suggest that the lesson to be learned from *eXistenZ* is that we should resort to a very stringent definition of what truth in a fiction amounts to: *nothing* is true in a fiction unless it is explicitly asserted by the fiction.[9] In comparison to the presumably infinite number of truths there are about the real world, this makes very little true in most fictions.[10]

It might be thought that this is too great a cost. My own view is that it is a desirable result. By adopting as minimal an account as possible of what truth in a fiction amounts to, we reduce the risk of prescribing unrealistic aesthetic regulations on the concept of a fiction. Such regulations are not likely to be followed by every fiction. The artistic nature of storytelling is such that innovative storytellers will not be constrained by such demanding regulations as those imposed on them by a model such as Lewis's. Cronenberg's *eXistenZ* is just one example where this is apparent. Another Cronenberg movie, *Videodrome,* also seems to fit this description. As with *eXistenZ*, as viewers of *Videodrome*, we undergo a shift in the course of the movie. We begin by appearing to be observing characters in the movie becoming uncertain as to what exactly is real, while we look on from a privileged position of certainty as to what is real (for them—i.e., in the fiction). As the plot develops, however, we lose that privileged position and find ourselves unable to locate a determinate world in which the fiction is true. Outside of the medium of film, there are almost definitely other examples. Numerous modernist works suggest themselves as candidates. James Joyce's *Ulysses* and *Finnegans Wake* and Djuna Barnes's *Nightwood*, to mention just three, are novels that may be plausibly interpreted in a way that would support the kinds of arguments I have given regarding *eXistenZ*. In each of these books, events are reported that do not appear to all be happening in the same fictional world, thus leaving us with no determinate answer to the question of which world is the world of the fiction. What all of these fictions have in common is that there is a level of ambiguity and indeterminacy, crucial to the fiction, that cannot survive being made to conform to the narrow prescription that they be true of any particular world. These works all steadfastly refuse to allow the audience to identify a particular world in which the narrative plays out.

If we adopt an analysis of what it is to be true in a fiction that evaluates sentences containing the fiction operator as true or false relative to a world that the fiction is related to, then we will have no choice but to classify works like these as anomalous. It is surely better to adopt an account of truth in a fiction that can accommodate them. Anyone who remains troubled by the fact that so little is true in most fictions on such an account would do well to remember that fictions, after all, are not real.

Notes

Thanks to Simon Riches for many helpful comments on an earlier draft of this essay.

    1. To avoid confusion, I italicize the name of the movie *eXistenZ* but not the name of the game eXistenZ that the film is named after.
    2. René Descartes, *Philosophical Writings*, ed. and trans. Norman Kemp Smith (New York: Modern Library, 1958).
    3. Some would deny this, holding that (3) and (4) are neither true nor false. The reasoning behind this view is that it is sometimes thought that nothing is true or false of a nonexistent thing. The view is first clearly articulated by Gottlob Frege in his 1892 paper "On Sense and Reference," reprinted in *Translations from the Philosophical Writings of Gottlob Frege*, ed. Peter Geach and Max Black (Oxford: Blackwell, 1952).
    4. David Lewis, "Truth in Fiction," reprinted in his *Philosophical Papers*, vol. 1 (Oxford: Oxford University Press, 1983), 261–80.

5. See Saul Kripke, *Naming and Necessity* (Oxford: Blackwell, 1980).
6. Lewis, "Truth in Fiction," 266.
7. See Mark Sainsbury, *Fiction and Fictionalism* (London: Routledge, 2010), 77.
8. There is an added complication with this example, as there is with all of Cronenberg's movies. *The Fly* is a work of science fiction that portrays events contradicting the laws of physics (and perhaps even metaphysics). One might think that this makes it impossible for there to be a world in which *The Fly* is a report of known fact. This is a different problem to the one I am discussing here, however. Lewis's original example discussed Arthur Conan Doyle's stories about the fictional detective Sherlock Holmes, for which this problem does not arise.
9. Should we also admit as true the logical consequences of what is explicitly asserted by the fiction? This might be argued for on the grounds that if the assertions of the fiction are true in the fiction, then their consequences ought to be true, by definition of logical consequence (a statement A is a logical consequence of a statement B just in case the truth of B guarantees the truth of A). This argument, however, begs the question. It assumes that logic behaves in the fiction as it does in reality, an assertion that is rarely made by any fiction and so not guaranteed to be true if what is true is what is explicitly asserted by the fiction.
10. Some fictions may also contain an infinite number of truths; for example, a fictional tale that explicitly stated that there are an infinite number of true arithmetical statements.

Re(ct)ifying Empty Speech
Cronenberg and the Problem of the First Person

Brook W. R. Pearson

And they can either paint it or draw it or write it down, right? And then pass it on to somebody. They read what you are saying, and then they are reexperiencing. That's the only connection that you have with that man. So you can't rewrite. 'Cause to rewrite is to deceive and lie, and you betray your own thoughts. To rethink the flow and the rhythm and the tumbling out of the words is a betrayal, and it's a sin, Martin. It's a sin.
—Hank in *Naked Lunch*

This ego . . . is frustration in its very essence . . . a frustration at one remove, a frustration that the subject—even were he to reduce its form in his discourse to the passivating image by which the subject makes himself an object by displaying himself before the mirror—could not be satisfied with, since even if he achieved the most perfect resemblance to that image, it would still be the other's jouissance that he would have gotten recognized there.
—Jacques Lacan

The life of a moviegoer is not always as simple as it seems, particularly when we step into the world of David Cronenberg. Like Beverly Mantle (Jeremy Irons) in *Dead Ringers* (1988), we can experience in ourselves a desire to dominate and control the films' interpretations, fashioning instruments for ourselves to allow access to their mysteries; at other times we become enmeshed in their narratives, sinking into them until it is difficult to determine where we end and the filmic reality begins. Our William Lee (Peter Weller) fingers mesh with our Clark Nova; we ingest the drug and fall under the spell of Interzone.

In this chapter, my purpose is to interrogate a thematic feature of Cronenberg's film oeuvre from the perspective of three different philosophical points of view. As my title suggests, this theme relates to the way in which Cronenberg treats the notion of identity—the first person, or the "I." There is a significant purposeful use of psychoanalytic categories throughout Cronenberg's output, beginning with his earliest feature work in *Stereo* (1969), and continuing through to his most recent and upcoming work.

In this chapter, we will hear from Jacques Lacan, controversial founder of the so-called French School of philosophically informed Freudian psychoanalysis; Ludwig Wittgenstein, the Cambridge philosopher of Viennese extraction whose later work, in particular, paid much attention to the logic of psychological discourse; and Gilles Deleuze and Félix Guattari, a philosopher-psychoanalyst team whose critique of Lacanian and Freudian thought has been very important in recent discussion of the internal structure of psychoanalytic theory. Each of these perspectives pays significant attention to the problems associated with understanding what a "self" is—what persons can mean when they say "I." These perspectives, at times, differ wildly from one another and can even be seen to be in diametric opposition. Cronenberg has consistently returned to the ground upon which these philosophical, psychological, or psychoanalytic perspectives have been founded. It is not just the case that Cronenberg's films can be pressed into service to demonstrate this or that philosophical concept, but rather that his work is constantly engaging with such concepts. If philosophy matters much in our world, it is where we can engage with it in the context of our own cultural lives, and Cronenberg is a significant player in this regard.

Not What People Expect from a Director's Couch

Lacan—who is a very subtle thinker, but sometimes an overly complicated writer—suggests that there is "no speech without a response, even if speech meets only with silence, provided it has an auditor, and this is the heart of its function in analysis."[1] This description of the therapeutic relationship evokes a well-worn picture of therapist on chair, patient on couch, with only, perhaps, the skritch-skritch-skritch of a pencil on pad as response to the patient's words. It is one with which we are very familiar, and the lack of response on the part of the therapist is not perceived negatively.

But what if we were to apply the structure of this relationship to our viewing of a film? In the same way that we recognize the value of the auditor in the therapeutic relationship, we could ask ourselves, "What is a film's existence without an audience?" Faced with a film screen, the audience becomes analyst, and Mr. Cronenberg's films the subjects that it seeks to understand. But then again, there is something in the moviegoing experience that is at once intimate and alienating. This is akin to what Lacan discusses in "The Function and Field of Speech and Language in Psychoanalysis" (quoted in part in the second epigraph to this chapter):

> This ego, whose strength our theorists now define by its capacity to bear frustration, is frustration in its very essence. No frustration of one of the subject's desires, but frustration of an object in which his desire is alienated; and the more developed this object becomes, the more profoundly the subject becomes alienated from his jouissance. It is thus a frustration at one remove, a frustration that the subject—even were he to reduce its form in his discourse to the passivating image by which the subject makes himself an object by displaying himself before the mirror—could not be satisfied with, since even if he achieved the most perfect resemblance to that image, it would still be the other's jouissance that he would have gotten recognized there. Which is why there is no adequate response to this discourse, for the subject regards as contemptuous any speech that buys into his mistake.[2]

Our experience in this regard is a "frustration at one remove." We watch the film as if viewing "the passivating image by which [a] subject makes himself an object by displaying himself before the mirror." Yet, despite this apparent intimacy, we "could not be satisfied with [it], since even if [we] achieved the most perfect resemblance to that image, it would still be the other's jouissance"—meaning the entire gamut of emotions and their interplay that make up the human experience—that "would have gotten recognized there." The moviegoer is quite familiar with this kind of alienation: all too often the lines in Neil Young's song "A Man Needs a Maid"—"I fell in love with the actress / She was playing a part that I could understand"—are a qualitative description of our experience with film. Our apparent understanding is made problematic by the fact that our "love" is for an image that sees only itself. The credits roll, the lights come up, and we crunch through popcorn sticky with sugar to the night or day of our *real* location. Even the most casual moviegoer has likely experienced this sense of displacement.

Still, the interpretive relation between moviegoer and film is made up of a set of predictable components: script, acting, sets, effects, lighting, editing, directing, and so on. Occasionally, though, a filmmaker comes along whose vision exceeds the sum of these parts, and we are challenged to think more deeply about our interface with his or her work. David Cronenberg has long been recognized to be such a director. For the most part, Cronenberg's films are anything but "passivating images," because they function on a level that thrusts the audience into an active role of consideration, of analysis that demands a response.

As I mentioned, the purpose of this chapter is to examine one particular strand of Cronenberg's complex oeuvre that is introduced in his first (rather short) feature film, *Stereo*, and that forms an important feature of many of his subsequent films: the possibility and function of a psychological or philosophical "statue" of the self—in other words, what does "I" mean? In philosophy, the first person, or "I" has a long history of discussion, and has important implications for theories to do with human identity, ethics, and even metaphysics. The psychoanalytic notion that a person's identity is formed from the interplay of different parts of the mind—the id, ego, and superego—has been of intense interest since Freud first posited his theories.[3] Intentionally or not, Cronenberg's treatment of this theme in films such as *Stereo, Crimes of the Future* (1970), *Naked Lunch* (1991), *Spider* (2002), and *A History of Violence* (2005) closely mirrors Lacan's development of Freudian psychoanalysis, but it also problematizes some of this theory in a way that mimics Wittgenstein's criticisms of psychoanalysis. Wittgenstein's wry comment that "the language game of reporting can be given such a turn that a report is not meant to inform the hearer about its subject matter but about the person making the report" signals this critique—namely, that the analysis of what it is to be a person, particularly what a human being means or denotes when he or she says "I," varies according to context.[4] In this chapter, to demonstrate this complexity, I will primarily explore a comparison between the presentation of the characters of Tom Stall/Joey Cusack (Viggo Mortensen) in *A History of Violence* and of Spider (Ralph Fiennes) in *Spider*.

A Modern Ovid

The Roman poet Ovid wrote a book called *Metamorphoses* that begins, "My mind leads me to speak now of forms changed into new bodies."[5] Throughout the book's epic sweep, Ovid describes the classical mythological emphasis on *transformation*, and, in so doing, engages in an analysis of Roman culture that is still being unraveled. Cronenberg's oeuvre is similarly marked by a fascination for, and exploration of, the transformation of bodies, whether by telepathic link (*Stereo, Scanners* [1981]), invading pathogen or organism (*Crimes of the Future, Shivers* [1975]), drugs (*Naked Lunch*), technology

(*Videodrome* [1983], *The Fly* [1986], *eXistenZ* [1999]), car accident (*The Dead Zone* [1983], *Crash* [1996]), or simply crime and violence (*Spider, A History of Violence, Eastern Promises* [2007]). Some of these, like his adaptation of J. G. Ballard's *Crash*, are less obvious as tropes of transformation than others, but even there, throughout the film, we watch bodies being altered, maimed, repaired, *transformed*. Our modern Ovid's preface might read:

My mind leads me to speak now of forms changed
into new bodies: O gods above, inspire
this undertaking (which you've changed as well)
and guide my films in their epic sweep . . .[6]

In fact, one can summarize all of the transformation in Cronenberg's films along two vectors: those changes engendered by technology, and those forced by the interface of the individual and society. Or, more simply still, we can see these two as inextricably linked. How the individual human subject *responds* to this transforming power is where Cronenberg sites much of the dramatic tension of his work. His most recent work, though—films such as *Spider, A History of Violence*, and *Eastern Promises*—has focused more directly upon characters undergoing an *inner* transformation. What could read as metaphor in earlier work, with the "body horror" that Cronenberg was so instrumental in developing, is now being addressed more directly.

The connectivity inherent in *Videodrome*'s "Civic TV, Channel 83: The One You Take to Bed with You" and *eXistenZ*'s organic computers that allow the linking of multiple minds in a shared hallucinatory game experience picks up on *Stereo*'s group telepathic experience. In each of these cases, we see a combination of sexuality, technology, and society—*Crash*, too, could be included in this nexus, as could the truly difficult and bizarre *Crimes of the Future*, and the grotesque but more comprehensible *Fly* and *Shivers*. In each of these cases, we see individuals undergoing transformation—willing or otherwise—learning to cope, somehow, with the effects of this transformation. The everyday human subject is drawn large for us on a two-story-tall screen, in a fashion similar to how the city of Plato's *Republic* acts as a thought experiment to discuss justice, in this case to examine *our own* responses to the (often technological) pressure of society.[7]

Lacan's development of Freud's psychoanalytic model, interrupted by the Second World War, led to schism within the ranks of Freudian psychoanalysis. Beginning in 1951 and becoming public in 1953, Lacan's hugely influential weekly seminars in Paris emphasized the linguistic identity of psychoanalytic pathology and espoused a "return to Freud" that rejected much of the development that had taken place in the intervening decades. The therapeutic model that Lacan describes—his version of Freud's "talking cure" (the primary locus of psychoanalytic therapy derived from the speech of the patient)—is one that recognizes and repositions the *conversation* as the central structure of the connection between patient and analyst.

Yet, it is a conversation wherein the subject is expected to present him- or herself in a fashion that is essentially *empty*. So, there are inherent dangers in this conversation. As Lacan states, "If the psychoanalyst is not aware that this is how [therapeutic] speech functions, he will experience its call all the more strongly; and if emptiness is the first thing to make itself heard in analysis, he will feel it in himself and he will seek a reality beyond speech to fill the emptiness."[8] So, in other words, if the "empty speech" that comes from the patient's pathologically damaged sense of "self" (or "ego") is answered uncritically, the analyst runs the risk of allowing the patient's "statue" of him- or herself to take the place of the actual person, and the "reality beyond speech" emerges from the response to a fantasy. Like falling in "love" with a phone-sex operator, the therapist ignorant of what Lacan discusses here may allow him- or herself to fill in the gaps in the fantasy, and so become embroiled in the patient's pathology.

This "reality beyond speech" is a theme addressed multiple times throughout Cronenberg's directorial oeuvre, both in those films he has himself written and in those that he has directed from adapted works written by others. From the early *Stereo* and *Crimes of the Future*, through, especially, his more recent work in *Spider* and *A History of Violence*, Cronenberg's study of human transformation has often emphasized what Lacan calls "the monument of [a subject's] narcissism." This narcissism leads individuals to cope with their place within the transformative structures around them by creating a purposeful "monument" to present to others, or themselves, as a way of avoiding more legitimate processing of the transformations they have themselves undergone. And, as I have suggested, this onscreen structure is both mimicked by and in service of this relation between film viewer and filmic discourse. *We,* armchair critics and philosophers who enter the movie house with intact statues of ourselves, discover that *we* have become interrogated by the film that we thought to analyze, pin down, and dissect. We came thinking to be analysts, aware only of the control that we have as viewer, but Cronenberg challenges us, and, reclining, we allow ourselves to be caught in the web of our patient's fantasy. We become interwoven with the "I" of the characters in the films, never entirely certain where we are seeing and where we are filling in what we cannot see.

Ruined Monuments

Many of the themes that Cronenberg pursues throughout his oeuvre are introduced in *Stereo* and *Crimes of the Future*. Both shot without synchronized sound, and presented as narrated filmic records, they make claims similar to what, as I have mentioned, Wittgenstein notes is the case with Freudian psychoanalysis: "The language game of reporting can be given such a turn that a report is not meant to inform the hearer about its subject matter but about the person making the report."[9] "Language game," explained simply, describes Wittgenstein's notion that language is not just vocabulary and grammar but also *use*. So, in this context, the idea that the purpose of making a report is to deliver the *content* of the report is turned on its side, and we have the psychoanalytic approach to the game emphasizing the *reporter* rather than the *reported*. For instance, *Stereo*, claiming from its opening credits onward to be a report forming part of a "mosaic" of educational resources by the Canadian Academy for Erotic Enquiry, is very clearly *not* filmed in such a manner, though the narrated commentary seems to be so constructed. The viewer is constantly drawn to make connections between the narration and the images. However, given that much of the film deals with telepathy and "psychic research," this demands more of the viewer than he or she perhaps realizes. We do work to interpret this film that *we do not realize we are doing*. There is significant *silence* in the way that this film communicates, and there is much that we observe without explanation, filling in our interpretations without any necessary basis for doing so. For example, at multiple junctures throughout the film, even where it is not discussed in the accompanying narrative, there is an emphasis on sexual interaction, and the characters often wear adult-size pacifiers on cords around their necks, or are pictured sucking on them. Even when the dominant controller character specifically notices one, and touches it, we are not treated to a narrative of it. Because of this, we, as viewers, cannot help but fill in the gaps in the narrative with our judgments, responses, and evaluations of the cultural expectations that inhere in the behavior of these characters. This, in turn, affects our interpretation of the more obviously connected words and images in the film.

Lacan argues that the "reality beyond speech" that the analyst seeks "leads the analyst to analyze the subject's behavior in order to find in it what the subject is not saying," and he recognizes in the ensuing process something of the erotic: "the ambiguous gap of an attempted seduction of the other by the means on which the subject manifests indulgence, and on which he stakes the monument of his narcissism."[10] The lack of awareness on the part of an analyst essentially allows the patient to market his or her vision of him- or herself to the analyst as if merely describing what is real. This coheres with what one of the narrators of *Stereo* (there are several, unidentified, narrative voices) says regarding parapsychological investigation:

> In psychic research, the emotional distance between the researcher and his subject is inevitably diminished until it is no more than the distance between any two persons. The acquiescence of the subject to the demands of the researcher becomes nothing more nor less than an individual act of faith, of love. If there can be no love between researcher and subject, there can be no experimentation.
>
> In conventional theories of scientific methodology, an experiment proves its validity when it can be universally repeated, in every aspect. In psychic research, such an approach is completely untenable. The existential circumstances of any experiment in parapsychology are inextricably mixed with the individuals and the phenomenological sets involved in that particular experiment, and cannot be extracted from those individuals or phenomenological sets. The conditions of experiments in parapsychology are unique, nonuniform, and nonrepeatable.
>
> A completely nonscientific burden is therefore placed upon the researcher, for if the personal relationship between researcher and subject deteriorates, the experiment cannot continue along its natural course. The sensitivity of the experimental parapsychological plexus requires new methods to help maintain the emotional momentum of certain experiments.

These ideas mirror the evolution of Freudian psychoanalysis (and its many successors) that was developed in the first place as a response to what are generally considered aberrant behaviors or attitudes because of their exception from a social norm. Joseph Breuer and Freud's seminal 1895 work *Studies in Hysteria* sought to develop a new approach to healing psychologically what were previously thought to be primarily *physical* maladies.[11] Freud's continued development of the "talking cure," first discussed in his work with Breuer, emphasized a picture of the human mind that was highly *structured,* with psychological problems being engendered by an *unbalancing* of these structures. Much of Freudian psychoanalysis depends upon attempts to describe and effect change in the various sorts of imbalance that are associated with categorizable *behaviors.* So, instead of thinking that there is some sort of inherent *physical* cause for behavior, the Freudian posits that there is an imbalance or damage that has been done to the structure of the patient's psyche. Without being too simplistic, a typical example is the notion of a Freudian slip: a use of a word that is not merely incorrect in a given situation but betrays a more deep-seated desire manifesting itself in the context of our speech.

Modeled from and mirroring human *physical* development, the growth of the psychological structures of the mind is thought by Freud to be associated primarily with the development of sexuality in the context of the nuclear family. This aspect of Freud's theory is infamous because of its assertion that incestuous feelings form the most basic and essential stages of growth in the psychosexual progress of the individual human. Many have also criticized aspects of Freudian theory because of, for instance, its prioritizing of *male* sexual development. The main area of focus for this critique has been the idea of the "Oedipus complex," in which a boy desires his mother and therefore seeks to destroy his primary competition for her affections—namely, his father. There is a concomitant realization that the mother does not have a penis, and therefore anxiety that the boy may then lose his penis, known as "castration anxiety." For a girl, this whole drama has an added layer because of her lack of a penis, which causes her to "envy" her father, and then to transfer her attachment to her father as a means of obtaining his penis, making the mother the focus of her competition. Another significant locus of critique for the Freudian model is its lack of experimental data to support its assertions concerning the structure of the mind. However, whatever its problems or strengths, the Freudian model has occupied the imaginations of many in the arts and other aspects of cultural production, and, as with the Christian story of the Passion that forms the substructure of much non-Christian literature, film, and art, so too does the "holy family" of the Oedipus complex find its way into much aesthetic output.

For my purposes in this chapter, a key element of the Lacanian development of Freud's psychoanalysis is his notion of the unconscious as a "censored chapter." He says that the "censored chapter" can be refound "in monuments: this is my body, in other words, the hysterical core of neurosis in which the hysterical symptom manifests the structure of a language and is deciphered like an inscription which, once recovered, can be destroyed without serious loss." So, once the *content* of an inscription has been recovered and preserved, the stone upon which it is inscribed is no longer necessary. The Lacanian treatment of the unconscious as *text* positions itself differently from a purely mechanistic implementation of the Freudian model of conscious/unconscious coupled with id/ego/superego. The unconscious is also recoverable "in its traces that are inevitably preserved in the distortions necessitated by the insertion of the adulterated chapter into the chapters surrounding it."[12]

Lacan's rather more thoroughgoing employment of the Freudian metaphors of text and interpretation positions the process of analysis *within* the arts. The metaphoric and interpretive dimensions of the arts are understood to be the location of the psychoanalytic discourse. When Lacan says that, in trying to understand the idea of "unconscious thought," we cast "the blame, in effect, onto the Word, but onto the Word realized in discourse that darts from mouth to mouth, conferring on the act of the subject who receives its message the meaning that makes this act an act of his history and gives it its truth," he could be describing exactly those acts that provide the central drama of *A History of Violence*.[13] Joey Cusack/Tom Stall embodies Lacan's idea that "the unconscious is the chapter of my history that is marked by a blank or occupied by a lie: it is the censored chapter. But the truth can be refound; most often it has already been written elsewhere."[14] His past—avoided through deceit—has bubbled up into the surface of his life. His reactions to the killers at the beginning of the film and to the appearance of the mobsters in his sleepy little town are, as Lacan puts it, hysterical symptoms that are manifesting themselves within the structure of the narrative of his new life.

This, too, was developed originally in *Stereo*—one female subject of the telepathic experimentation is said to have developed a

> sophisticated intrusion avoidance device, known as schizo-phonetic partition. . . . In order to subvert attempts by fellow subjects to establish potentially intrusive telepathic rapport, she completely separated her telepathic nonverbal self from her oral-verbal self. Her telepathic self functioned as a false self, diverting fellow telepathists from the real or true self which manifested itself only in occasional, deliberately confused verbal utterances. She thus protected her true self from telepathic intrusion by abandoning her telepathic faculty to a false self. Not surprisingly, repeated telepathic probes undertaken by other subjects could not discover the true nature of her experiential space-continuum. The danger inherent in the use of schizo-phonetic partition as a telepathic intrusion avoidance device is that the false telepathic self tends to become increasingly parasitic on the true oral-verbal self. The true self begins to suffocate, inasmuch as it is starved of contact with the outside, and the false self gradually becomes the only self to interact with other selves.

This theme of "schizo-phonetic partition" is most obviously worked out subsequently in Cronenberg's production of Patrick McGrath's 1990 novel *Spider*. The eponymous main character's apparent dissociative response to his childhood killing of his mother is brought to visual life in this film. The obsessive actions of Spider—writing in his notebook in an apparent non-language, wearing multiple layers of clothing, the apparently purposeful layering of the location of his halfway house over his childhood neighborhood—combine as they unravel into the complex Oedipal story of Spider's fixation on his mother. The subsequent psychotic break in response to his recognition of her as a sexual being is channeled initially against the father but then into his visual dissociation of her from what he begins to perceive as his father's replacement for her (and, indeed, the imagined murder of the mother to enable this replacement). This dissociative response in Spider closely mirrors that described in *Stereo*—a "schizo-phonetic partition." The grown Spider—the verbal self described in the quotation from *Stereo*—has "protected [his] true self from [psychological] intrusion by abandoning [his rational] faculty to a false self." This false self continues to replicate the conditions associated with his mental break, reliving, and even finding people to play the important roles in his particular Oedipal tragedy. As for Tom/Joey in *A History of Violence*, the past has become Lacan's "censored chapter," yet the suppression of this chapter, as Lacan suggests, has "already been written elsewhere."

In Tom/Joey's case, the suppression of a violent past bubbles up in response to violence, and his capabilities and rejected Joey persona appear throughout the initial stages of the film to be almost unconscious. Without having been present for the filming, and so on, it is impossible to know, but one gets the impression that Viggo Mortensen's performance in this regard is *very* carefully directed by Cronenberg. It is not until Carl Fogarty (Ed Harris) shows up at the Stall house with Tom's son, Jack (Ashton Holmes), held hostage that we begin to see the Tom veneer/persona shift into the background and the Joey persona come out. Facial expressions, voice, and accent all shift, and Tom/Joey uses the pronoun "I" as the subject of a sentence involving Joey's actions. When Tom/Joey drives back to Philly and meets with his brother's henchman in the Track and Turf bar, his response to "You Joey?" is the completion of this subtle transformation. Even Mortensen's vocal register shifts at this point.

Subsequently, in the hospital when his wife, Edie (Maria Bello), confronts him, saying, "Tell me the truth," Tom/Joey responds by asking her, "What do you think you heard?" She responds, "It's not what I heard. It's what I saw.

I saw Joey. I saw you turn into Joey right before my eyes. I saw a killer—the one Fogarty warned me about. You did kill men back in Philly, didn't you? Did you do it for money, or did you do it because you enjoyed it?" Tom/Joey stumbles in his response—the repression of Joey is no longer possible, and the statue of Tom Stall is suddenly no longer on its pedestal. He says, "Joey did, both. I didn't. Tom Stall didn't." Joey/Tom is in the crisis of his own unity, in keeping with Nietzsche's comment regarding the pronoun "I": "You say 'I' and you are proud of this word. But greater than this—although you will not believe in it—is your body and its great intelligence, which does not say 'I' but performs 'I.'"[15]

Lacan's notion that the truth of the censored chapter can be refound in the monuments of one's body, that "the hysterical symptom manifests the structure of a language," is clearly seen in Tom/Joey's awkward positioning of dual selves via names and the pronoun "I," as well as in Spider's painstakingly edited written nonsense. In both of these films, we witness the reestablishing of the meaning of the censored chapter, of its relations with those chapters surrounding it, and hence also its relations to the sense of those chapters individually and therefore of the entire text—that is, of one's whole consciousness/self.[16]

Seeing *As:* Wittgenstein Tilting at Unconscious Windmills

Yet, the existence and understanding of the "unconscious" that has been so important to my analysis of these two films so far—and, of course to Freudian psychoanalysis in general—are by no means a done deal. Even in my interpretation here, this perspective leaves unanswered questions, questions that might be easier to include in my analysis if Wittgenstein's perspective on psychology and psychoanalysis is taken into account.

Famously the subject of many of his unpublished works, including the second section of *Philosophical Investigations,* Wittgenstein remained fascinated with Freudian psychoanalysis throughout his career. Recent work by Jacques Bouveresse has very helpfully drawn together—in a way that Wittgenstein never does himself—all of the scattered comments on Freud and psychoanalysis, but I will introduce here only a single Wittgensteinian concept: the language game.[17] As Wittgenstein explains it:

> How many kinds of sentence are there? Say assertion, question and command?—There are *countless* different kinds of use of what we call "symbols," "words," "sentences." And this multiplicity is not something fixed, given once for all; but new types of language, new

language-games, as we may say, come into existence, and others become obsolete and get forgotten. (We can get a *rough picture* of this from the changes in mathematics.)

Here the term "language *game*" is meant to bring into prominence the fact that the *speaking* of language is part of an activity, or of a form of life.[18]

In the second section of *Philosophical Investigations*, Wittgenstein develops a long argument concerning what it means when we say that we "see" something "as" something else. A constant interest throughout this section of the book is psychoanalysis, in particular its approach to the unconscious. He sees the Freudian (and would have seen the Lacanian) approach to the unconscious and its role in the formation of the ego's identity as a special form of what we call "doxastic logic" (from the Greek verb *doxadzo*, "I believe"), or sometimes "Moore's paradox" (after the analytic philosopher G. E. Moore, who gave it a lot of attention).[19] It goes something like this: "It is raining outside, but I don't believe that it is raining"; this raises questions concerning what relation the idea of "belief" has to knowledge. Wittgenstein says that "Moore's paradox could be put something like this: the expression 'I believe that this is the case' is used like the assertion 'This is the case'; and yet the *hypothesis* that I believe this is the case is not used like the hypothesis that this is the case." From this beginning, Wittgenstein reasons that the grammar of "belief" is not like that of verbs like "cut," "chew," or "run": "'Hence it *looks* as if the assertion "I believe" were not the assertion of what is supposed in the hypothesis.'—So I am tempted to look for a different development of the verb in the first person indicative."[20] In other words, the use of "I" is not always doing the same thing. It has a more complex role to play in the various language games in which we participate as humans than merely indicating the first person. The "I" that says "but I don't believe that it is raining" is a construct, complexly dissimilar from the "I" that can be presumed to observe that it is raining.

In the scene at the end of *A History of Violence*, from a Lacanian point of view, Tom, now excised fully from the repressed unconscious of his own history, has responded finally to the displaced Oedipal rage of his brother, who (instead of competing with the *father* for his mother's attachment) admits having tried to strangle Joey in his crib. He arrives back home and enters the Stall house, where his family has just begun dinner. No words are spoken for the full three minutes of this closing scene. Each member of the family is now aware of the contents of his censored chapter. As Lacan states, "What we teach the subject to recognize as his unconscious is his history"—if it is accepted as the subject's *own* history, it will no longer be something coming as if from an external source to trouble the subject.[21]

His plate is brought to the table by his young daughter (Heidi Hayes), and he sits. He is offered meatloaf by his son, and then, no longer a muddled "I," he meets the searching gaze of his wife, and the screen goes dark. He is now Tom who *was* Joey: "At every instance... from then on, they will more easily grasp the fact that these metaphors—like negation, whose doubling undoes it—lose their metaphoric dimension."[22]

Yet, from a Wittgensteinian perspective, the important moment in the film comes earlier, in the hospital scene described previously, when Tom/Joey cannot locate him*self* in relation to the pronoun "I": "If I listened to the words of my mouth, I might say that someone else was speaking out of my mouth. 'Judging from what I say, *this* is what I believe.'"[23] Or, to translate this into terms more immediately recognizable to Lacan, "It seems to me that my ego believes this, but it isn't true." From this perspective, Tom/Joey is playing a language game that has different rules from what those around him expect. Instead of acknowledging the role that the pronoun "I" plays in ordinary language, he has attempted to create a complicated *private language* in which "I" has a different meaning. This attempt to play a private game is, in essence, parasitic on ordinary use. Fogarty (the gangster from Philly who comes to collect Joey for retribution after Tom's accidental celebrity causes him to be rediscovered) and Tom's wife, Edie, represent players from both of his lifestyles who don't accept the validity of this private game—who both, in fact, see his actions equally as *cheating*. When we see the subtleties of Tom's transformations "back into" Joey, we are faced with a portrayal of someone whose rule sets are shifting. In the end, Tom's return to his family is then not the result of some Oedipal allegory, but a full disclosure and relief of the hidden complexification that was, as Wittgenstein would put it, a kind of "mental cramp."[24] As Wittgenstein says concerning the idea of a "private language": "The words of this language are to refer to what can be known only to the speaker; to his immediate, private, sensations. So another cannot understand the language"—the implication of which, Wittgenstein goes on to argue, is that a truly *private* language cannot exist.[25] In the case of Tom/Joey, his desire to suppress his past and erase its significance, to distance himself from himself, is not *private* at all, but actually only evidence of the shifting between one language game and another, that Joey/Tom or Tom/Joey has further complexified by shifting the way that he understands the role of "I" with regard to each game.

For Spider, the denouement is less hopeful, but therapeutically similar. As the film progresses, Spider's childhood activities are apparently observed and recorded by the adult Spider, who also experiences their effects spilling out into the world in which he physically lives. The matron of the halfway house to which he has been released takes on, alternately, the visage of his mother and of "Yvonne" (Miranda Richardson), the woman he imagined to be his mother's replacement. With Spider poised over the matron's head with hammer and chisel, we then "witness" his murder of his mother, with the adult Spider standing no longer as observer in the Oedipal tragedy, but as actor. His father (Gabriel Byrne), having dragged the corpse of Spider's mother from the gas-filled house, looks up at him—now no longer Spider-the-child, but rather the grown Spider and says, "You did this. You did this. You did your mum in. You killed your mother. You murdered your mum." Immediately, the scene shifts back to the physical world, and the matron, now again appearing as Mrs. Wilkinson (Lynn Redgrave), wakes, saying, "What have you done? What have you done?" Spider drops the hammer, realizing that he has mistaken her identity.

As Spider is driven by his psychiatrist back to the mental hospital where he has spent most of his life, the scene returns to the child Spider, also being driven to the mental hospital where he is about to spend most of his life, yet the bewildered confusion of the adult Spider is not mimicked in the face of his youthful counterpart. Instead, we see only passivity, and possibly the hint of a smile. This Oedipal tragedy, from a Lacanian perspective, remains at the level of metaphor that has not lost its metaphoric dimension at all. Perhaps we can imagine a future in which Spider can recover this space, but, as with the previously discussed female subject from *Stereo* who had undergone "schizo-phonetic partition," Spider's current reality is one in which "the true self begins to suffocate, inasmuch as it is starved of contact with the outside, and the false self gradually becomes the only self to interact with other selves." Spider is the clearest example of "schizo-phonetic partition" in the whole of Cronenberg's oeuvre, and perhaps the best example of Lacan's reading of Freud's notion of the Oedipus complex:

> The Oedipus complex ... mark[s] the limits our discipline assigns to subjectivity: namely, what the subject can know of his unconscious participation in the movement of the complex structures of marriage ties, by verifying the symbolic effects in his individual existence of the tangential movement toward incest that has manifested itself ever since the advent of a universal community.
>
> The primordial Law is therefore the Law which, in regulating marriage ties, superimposes the reign of culture over the reign of nature, the latter being subject to the law of mating.[26]

Spider's entire existence is governed by his Oedipal rage. The tragedy of his accidental murder of his mother continues to play itself out as the people in his life fill the roles of those primordial characters, and we receive the impression that the events in this film are only the latest iteration in a series. Spider's killing of his mother unfolds as a tragedy of mistaken identity, but, as we learn, the mistaken identity is Spider's own.

Spider's experience also evokes the rather different treatment of the Oedipus complex by the French philosopher Gilles Deleuze and his psychoanalytic colleague, Félix Guattari. Antagonistic to many of Freud's and Lacan's basic ideas (including the Oedipus complex), these two (and sometimes just Deleuze or Guattari alone) produced an important body of work that repositions the relation between psychoanalysis and philosophy, and concentrates much attention on the problem of the "I." In *What Is Philosophy?* (originally published in French in 1991), following on from their earlier two-part work *Capitalism and Schizophrenia* (*Anti-Oedipus* [1972] and *A Thousand Plateaus* [1980]), the pair continue to take aim at (particularly Lacanian) psychoanalytic conceptions:

> Let us proceed in a summary fashion: we will consider a field of experience taken as a real world no longer in relation to a self but to a simple "there is." There is, at some moment, a calm and restful world. Suddenly a frightened face looms up that looks at something out of the field. The other person appears here as neither subject not object but as something that is very different: a possible world, the possibility of a frightening world. This possible world is not real, or not yet, but it exists nonetheless: it is an expressed that exists only in its expression—the face, or an equivalent of the face. To begin with, the other person is this existence of a possible world. And this possible world also has a specific reality in itself, as possible: when the expressing speaks and says, "I am frightened," even if its words are untruthful, this is enough for a reality to be given to the possible as such. This is the only meaning of the "I" as linguistic index.[27]

Deleuze's fascination with film is clearly in view in this conception—the frightened face gazing at something "out of the field" of the cinema screen is a possible world, and our relation to this possible world is simply that we experience that it exists somehow. Yet, this screen is also a mirror, and the linguistic index of "I" is formed in relation to this mirror, this screen, this field of view, and this experience as a set of possible worlds.[28] For both

Joey/Tom and Spider, "the other is a possible world as it exists in a face that expresses it and takes shape in a language that gives it a reality." Each of these characters manifests the "I" as a bubbling through of Oedipal violence, not yet brought into coherence with the language of the unconscious.

Yet, Spider, too, is playing games with language. His notebook is a wonderful example of the Wittgensteinian idea of private language. Consider Wittgenstein's restatement of this in part 2 of *Philosophical Investigations:*

> If I were to talk to myself out loud in a language not understood by those present my thoughts would be hidden from them.
> Let us assume that there was a man who always guessed right what I was saying to myself in my thoughts. (It does not matter how he manages it.) But what is the criterion for his guessing *right*? Well, I am a truthful person and I confess that he has guessed right.—But might I not be mistaken, can my memory not deceive me? And might it not always do so when—without lying—I express what I have thought within myself?—But now it does appear that "what went on within me" is not the point at all.[29]

Spider's complex interweaving of interior and exterior, real and imagined, memory and experience is a compelling portrait of a subject whose damage is, perhaps, too easy to interpret through a Freudian/Lacanian lens, or rather, too difficult not so to interpret. Yet, from the perspective of the notion of the non-sense of private language, could it not also be the case that the temptation to explanation that the Freudian/Lacanian model satisfies is a species of the model that Wittgenstein introduces in the quotation just given? On this reading, Spider's multiple obfuscations of his own childhood actions are an attempt to hide behind his own private language. Like Tom/Joey's repositioning of the pronoun "I," so too with Spider's deliberate repositioning of his ego with regard to memory. If we are "the man who always guessed right" with regard to the "story" of Spider that unravels throughout the film, then we, too, may be caught in his web of "memory" that always attracts, always deceives, always traps.

The Activating Image

In conclusion, I think—and hope—that it is fair to say that Cronenberg's oeuvre is far from complete. Given that his most recent work displays his continued outworking of ideas first explored in the late 1960s, there is a good chance that, for instance, the upcoming *A Dangerous Method* (2011), dealing with the relationship between Freud and Carl Jung, might give significant insight into the meaning and sense of many of the themes that I have chosen to discuss here.[30] However, on another level, the complexity and honesty with which Cronenberg's films tell stories will likely always lend itself to the comparison with equally complex philosophical and psychological categories, and make discussion of them together an ongoing process, whatever the future may hold.

There is significant attention already in Cronenberg's oeuvre, as we have seen, to the problem of the "I," covering ground that philosophers and psychoanalysts have long disputed. A particular value in Cronenberg's treatment of the issues, as I have intimated at several points in this chapter, derives from their treatment *in film*. The immersive identity of our experience of film is not merely a bit of benign fun on a Friday night. Film is a different form of experience altogether from typical philosophical or psychoanalytic discourse. The realities and claims to reality that are presented by the flicker of the silver screen interpenetrate with the day-to-day logic of our lives. The momentary loss of identity in the anonymity of immersion in filmic reality is akin to a baptism, except that it is a baptism—in the best of films—of *ideas*.

And I say, "Bring me to the waters, Brother Cronenberg."

Notes

1. Jacques Lacan, "The Function and Field of Speech and Language in Psychoanalysis" (1953), in *Ecrits: A Selection,* trans. Bruce Fink, Héloïse Fink, and Russell Grigg (New York: Norton, 2004), 40–41.

2. Lacan, "The Function and Field of Speech," 43.

3. Of particular interest to this chapter is the early interest in Freud by his fellow Viennese Ludwig Wittgenstein. On this, see Jacques Bouveresse, *Wittgenstein Reads Freud: The Myth of the Unconscious,* trans. Carol Cosman (Princeton, N.J.: Princeton University Press, 1995). For early work by Freud, see Sigmund Freud, *On Dreams,* standard ed., trans. and ed. James Strachey (New York: Norton, 1990).

4. Ludwig Wittgenstein, *Philosophical Investigations,* 2nd ed., trans. G. E. M. Anscombe (Oxford: Blackwell, 1958), 190e.

5. Ovid, *Metamorphoses,* trans. Charles Martin (New York: Norton, 2004), Book 1, lines 1–2 (p. 15).

6. Ovid, *Metamorphoses,* Book 1, lines 1–4 (p. 15), last line slightly modified.

7. Plato's character Socrates, in *The Republic* 368e–69a, is, at this point in the dialogue, stymied by the difficulty of discussing the idea of justice in a single individual. He suggests to his dialogue partners that, as they inscribe important laws in "two-foot letters" on stone for all to see, making them easier to read and more accessible, they

should discuss the idea of justice in the context of an entire city. For a translation of this work, see Plato, *Republic*, trans. Desmond Lee (London: Penguin, 2007).
    8. Lacan, "The Function and Field of Speech," 41.
    9. Wittgenstein, *Philosophical Investigations*, 190e.
    10. Lacan, "The Function and Field of Speech," 41.
    11. Joseph Breuer and Sigmund Freud, *Studies in Hysteria*, trans. Nicola Luckhurst (London: Penguin, 2004).
    12. Lacan, "The Function and Field of Speech," 50–51.
    13. The use of capitalization for "Word" here reflects the Greek word *logos*, which can mean "word," "argument," or even "reason." It has a complex history of use in ancient philosophy, particularly in Stoicism, and found its way into the Christian New Testament through this influence, particularly in the Gospel of John.
    14. Lacan, "The Function and Field of Speech," 50.
    15. Friedrich Nietzsche, *Thus Spoke Zarathustra*, trans. R. J. Hollingdale (London: Penguin, 2003), 62.
    16. Lacan, "The Function and Field of Speech," 50–51.
    17. Bouveresse, *Wittgenstein Reads Freud*.
    18. Wittgenstein, *Philosophical Investigations*, 11e.
    19. G. E. Moore, "Moore's Paradox," in *G. E. Moore: Selected Writings*, ed. Thomas Baldwin (London: Routledge, 1993), 207–12.
    20. Wittgenstein, *Philosophical Investigations*, 190e, 191e.
    21. Lacan, "The Function and Field of Speech," 52.
    22. Lacan, "The Function and Field of Speech," 51.
    23. Wittgenstein, *Philosophical Investigations*, 192e.
    24. "In philosophy one feels forced to look at a concept in a certain way. What I do is suggest, or even invent, other ways of looking at it. I suggest possibilities of which you had not previously thought. You thought that there was one possibility, or only two at most. But I made you think of others. Furthermore, I made you see that it was absurd to expect the concept to conform to those narrow possibilities. Thus your mental cramp is relieved, and you are free to look around the field of use of the expression and to describe the different kinds of uses of it." This is from a 1946 lecture by Wittgenstein relayed in Norman Malcolm, *Wittgenstein: A Memoir*, with a biographical sketch by G. H. von Wright, 2nd ed. (Oxford: Oxford University Press, 1984), 43.
    25. Wittgenstein, *Philosophical Investigations*, 243e.
    26. Lacan, "The Function and Field of Speech," 65–66.
    27. Gilles Deleuze and Félix Guattari, *What Is Philosophy?* trans. Hugh Tomlinson and Graham Burchell (New York: Columbia University Press, 1994), 17. See also Gilles Deleuze and Félix Guattari, *Capitalism and Schizophrenia: Anti-Oedipus*, trans. Robert Hurley, Mark Seem, and Helen R. Lane (New York: Viking, 1977), and *Capitalism and Schizophrenia: A Thousand Plateaus*, trans. Brian Massumi (Minneapolis: University of Minnesota Press, 1987).
    28. Most likely a reflection of Lacan's famed "mirror stage," in which he argues that, in observing an infant's initial recognition of him-"self" in a mirror, we garner empiri-

cal data that prove the existence of Freud's notional structures of the human mind. See Lacan, "The Mirror Stage as Formative of the *I* Function as Revealed in Psychoanalytic Experience," in *Ecrits: A Selection*, 4–9.

29. Wittgenstein, *Philosophical Investigations*, 222e.

30. This is a film version of Christopher Hampton's play *The Talking Cure*, based on John Kerr, *A Most Dangerous Method* (New York: Vintage, 1983).

The Politics of Mad Science in *The Fly* and *Dead Ringers*

R. Barton Palmer

A Literary Filmmaker?

Surely the most provocative recent study of director-screenwriter David Cronenberg's varied cinematic oeuvre is Mark Browning's *David Cronenberg: Author or Filmmaker?*[1] Although Browning never definitively answers the question posed in the book's title, his assessment is that the most useful approach to Cronenberg's filmmaking is through a complex web of literary intertexts, the other works to which his films refer and that they often remake or recycle, ranging from those authors whose works the writer-director has adapted for the screen (notably J. G. Ballard, William S. Burroughs, and Patrick McGrath, each a practitioner of what we might call scandalous modernism) to such lesser novelists as Rose Tremain and Bruce Chatwin. Even film composer Bernard Herrmann is invoked as an influence in a move that strains the meaning of "literary" if not of "intertext." Browning casts a wide net, to be sure, but he seems, and there is justification for this view, most fascinated by Cronenberg's undeniable interest in writers who have elicited their fair share of controversy, *écrivains maudits* whose themes suit his interests in shock and offense. Doubtless, there is an outlaw quality shared by the fiction of McGrath, Ballard, and Burroughs. And it is exactly their air of taboo breaking and carefully cultivated bad taste that Cronenberg himself has aimed at throughout much of his career.

But in emphasizing this particular set of influences, Browning seems to have missed the taller trees in this literary forest, ignoring the importance for an assessment of Cronenberg's filmmaking of the larger nineteenth-century tradition of what may usefully (to take account of both its themes and its intended effect on readers) be called science horror fiction. The principal character of this tradition is a megalomaniacal scientist.[2] Science horror

175

fiction, along with its various cinematic incarnations, arguably constitutes the intertext that defines the cultural politics of Cronenberg's horror films. In examining the discontents of modern science, the director comes to share much with twentieth-century anti-Enlightenment critique, particularly that of the Frankfurt School thinkers. In this essay, I will also show that Cronenberg's most penetrating dramatizations of that critique are to be found in the particular forms that "mad science" assumes in *The Fly* (1986) and *Dead Ringers* (1988).

Monstrous Doubleness

Conspicuously absent from Browning's idiosyncratic grouping of influences is Mary Shelley, whose *Frankenstein; or the Modern Prometheus* (1818) constitutes the distant but palpably resonant source of Cronenberg's 1970s and early 1980s films (all of which feature mad scientists in the Frankenstein tradition).[3] More important for our purposes here, however, Browning makes no mention of Robert Louis Stevenson, whose *The Strange Case of Dr. Jekyll and Mr. Hyde* (1886), mediated by its many influential screen adaptations, furnishes much of the narrative patterning, as well as many of the thematic concerns, of both *The Fly* and *Dead Ringers*.[4] These two films effect, in terms not only of influence but also of style and intellectual sophistication, an important break from the Frankenstein-inspired early productions. In fact, they constitute a diptych devoted to the dramatization of horrifying self-destruction, as the protagonists in each case turn the investigatory or medical gaze on themselves, in the process becoming nothing less than experimental patients. In this way, Cronenberg dramatizes the collapse of the intellectual distance between subject and object established for modern science by Francis Bacon. In turning toward a conception of the monster as the self, *The Fly* and *Dead Ringers* meditate in different but related ways on the imbricated central themes of Stevenson's novel: both the paradox of twinness (in which ostensibly separate identities mask the sense in which two selves are physically and psychically inseparable) and moral doubleness. These are "those provinces of good and ill," as Dr. Jekyll so tellingly puts it, "which divide and compound man's dual nature."[5] It is the transformative technologizing of those "provinces" that Stevenson's fictional physician and medical researcher fails so signally to achieve. This failure exemplifies the resistance of the human nature in all its paradoxical complexities to the sort of rationalization and rectification imagined by Jekyll, who, at least at the outset, shares with the Enlightenment philosophers an unquestioned belief in the transformative powers of scientific method and practice. *The Fly* and

Dead Ringers stage similar failures of this urge toward the betterment of the human condition and, by extension, the mastery of self or identity.

The critique offered in these two later films extends and deepens the antiestablishmentarianism of Cronenberg's 1970s features. Following the Frankenstein tradition, these earlier films portray the reckless experimentation of mad scientists, which threatens their worlds with apocalyptic destruction, as dangerous, perhaps unstoppable forces are set in motion through a monstrosity that resonates with what emerge as already potent discontents of human experience. This scenario is thoroughly traditional. A major theme of the Victorian Gothic, followed closely by Cronenberg, is, in the description of Judith Halberstam, the deployment of "a catalogue of perverse sexuality," which is characterized by its "production . . . as identity and as the inversion of identity." This splitting or doubleness of the sexualized self can be readily figured as the contrast between the conventionally respectable and the morally (and physically) monstrous.[6] Such a thematizing of the doubleness inherent in perverse sexuality can also be seen in both *The Fly* and *Dead Ringers,* which in part stage the liberation of repressed sexual energies. Initially, these films enact something like the psychic victory promised by the optimistic neo-Freudianism that is such an important element of postwar American therapeutic culture, as defined by works such as Herbert Marcuse's *Eros and Civilization* (1955).[7] We remember that in devising a potion that will allow his two natures to go their separate ways, Jekyll hopes for something similar to the lifting of repression later envisioned by Marcuse and his contemporaries—namely, that "the unjust might go his way, delivered from the aspirations and remorse of his more upright twin."[8] And yet Cronenberg's two films climax not with a celebratory overturning of a bankrupt, repressive world order, but instead, in the manner of *Dr. Jekyll and Mr. Hyde,* with the display in the same subject of the now unbalanced and unsustainable coexistence of monstrosity and respectability. After the critical and popular success of *Dead Ringers,* Cronenberg abandoned this focus on horrific forms of doubleness, turning for inspiration to writers like Ballard and Burroughs who take a modernist pleasure in imagining a desire still eager to discover its proper object and limits (if any). But in these two earlier films, the director's intellectual perspective seems more neo-Victorian in depicting with unflinching thoroughness the effects of an abandonment of self-control and repression. In each case, the narrative traces the emergence of the monstrous from within.

The finales of *The Fly* and *Dead Ringers* stage the only kind of triumph that the will to power transformed by misguided science can achieve. Ironically, that triumph is self-destruction. In Stevenson's novel, Jekyll's desperate attempts to return to what he would rather think of as his real self are thwarted by the persistence of his evil twin, who continually gains power after being constituted as a more or less separate identity. Unable to exchange any longer at will this originally second self for his official, preferred identity, Jekyll finds himself with no alternative but to end his life. Similarly, both Cronenberg films conclude with failed gestures of separation, disentanglement, and restoration. For Seth Brundle (Jeff Goldblum) in *The Fly* and (even more ironically) the Mantle twins (Jeremy Irons) in *Dead Ringers*, Jekyll's prediction of his own irrevocable slide into permanent, unsupportable monstrosity proves a fitting epitaph: "I was slowly losing hold of my original and better self, and becoming slowly incorporated with my second and worse."[9] In *The Fly*, this slide is phylogenetic, a reversing of the evolutionary trajectory that has produced the genus *Homo* as *sapiens*, yet, as in Stevenson's novel, this decline asks to be read morally as well. Brundle's gradual revelation as an *unheimlich* or monstrous amalgamation of man and insect also signals, as Cronenberg scholar William Beard points out, "the emergence of a corrupt and ill-mannered Mr. Hyde whose lurking existence must always be circumscribed through vigilance and self-control." It is significant that Brundle's respectability disintegrates before his body completes its horrific metamorphosis.[10]

Dead Ringers also traces a social and moral decline in the tradition of Stevenson's novel. The Mantles fall into drug addiction and psychopathology from their eminent positions as a brother team of acclaimed medical researchers and practitioners. The double singleness of their identity has led them to the heights of their profession, but their twinness becomes unsustainable and then untransformable, even in extremis. This form of monstrousness, the result of procreative chance and upbringing, is natural rather than uncanny. The example of the original Siamese twins is invoked by the Mantles themselves to explain their destructive connection to each other. In the film, monstrousness, however, also expresses itself through the brothers' scientific and medical practice. The urges to understand, dominate, and cure (which the Mantles are shown to possess as precocious adolescents) lead in the beginning to the acclaim of their peers and considerable wealth. Yet their ostensible respectability conceals a dark side, more sadistic and misogynistic than therapeutic. In the manner of Dr. Jekyll's recreational adventures as Mr. Hyde, the Mantles indulge their unjust "province" in a conscienceless predation: taking sexual advantage of attractive patients and even sharing seriatim these conquests with each other through identity switching when the woman in question is unaware that there are two of them. Such illicit and exploitative sharing, in fact, seems the very ground of their twinned being, a form of sexual intercourse that they are able through the medium of a third party to share with each other. As Elliot tells his brother, "You don't have any experience until I have it too." Disaster looms only when Beverly's growing emotional attachment to one of their unwitting victims, the actress Claire Niveau (Genevieve Bujold), makes him desire a separation from his brother that, it turns out, neither one can survive.

In *Dead Ringers,* a Stevensonian double singleness figures in yet another intriguing fashion, one even more closely connected to the film's critique of Enlightenment thought and practice, especially its reliance on a supposedly objective, observing self. Later in the film, and more eerily, both scientific research (especially the invention of surgical instruments, an endeavor for which the pair achieves an early and much-celebrated success) and medical practice become, especially for Beverly, a self-deceptive displacement. Beverly begins to project his increasing pathology, including intimations and fears about what he comes to see as his freakish fraternal relationship, onto both the gynecological maladies he is called on to treat and also the patients who suffer from them. His deeply disturbed private self begins to break into his hitherto carefully compartmentalized professional identity. Ethical, therapeutic medical practice quickly becomes impossible as Beverly begins to see his patients as "mutants" requiring surgery with a set of bizarre medical instruments that he has specially designed and had manufactured. These seem suited better to torture than to healing, revealing a deep-seated dread of difference as Beverly begins to complain to Elliot that the women are "all wrong." In the end, Beverly uses these same instruments to attempt a separation from his brother, even though there is of course no physical structure that joins them, disemboweling and killing the compliant Elliot, by the side of whose corpse he himself eventually curls up and dies.

Such an irresolvable double singleness, of course, is Jekyll's condition as well. Despite the seeming contradiction, his suicide occurs when the doctor can no longer abandon the identity of Hyde, even though Jekyll's conscience and his sense of shame can still master that other self. To put this another way, Hyde is always already Jekyll as well, not a fully independent being; his selves are conjoined twins, incapable of both moral and physical separation. As Vladimir Nabokov aptly observes, above Hyde "floats aghast, but dominating, a residue of Jekyll. . . . This ring of good still remains."[11] Similarly, in *The Fly,* Brundle becomes at the end genetically, and hence irrevocably, linked not only to an ordinary housefly but also, ironically enough as a result of his own misguided attempt to rid himself of his insect DNA, to the very machine, the telepod, he has invented. Only by an immense strength of will can he overcome his increasing insectness and thingness in order to bring about his own death, as he convinces the woman who loves him, Veronica (Geena Davis), to blow him apart with a shotgun blast. Jekyll's suicide by swallowing poison, the only solution to the dead-endedness of his now increasingly inexorable (and ever diminishing) presence in the transgressive alter ego that is Hyde, recalls his devising and then self-medicating with a transforming potion. It seems morally fitting that his death recapitulates the transgression that it seems to punish. This ironic, but also poetically just, finale is tellingly refigured in *Dead Ringers* as the Mantles both impose (as subjects) and endure (as objects) their own deaths in a bizarre and horrifying reenactment of their twisted, self-serving careers in gynecological surgery. The finales of both films thus emphasize a kind of Dantean *contrapasso* in which punishment follows the form of the sin in question, with "body horror" figuring as the physical result of those moral failings that emerge through the practice of a science that goes mad and destructive.

Cronenberg and the Body Horror Tradition

The intellectual importance of mad science to Cronenberg's overall career can hardly be overemphasized. The director's early projects made him an interesting (if commercially marginal) figure in the horror film revival that was such an important element of 1970s and early 1980s Hollywood independent filmmaking. Thematically, *Crimes of the Future* (1970), *Shivers* (1975), *Rabid* (1977), *Scanners* (1981), and *Videodrome* (1983) resemble other horror films of the period because they feature striking forms of physical abjectness designed to "gross out" the audience, thus taking full advantage of advances in makeup design (including the extensive use of prosthetics) as well as various other forms of special effects. As in the works of other contemporary directors who specialized in what soon became known as body horror (the central figures here are probably Tobe Hooper, Larry Cohen, Wes Craven, and George Romero), Cronenberg's early films, if on some level playfully antirealist and hence shocking only in a carefully delimited sense, deploy physical abjectness to evoke truths of psychology or cultural values that are customarily not discussed directly. In general, the body horror films of the period ask to be read as serious engagements with rather than escapist flights from contemporary politics, as Robin Wood has demonstrated. Wood traces convincingly the emergence of the cycle to the wider cultural and political instabilities of the era, particularly the ongoing interrogation in the 1970s of technological progress, as well as the abandonment of traditional sexual and gender norms that accelerated as conventional forms of authority lost at that time much of their collective purchase.[12]

In terms of group practice, this political tendentiousness was largely abandoned in the 1980s as America turned sharply toward the right. But Cronenberg's body horror films from the 1980s escape the overall developing history of the genre, in which the "apocalyptic" productions of the previous decade that, if indirectly, signal "the end of the highly specific world of patriarchal capitalism" make way instead for a reactionary revisionism.[13] In these revisionist productions, such as John Carpenter's *Halloween* series (debuting in 1978) or the star-driven *Omen* (1976 and several sequels), the monster becomes more obviously "evil" and very often less than human, while religion is sometimes invoked to offer a metaphysical explanation for the monster's depredations, now often resulting from some Manichean opposition of good to evil.

In Cronenberg's career, however, no such shift in genre politics can be glimpsed. He does not move toward the era's mainstream horror filmmaking that, in Wood's dismissive characterization, centers on a "series of empty anecdotes in which nasty people do nasty things to other people, the nastiness being the entire point and purpose."[14] In contrast, the director's 1980s productions continue in a highly individualized fashion the generalized critique of the "world of patriarchal capitalism." What these films engage is the dependence of the modern world on the central Enlightenment values of rationalization and reification (which are nothing less than the intellectual underpinnings of modern culture's promotion of science as an indispensable social technology and tool of global domination). Now in the later stages of a distinguished career, Cronenberg has hardly abandoned political partisanship and wide-ranging critique, as bear witness his rich forays beyond body horror into examining intractable questions of moral identity in two exceptional neo-noirs (*A History of Violence* [2005] and *Eastern Promises* [2007]). Through the embrace of an avant-garde literariness, moreover, the director has been instrumental during the past fifteen years or so in extending the limits of the cinematically and culturally permissible (most stridently in the three outlaw adaptations *Naked Lunch* [1991], *Crash* [1996], and *Spider* [2002]).

Looking both backward and forward, the direction that his career took in the 1980s is hardly surprising. Cronenberg's contributions to the horror revival during the previous decade already differed from those of contemporaries in sustaining a political *engagement* that always glimpses the apocalyptic collapse of the dominant social, political, and, especially, psychosexual order. With their emphases on fantasies of biological disaster (often resulting from plots to effect some kind of revolution), these films, as mentioned earlier, connect more deeply to various literary and cinematic strains of science fiction than to cinematic horror in the strict sense. As not in the works of Hooper, Romero, or Craven, Cronenberg's key figures are mad scientists drawn from the antiscience traditions of popular culture. Cultural historian David J. Skal usefully emphasizes the ambivalent character of this cultural stereotype, who gives personal form to the success undeniably achieved by the objectification, measurement, anatomizing, and, in the end, technologizing of nature. Because of the destruction he brings on himself and others, the mad scientist also exemplifies the perhaps inescapable failure of such interventions, which are customarily portrayed as overreaching: "A prototype outsider, shunted to the sidelines of serious discourse, to the no-man's-land of B movies, pulp novels, and comic books, the mad scientist has served as a lightning rod for otherwise unbearable anxieties about the meaning of scientific thinking and the uses and consequences of modern technology.... He reveals himself (mad scientists are almost always men) to be a far more complicated symbol of civilization and its split-level discontents."[15]

In Cronenberg's early films, the threat to the social order issues from the science that is ostensibly the very basis of modern culture. His mad scientist figures, true to the type identified by Skal, press us through their transgressiveness "to confront the serious questions of ethics, power, and the social impact of technological advances." In such characters, we are forced to contemplate how "science might occasionally be the handmaiden of megalomania, greed, and sadism," a critical perspective that comes to dominate in both *The Fly* and *Dead Ringers*.[16] This obsession with the discontents of scientific practice and the practical fruits of scientific inquiry marks Cronenberg out as a body horror director with a difference. In New Hollywood body horror more generally, society is threatened by either the psychologically/morally depraved (as in Hooper's widely influential *Texas Chainsaw Massacre* [1974] and its various sequels or appropriations, the most notable of this latter category being *Silence of the Lambs* [1991]); or, conjuring up a fearfulness with deeper atavistic roots, the unaccountably revivified dead, who return to wreak a terrible, final destruction on the living, with the key film here being Romero's *Night of the Living Dead* (1968) and its several sequels and imitations. In such works, abjectness figures as flesh destroyed by the inherent discontents of human nature: inexplicable perversity or the death instinct. For Cronenberg, by way of contrast, it is the misguided energies and brilliance of the mad scientist that bring about the unseemly transformation and, often, subsequent destruction of the body, which becomes, with generic faithfulness, an object of both loathing and fascination.

Though dominated by a self-consciously fantastic antirealism that is hardly devoid of whimsy and humor, Cronenberg's early films construct the enemy of normality as the uninstitutionalized individual research of an antisocial genius, whose dangerous derangement finds expression in his intention to go "beyond nature," usually in order to instrumentalize others for his own dubious purposes. *Crimes of the Future* conjures up a future society suffering from a disease called "Rouge's malady," an illness named after its "creator," the mad dermatologist Antoine Rouge, whose experiments have somehow gone awry. Most of the women in this culture have already died off, and the men are left to suffer a disgusting effluence of something like mucous from the ears and nose and, in the end stages, a nauseating semen-like flow from the mouth. In *Shivers*, it is the mentally unbalanced university professor and researcher Dr. Emil Hobbes (Fred Doederlin) who opens up a medical Pandora's box by attempting to create substitutes for diseased bodily organs. In the process, Hobbes unwittingly creates parasites that turn their victims into insatiable sex maniacs; the disease rapidly turns into an epidemic, spreading from one of Hobbes's patients to the other inhabitants of an apartment complex and, it seems at the film's end, soon thereafter to society at large.

Rabid relates the story of yet another medical experiment gone wrong, as Dr. Dan Keloid (Howard Ryshpan), attempting a radical form of plastic surgery on a traffic accident victim, unwittingly turns her into a vampire; she awakens with a thirst for blood and a phallic spike residing in a kind of vaginal opening in her armpit, whose purpose is to extract that blood from unwitting victims. These unfortunates are subsequently infected with something like rabies, which transforms them into raging monsters. In *The Brood* (1979), therapy rather than medical research brings on disastrous consequences, as psychiatrist Dr. Hal Raglan (Oliver Reed), putting a different twist on Freud's talking cure, encourages his patients to express physically their secret discontents. In one disastrous case, the result is the "hatching" of a "brood" of angry, aggressive childlike beings produced from the body of Nola Carveth (Samantha Eggar) that go on a murderous rampage. Similar scenarios of destructive Faustian science play out in both *Scanners* (mad scientist Darryl Revok [Michael Ironside] attempts to take over the world through the creation of telepathic "scanners," brought into this world by injecting pregnant women with the drug Ephemerol) and *Videodrome* (Dr. Brian O'Blivion [Jack Creley] attempts to control the world by broadcasting a television signal that gives rise to tumors and hallucinations, converting the victims into assassins whose mission is to overturn the existing social order). In speaking of *The Brood*, William Beard neatly captures the apocalyptic bleakness of all these narratives, which "express a cold, sad helplessness at the end of the road, a flat defeated finality." "Is it necessary," Beard asks, "to point out how unusual this emotional paradigm is for a horror movie, or indeed any kind of commercial film?"[17] Hardly.

Directorial Ontogeny Recapitulates Cultural Phylogeny

The desolate endings of his body horror films certainly reflect Cronenberg's auteurist vision, his unflagging interest in works that are anti-Hollywood in formal, political, and intellectual terms. If the essence of American commercial filmmaking is the concept of the happy ending that recuperates the discontents and disruptions that drive the narrative, then Cronenberg's body horror films can usefully be seen as disputing the soothing conservatism of conventional closure. But Cronenberg's consistently negative view of science connects his work to broader intellectual currents in ways that become increasingly less fantastical as his career progresses. These currents are best exemplified in the twentieth century by the anti-Enlightenment critique of the Frankfurt School thinkers, especially Theodor Adorno, Max Horkheimer, Erich Fromm, and Herbert Marcuse, with whom Cronenberg as cultural critic shares much in common.

In their influential *Dialectic of Enlightenment* (first published in 1944), for example, Adorno and Horkheimer trace the essence of modern science as a discourse and worldview to Francis Bacon, who, they argue, had in mind "a concordance between the mind of man and the nature of things . . . [that] is patriarchal," with "the human mind, which overcomes superstition . . . to hold sway over a disenchanted nature." And so "knowledge, which is power, knows no obstacles." Interested in the turning of brute reality to human purposes, Bacon viewed "technology . . . [as] the essence of this knowledge." The problem is that science, particularly in its practical incarnation as technology, conceives itself in strictly utilitarian rather than moral or intellectual terms. Unconcerned with "concepts and images," technology thus works strictly by "method." Science only seems committed to making discoveries for the sake of advancing knowledge; its actual agenda is the "exploitation of others' work and capital." And so nature, demythologized and decontextualized, becomes an object of domination instead of either intellectual or spiritual inquiry, as "men renounce any claim to meaning."[18] It is easy enough to see that Cronenberg's mad scientists, much like their generic ancestors Drs. Victor Frankenstein and Henry Jekyll, are eager to know things only "in so far as [they] can manipulate them," turning "their potentiality to [their] own ends."[19] Yet Cronenberg's would-be dominators lose control over their creations and so suffer the iron law of unintended consequences. Or, in the more poetic formulation of Horkheimer and Adorno, "the reduction of thought to a mathematic apparatus conceals the sanction of the world as its own yardstick." The epistemological result is that "what is abandoned is the whole claim and approach of knowledge, to comprehend the given as such," as science's promise to produce a valid, consistently exploitable understanding of the world proves hollow.[20]

Victims of a failure that can be seen as inherent in their worldview and professional practice, Cronenberg's mad scientists unwittingly bring about the collapse of the objectified natural and social order it had been their intention to keep in perpetual subordination. For Cronenberg, and the other body horror directors of the 1970s and '80s, it is through the figure of the uncontrollable monster that some repressed other of American experience, some Mr. Hyde of the national consciousness, comes into view. In Cronenberg's early films, as Mary B. Campbell suggests, this other is located "in those strands of our experience and ourselves which are in fact the least personal and individual"—namely, "the new diseases we fear that genetic research will create." These diseases are metaphorized by the pervasive theme of "meaningless and uncontrollable reproduction."[21] In the director's early films, the repressed power of sexuality is rendered deadly once perverted by science, and, as noted previously, this theme occurs in both *The Fly* and *Dead Ringers* as well, albeit in less fantastic forms.

In the genre of science horror fiction inaugurated by Shelley's *Frankenstein*, the monster and his creator constitute a complex dialectic, but Stevenson's novel interiorizes and psychologizes this tension. As Judith Halberstam observes, "If the monster's monstrosity in *Frankenstein* depended upon the fragility of his maker's humanity, the hideous nature of Mr. Hyde can only be known through the failed respectability of Dr. Jekyll."[22] As a result of the structural and thematic break Stevenson's novel effected in the genre, creator and monster come to share a single though multiple, indivisible though fragmented, identity. A striking oneness is the ground of being of their two-ness. What Hyde does, Jekyll knows; what happens to the one happens to the other as well, indicating that in terms of substance they are one and the same even as they differ in person. The boundary between these at least theoretically separable selves becomes undecidable (a theme that dominates in *Dead Ringers* as well). In any event, through its introversion of monstrousness, Stevenson's narrative rejects decisively the epistemological premise of modern science—the constitution of external reality as a series of objects to be known, with the observer always distinct from what is observed. Science is thus critiqued not only for its ends (the Frankenstein monster as undead and uncontrollable corpse) but also for its means (a faux objectivity that only theoretically separates the practitioner from his practice). In the view of Adorno and Horkheimer, science lacks the intellectual resources to recognize and correct this particular form of blindness, having, like Enlightenment thought more generally, "extinguished any trace of its own self-consciousness."[23]

Jekyll, we are reminded, attempts to turn what he perceives as the divisions of his self into two discrete objects, hoping that "each could be housed in separate identities." He believes that such a transformation would be morally and constitutionally therapeutic because, if properly effected, it would relieve "life of all that was unbearable."[24] Here is a tale that no longer is interested, Halberstam points out, in dramatizing some Frankensteinian "fear of the other," locating the discontents of the scientific impulse in the technologized object that rebels against its creator. Instead, Stevenson's novel evokes the horrifying possibility of an innate human resistance to the prospect of "reformed" character, emphasizing, as Halberstam puts it, "a paranoid terror of involution or the unraveling of a multiformed ego."[25] Such an unraveling, with its revelation of innate depravity, could be provided with a traditional Christian interpretation, but Stevenson refuses any such metaphysical gesture, opening the door for the seemingly unlimited host of possibilities that have been advanced by modern critics (most prominently, understandings of Jekyll's double life as that of a drug addict, alcoholic, or closeted compulsive homosexual).

Cronenberg follows the novelist down this same thematic path, promoting what we might call a secular moralism that focuses psychologically and physiologically on the problematically divided (or, perhaps better, multiform) self. This is an issue that the director later explores in two nonhorror films, *Spider* and *M. Butterfly* (1993), which focus on the involutions of schizophrenia and gender disguise, respectively. Probing in the course of the 1980s the problematic constitution of a supposedly solid identity, Cronenberg thus turns away from "the least personal and individual" themes that define his engagement with mad science during the 1970s. With its abandonment of the Frankenstein tradition for that of *Dr. Jekyll and Mr. Hyde*, the trajectory of the director's early career comes to reflect the history of the science horror genre itself. Monstrosity is no longer located in an unknowable, hence unreformable external reality, but rather in an unstably divided self that can escape neither its subjection to nature nor the deadly web of power relations in which the urge to objectify and dominate entraps it.

The Descent into Self

In his narrative, which closes out the formally disconnected series of testimonies that constitute Stevenson's "strange case," Jekyll acknowledges that it was the moral struggle taking place within his own "agonized womb of consciousness" that made him reflect on the "trembling immateriality" of the body and subsequently aim at concocting a potion that would allow a "second form and countenance" to be substituted for the internally divided self he had hitherto occupied.[26] This discovery is a response to what he terms the "impatient gaiety" of his disposition, which makes him only barely tolerant of the "primitive duality" he shares with all his fellows. And so his invention has nothing to do with either its creator's medical practice or the professional inquiries in which he is engaged and for which he has hitherto employed his well-equipped laboratory.[27] Interestingly, a persistent theme in the subsequent adaptations and reimaginings of the story has been to alter Jekyll's motives for the research that leads him to the invention of the drug. In these other versions of the story, Jekyll becomes a scientist who, though initially altruistic, is seduced by the possibility of technologizing his own self. For example, what is arguably the most influential of the numerous film adaptations, the 1941 Hollywood production directed by Victor Fleming, portrays Jekyll (Spencer Tracy) as a researcher opposed to a hide-bound medical establishment who has dedicated himself to discovering a drug that can resolve an unbalanced orientation toward evil that, in his view, has an organic cause. His experiments with animals have proved successful, as Jekyll, after a number of failures, finally turns a rabbit violent and a rat into a house pet. But he still needs an appropriate human subject to prove the efficacy of the drug for medical use.

It seems providential, therefore, that while listening to a Sunday sermon about the triumph of moralism during Queen Victoria's reign, the good doctor comes across a formerly law-abiding and respectable man who objects wildly to the preacher's message, extolling the virtues of evil and thus showing that he suffers from such an imbalance (it turns out to be the result of an industrial accident). But the man dies before treatment can begin, and, dedicated to his profession, Jekyll tests his discovery on himself, with his immediate physical transformation into the creature he will subsequently name Hyde ratifying his success. The good doctor, however, quickly resumes his customary identity. Only later does Jekyll take the drug recreationally, after finding himself tempted by Ivy (Ingrid Bergman), a music hall waitress. After recognizing the urgency of his desires, he is then thwarted from quickly marrying his true love, Beatrix (Lana Turner), whose father

(Donald Crisp) resents the barely concealed ardor of his prospective son-in-law. In the person of Hyde, Jekyll proves able to seduce the hapless Ivy in an act of appropriation and the transgression of class boundaries that is not permitted either morally or socially to the good doctor. In a mockery of the patrician's exploitation of a hapless underclass, his wealth makes Ivy a prisoner of his lust, which manifests itself less in desire than in continuing verbal and physical abuse.

If the novel remains vague about the depravity in which Hyde indulges, the theatrical and film versions of the story invariably depict it as a sadistic sexual excess, and Fleming's film is no exception. The dream vision that accompanies the emergence of Hyde puts both women on erotic display and offers a vivid image of Jekyll's hitherto repressed misogyny. In the dream fiction, he assumes the guise of a maniacal coachman furiously whipping his two horses, who bear the thoroughly terrified likenesses of Ivy and Beatrix. This vision presages the cruelly manipulative treatment that, under the cover of Hyde's identity, the ostensibly respectable doctor will mete out first to Ivy (in the end beating the unfortunate woman to death) and later to Beatrix (who, though abducted, is rescued before the worst can happen). What begins as a tale of medical research meant to serve humanity ends in the release of the inventor's darkest and most transgressive desires as he becomes first attracted to and then dominated by the very beastliness he had in his idealism hoped to eradicate.

The Fly features a similarly horrific turning away from science and subsequent liberating but ultimately destructive descent into the darker recesses of the self. Like Fleming's Dr. Jekyll, Cronenberg's Seth Brundle is an archetypal figure who falls from grace: a scientist who, disputing the restrictions of conventional thinking, has made an important discovery, one whose technological application promises an overturning of "the world as we know it," in his own hardly modest assessment. Transportation of physical objects, including living bodies, has hitherto meant their actual moving through space. But Brundle has developed a form of computer-driven analysis that reduces objects to a code that, in the manner of the Internet, can be transmitted from one computer to another. At the receptor terminal, the object is reconstituted as itself by the second computer, thus defying the inevitability of Newtonian mechanics and conventional notions of both movement and matter. Brundle's computer system, which drives the pair of devices he terms "telepods," corresponds in an interesting fashion to both Jekyll's discovery of the "trembling immateriality" of human flesh and then, as the theoretical becomes practical, his subsequent technologizing of the twinned possibilities of flesh's dissolution and transformative reconstitution.

What practical applications Brundle's device might have are rather unclear at best. It seems, however, that his hope is to overcome one of the central discontents of human existence: the seemingly inescapable materiality of bodies, as well as their limitation by the laws of motion and movement. Through Brundle's technological breakthrough, the solid fleshly real reveals itself as always already immateriality. His discovery demonstrates that objects, including living beings, may be forced to yield to both analysis (the anatomizing of their constituent parts by a machine that extends human capacity, reducing physical complexities to a series of formulas) and also transformation (the intended, predictable, and repeatable reconstitution of the object in another space). This process is premised on key elements of Baconian science, offering as it does something like a paradigm of the discovery of a physical truth and its nearly simultaneous practical application in aid of mastering nature.

But is the apparently smooth progress of this process deceptive? Is the predictability of the process simply a mirage? To echo the criticism raised by Adorno and Horkheimer and quoted earlier, we might ask if what is here involved might be some form of the failure of rationalizing Enlightenment thought to "recognize the given as such." Dependent on abstractions, technology might prove unable to incorporate the truths that common sense (and, on a more sophisticated level, chaos theory) reveal, most important the central point that in some natural systems an apparently infinitesimal deviation entails large-scale, unpredictable consequences. This would happen, for example, should the telepod prove unable to recognize all the ultimately significant ways in which a particular given does not conform to a governing abstraction. And, of course, in yet another movement parallel to the experience of Dr. Jekyll, this is precisely the horrific consequence of Brundle's experimentation, as disaster results precisely from the telepod's following its protocol (interpreting what it is intended to teleport as a singularity). Separating his two "provinces," Stevenson's doctor similarly fails to take into account that his evil side, although initially smaller and weaker than its virtuous counterpart, might through the very act of being separated come to dominate its erstwhile master. Brundle comes to be similarly dominated at the genetic level by the small fly that inadvertently shares the telepod with him. The rematerializing of immateriality proves disastrous in both cases. Tellingly, this tragic finale is presaged earlier in the narrative by the fact that the telepod system, while spectacularly successful with inanimate objects, fails initially both to read and to reconstitute living tissue correctly.

Only when Brundle becomes romantically involved with Veronica does he manage, with her help, to fine tune the system in order to accommodate living things without transforming them into disgusting, quivering lumps (the disastrous result of his first attempt to teleport a baboon). Brundle's fall into sexuality, ironically enough, connects to both his breakthrough in learning how to deal with the flesh in his research, and also to his foolish decision one night when, half drunk and momentarily abandoned by Veronica, who has left the lab to end her relationship with a previous lover, he decides to teleport himself simply for the thrill of it. And the process does indeed give him a thrill, recalling what happens to Stevenson's hero the first time he brings forth Hyde. After the initial dose of his potion, Jekyll confesses to having felt "younger, light, happier in body."[28] Brundle too feels a burst of physical vitality, discovering that, apparently, the technologizing that his body has undergone is the source of the newfound sexual potency he comes to experience with Veronica, whose eventual inability to match his now insatiable libido soon frustrates him.

Abandoning his accustomed professional demeanor as the shy, reclusive, and intellectually obsessed researcher, he leaves the apartment to cruise the bars in a rougher part of the city. There he meets up with a woman who has promised herself for the night to whichever of two toughs wins the arm-wrestling match in which they are engaged. Brundle is now not only swaggeringly self-confident but also aggressively macho, qualities the young woman immediately recognizes and values. With her hardly reluctant consent, the initial contest between her two friends is abandoned as Brundle contends with the stronger of them for her sexual favors. Possessed now of an amazing strength, he wins easily, breaking his opponent's arm in the process. When Veronica later discovers the two together, Brundle seems cruelly indifferent, strangely detached. She quickly realizes that something is wrong. But the problem is neither essentially psychological nor moral, as Brundle begins to suspect. Increasingly horrified by the seemingly inexplicable changes in his body and physical being, he consults the telepod's computer and learns that he has been merged at the genetic level with a fly. Nothing but death can save him from a DNA that has greater power than his own. His sudden descent into mindless violence and the exploitation of women (which are Hyde's crimes) offers only the first glimpse of the unimaginably horrible dark side that is soon to dominate him completely.

The Fly reduces the scientific enterprise to a bitter irony. Brundle's invention leads not to a transformation of "the world as we know it," but rather, through a disastrous introversion, to his own destruction, as he finds himself victimized by his arrogant assumptions about the unproblematic repeatability of his conquest of materiality. Nature, to be sure, is transformed, but this transformation turns out to be monstrous, as it produces an amalgamation of two beings that had been hitherto separated by the processes and principles inherent in the order of things. The scientist who had hoped to wield a power over himself and his world comes to be dominated by a bruteness to whose terrifying potential he had previously paid no attention. Nature, untranscended, remains the ground of being, with the human restored to its basis in the animal. Science's promise of disinterested inquiry proves deceptive, as the researcher finds himself surrendering caution and objectivity for misguided, frivolous self-indulgence.

As in the various adaptations of *Dr. Jekyll and Mr. Hyde,* the turn toward the technologized self affords free play to the darker forces of human nature, which are always sexualized in Cronenberg's films as well. The insect DNA prompts the crueler, less civilized, and less altruistic elements of masculinity to emerge and dominate the once demure scientist, whose moral degradation presages an even more transformative fall into the very materiality it had been his intention to overcome. In a literal sense, *The Fly* thematizes a monstrousness that could emerge only from some hypothetical (that is, fictional) power of modern technology to create a genetic merger of radically different organisms. Allegorically speaking, the film's message seems darker. Because its hopeful promotion of an immaterializing that would overcome both time and space proves a disaster, the film can be read as a bitter indictment of the urge toward any form of transcendence that fails to take into proper account the inescapable, if alienating, thingness of the body, whose claims to constitute our true self cannot, the film seems to say, be ignored. In deconstructing the subject/object relations of science—that is, the rigid distinction between experiment and experimenter as Brundle becomes his own experiment— *The Fly* also disputes the founding dualism of such inquiry, with its customary separation of minds (observing and technologizing selves) from bodies (the physical presences that can be technologized). As the film's apocalyptic ending seems to suggest, the body can also be seen as constituting the mind's ground of being, for Brundle (reduced to only mind inside the body of a fly-telepod) is driven to suicide in order to escape an imprisonment that becomes increasingly horrific.

The Handmaiden of Sadism

Allegory is abandoned in *Dead Ringers* as the multiform nature of human identity is examined more directly. Because monstrousness in this film manifests itself initially as natural rather than, as in *The Fly,* a technologized horror, Cronenberg here raises the unanswerable question of what is truly unnatural if the unnatural is manifestly a part of nature. In the film's terms, multiplicity rather than a customary singularity, however freakish or abnormal it might seem, is revealed as a fact of the human condition, with the twinness of the Mantles finding an asymmetrical reflex in Claire's trifurcate uterus, an anomaly that, like their own, makes ordinary life in some sense impossible for her. And this multiplicity is something that medical science proves unable to cure: the Mantles cannot restore to fertility a patient like Claire who, ironically enough, finds herself with an excess of reproductive parts, and they can separate themselves only by a surgery that ironically leads to their deaths.

Dead Ringers, in consequence, is more heavily invested than The Fly in psychological realism, without any need to evoke the abject as surreal or hyperreal, except in one striking dream sequence where the departure from the plausible is provided with a subjective motivation. In Beverly's nightmare, he awakes in bed with Claire, who offers to separate him from Elliot, to whom he is joined by something like a thick placenta pulsing with veins. Biting into this fleshy bridge, to Beverly's horror and intense pain, Claire removes something like a penis from its interior. In The Fly, the abject appears as the disgusting display of a human body turning into an insect; in Dead Ringers, the abject makes its most characteristic appearance in the less dramatic and yet still shocking form of a doctor's office filling up with used needles, meal leftovers, and all manner of paper debris, a mess that serves as a metonymy (of a particular bourgeois sort) for the decaying minds and lapsing professionalism of the two doctors that practice there. Horror in this film can be glimpsed not only in the unconscious revelation of dreams but also in the collapse of order and neatness, of professional ethics and decorum, with monstrousness of this kind (bad manners and a disregard for the good opinion of others) first appearing in Dr. Beverly Mantle's unexpected and drunken appearance at an award ceremony honoring his brother Elliot. Beverly offends the group by revealing, in language that can hardly be called professional, the secret of the brothers' professional partnership: "I slave over the hot snatches, while Elliot makes the speeches," a remark that finds an interesting, if contrasting, correlative in what Claire, who has unwittingly bedded them both, opines about the twins. Beverly, she says, is the "nice one," while Elliot is the "shit."

In its emphasis on "found" forms of multiplicity, Dead Ringers focuses more on the Stevensonian problem (the doctor's increasingly unbearable, if perfectly natural, inner doubleness) than on his radical solution and its consequences, an element of the story pattern that, if foundational for the novelist, figures only at the very end of Cronenberg's film. The solution, of course, is the horrifying and fatal surgery that Beverly performs and to which Elliot submits. In a sense, the Mantles fail where Jekyll, who manages to bring about a separation of some viability, provisionally succeeds. The deepest irony of that success, of course, is that the transformed self (Hyde) is predominantly evil, indicating, as the doctor himself theorizes, the greater forcefulness and presence of that part of his soul. His expectation was that a purely virtuous form of himself—the "upright" province—would have been just as likely to emerge from the twin processes of dematerialization and reconstitution. Hyde's appearance is thus something of a shock and surprise, as in a sense is Jekyll's continued interest in achieving this particular form of separation, which, he realizes, gives him the cover to indulge his disreputable urges.

Despite its determined secularism, Stevenson's novel, in fact, follows a traditional Christian trajectory in demonstrating the greater power of evil; Hyde's bent for mindless destruction and mayhem seems to confirm Augustine's view of a postlapsarian human depravity.[29] In *Dead Ringers,* by way of a bitter reversal, it is Beverly, the "nice one," whose moral and psychological degeneration destroys both Elliot and himself. Beverly is eager to terminate the fraternal partnership because he wishes for normalcy (a form of interconnection that offers the possibility of deep companionship and sexual satisfaction). Unquestionably normal is his desire to establish a committed relationship with Claire, whom he has come to love deeply. It is the very conventionality of that desire, however, that leads to his moral, professional, and psychological deterioration. Separating from Elliot to live with Claire, Beverly soon finds himself drawn to the tranquilizing drugs that Claire is dependent on; he quickly becomes a hopeless addict and occasional drunk.

When Claire departs for a film shoot, Beverly's deterioration accelerates, fed by jealousy and a misunderstanding that makes him think his lover has been unfaithful. (An interesting connection with *The Fly* is that Seth's self-pitying drunkenness and subsequent disastrously reckless decision to transport himself result from similar feelings of sexual jealousy and abandonment.) Left in charge of the medical practice while Elliot is traveling, Beverly's performance of his professional duties comes to be poisoned by a delusionary antifeminism. During the physical examination of one patient, he insists to her dismay and horrible pain on using that famous "Mantle retractor" designed for use only during surgery. Beverly starts to see women as "all wrong" and as "mutants," designing for their rectification that set of truly terrifying instruments mentioned earlier. Attempting to use these during surgery, with his body at near collapse from drug abuse, Beverly almost kills his unwitting patient. Called to the medical board to explain his actions, Elliot, posing as his brother, is unable to prevent the suspension of their hospital privileges. And the Mantles' medical practice comes to an effective end when his medical assistant walks in on Beverly shooting up hard drugs in his garbage-strewn office.

Science, David Skal suggests (in a passage quoted earlier), can become the "handmaiden of sadism" for the simple reason that the researcher/observer/therapist assumes a position of power over the objects of his or her gaze and practice that can readily turn abusive and destructively self-serving, as is an unfortunate tendency in all relations of unequal power. Such cultural sadomasochism, according to Lynn S. Chancer, is one defining feature of a modern society that "bombards us with experiences of domination and subordination far more regularly than it exposes us to sensations and inklings of freedom and reciprocity."[30] Beverly's unintentional but very real cruelty toward his patients, however, indexes his feelings of alienation from yet desire for women. These ambivalent feelings are revealed as a signal part of his personality, evident in the comment of his adolescent self that he would have preferred a form of sexual congress without the touching of bodies. Elliot proves more healthy, in a rather perverse sense, because he can treat women only as sexual objects, desiring nothing else from them but physical release and the mediated connection to his brother they can provide.

Beverly's sadistic treatment of his patients, an uncharacteristic surfacing of repressed anger and fear, more importantly serves as a displacement for the disconnected connection he experiences with his twin brother. Their relationship is sadomasochistic in the sense identified by Chancer, namely that "an excessive attachment exists for both parties," with dependence being "of a symbiotic character in that both sadist and masochist feel a compulsive need for physical, but most critically for psychic, connection to the other."[31] Yet these roles are inherently dynamic, often interchangeable because the relationship is inherently unstable, devoted as it is to satisfying shifting needs and desires. Elliot nurses Beverly through his drug addiction and professional collapse, but when Beverly manages to get himself straightened out enough to visit Claire, Elliot himself collapses. Reuniting, the brothers descend as one into a pathology that finds its ironic final expression in a failed gesture of separation. As in the final scenes of *The Fly,* which feature Brundle's frustrated attempt to disentangle himself from the insect within, the closing images of *Dead Ringers* evoke a technologizing science that cannot simplify the multiplicity that is human nature, never solving the existential problem that Dr. Henry Jekyll, speaking of the contraries within his psyche, identifies: "that in the agonized womb of consciousness these polar twins should be continuously struggling."[32]

Notes

1. Mark Browning, *David Cronenberg: Author or Filmmaker?* (Bristol: Intellect, 2007).
2. Here I follow the definition of the science horror film propounded in J. P. Telotte, *Replications: A Robotic History of the Science Fiction Film* (Urbana: University of Illinois Press, 1995). Telotte observes: "In these works a mad scientist typically turns the body into a piece of artifice, making of it not something to be desired but something from which we almost instinctively recoil" (72).
3. Mary Shelley, *Frankenstein; or The Modern Prometheus*, 1818 ed. (Oxford: Oxford University Press, 2009).
4. Robert Louis Stevenson, *The Strange Case of Dr. Jekyll and Mr. Hyde*, ed. Katherine Linehan (New York: Norton, 2003).
5. Stevenson, *The Strange Case of Dr. Jekyll and Mr. Hyde*, 48.
6. Judith Halberstam, *Skin Flicks: Gothic Horror and the Technology of Monsters* (Durham, N.C.: Duke University Press, 1995), 17.
7. Herbert Marcuse, *Eros and Civilization: A Philosophical Inquiry into Freud* (New York: Vintage Books, 1962).
8. Stevenson, *The Strange Case of Dr. Jekyll and Mr. Hyde*, 49.
9. Stevenson, *The Strange Case of Dr. Jekyll and Mr. Hyde*, 55.
10. William Beard, *The Artist as Monster: The Cinema of David Cronenberg*, rev. and expanded ed. (Toronto: University of Toronto Press, 2006).
11. Quoted by Linehan, in Stevenson, *The Strange Case of Dr. Jekyll and Mr. Hyde*, 185.
12. Robin Wood, *Hollywood from Vietnam to Reagan* (New York: Columbia University Press, 1986).
13. Wood, *Hollywood from Vietnam to Reagan*, 192.
14. Wood, *Hollywood from Vietnam to Reagan*, 191.
15. David J. Skal, *Screams of Reason: Mad Science and Modern Culture* (New York: Norton, 1998), 18.
16. Skal, *Screams of Reason*, 18.
17. Beard, *The Artist as Monster*, 95.
18. Max Horkheimer and Theodor W. Adorno, *Dialectic of Enlightenment*, trans. John Cumming (1944; New York: Continuum, 1995), 4, 5.
19. Horkheimer and Adorno, *Dialectic of Enlightenment*, 9
20. Horkheimer and Adorno, *Dialectic of Enlightenment*, 26.
21. Mary B. Campbell, "Biological Alchemy and the Films of David Cronenberg," in *Planks of Reason: Essays on the Horror Film*, ed. Barry Keith Grant (Lanham, Md.: Scarecrow, 1996), 318.
22. Halberstam, *Skin Flicks*, 53.
23. Horkheimer and Adorno, *Dialectic of Enlightenment*, 4.
24. Stevenson, *The Strange Case of Dr. Jekyll and Mr. Hyde*, 49.

25. Halberstam, *Skin Flicks*, 55.
26. Stevenson, *The Strange Case of Dr. Jekyll and Mr. Hyde*, 49.
27. Stevenson, *The Strange Case of Dr. Jekyll and Mr. Hyde*, 49.
28. Stevenson, *The Strange Case of Dr. Jekyll and Mr. Hyde*, 50.
29. Augustine, *On Free Choice of the Will* (New York: Hackett, 1993).
30. Lynn S. Chancer, *Sadomasochism in Everyday Life: The Dynamics of Power and Powerlessness* (New Brunswick, N.J.: Rutgers University Press, 1992), 2.
31. Chancer, *Sadomasochism in Everyday Life*, 3.
32. Stevenson, *The Strange Case of Dr. Jekyll and Mr. Hyde*, 49.

From "Impassioned Morality" to "Bloodless Agnosticism"
A Philosophy of David Cronenberg through the Burroughs/Ballard Axis

Jones Irwin

In this essay I will provide an analysis of the vision that lies behind two key films in the Cronenberg canon, *Crash* (1996) and *Naked Lunch* (1991), so as to open up a macroanalysis of the philosophical themes that provide a framework for Cronenberg's enigmatic art. I will explore such themes as the relationship between the social and the individual, the experience of mortality, the nature of artistic integrity, and the distinction between morality and immorality. Cronenberg has professed a long-standing obsession with William S. Burroughs as a writer (and figure of cultural myth);[1] and Burroughs's subversive approach to existence and to philosophical problems is traceable as an influence all the way back to Cronenberg's first films (e.g., *Stereo* [1969], *Crimes of the Future* [1970]), as well as heavily determining the mood and direction of *Videodrome* (1983). Burroughs has likewise expressed admiration for Cronenberg, citing him as "the only filmmaker who could take on *Naked Lunch*."[2] Nonetheless, there are crucial differences in the respective visions of Cronenberg and Burroughs—not simply with regard to a heterosexual (Cronenberg) versus "queer" (Burroughs) style but also, more fundamentally, in terms of their self-conception with regard to the ethical import of their work. If Cronenberg sees his work as amoral, or at least nonmoral, Burroughs certainly sees a moral vision as central to his thinking and art. Despite all the appearances to the contrary, Burroughs consistently views his art as "telling the truth," in commentator Mitch Tuchman's phrase, as an "impassioned moralism," while Cronenberg (who might have more obvious claim to the title "impassioned moralist") sees himself more as a kind of "bloodless agnostic."[3] Here, we can understand "impassioned moralism" to designate an unequivocal commitment to moral values that is also highly emotive, while "bloodless agnosticism" seems to signify a sense that Cronenberg disavows any knowledge of a moral dimension to his work.

Moreover, "bloodless" signifies an apathy in this regard. That is, Cronenberg wouldn't seem to care whether his work is moral or amoral. Again, paradoxically, this same distinctiveness of vision (impassioned moralist vs. bloodless agnostic) is played out in the encounter between Cronenberg and another writer whose work he adapts, J. G. Ballard.

In this essay I will seek to untangle the knots of this complex set of interconnected relationships and visions. Through analyzing the triangular relationship between Burroughs, Ballard, and Cronenberg, and particularly the metamorphosis that the original literary texts of *Naked Lunch* (Burroughs) and *Crash* (Ballard) undergo as adapted for Cronenberg's cinema, I will seek to determine the respective philosophical and/or moral commitments of these three controversial artists.

Cronenberg on Cronenberg

In a satirical foreword that David Cronenberg seems to have written himself—under the name "Dr. Martyn Steenbeck"—to a collection of interviews on his work, there is a reference to the "Cronenberg condition . . . an audiovisual virus" that the author caught in a cinema in 1976 and that overwhelmed him in the measure to which his immune system had become weakened by a "diet of polite imagination, subtle subtext and decorative gore."[4] Now, life would never be the same again. Describing this condition as a "parasite" of the horror genre, Steenbeck names it as "body horror . . . Cronenbergesque," and notes, "His practice has no other cinematic parallel that I am aware of."[5] The meta-level description (that is, a view of Cronenberg's work as a whole) goes on to speak of the fundamentally "scientific" aspect of Cronenberg's practice: "The films are experiments, conducted in a pure sense, with little or no regard for the consequences; the point is to follow the experiment or hypothesis thru to the end, unrestrained by social or political considerations."[6] Unlike the work of other previously avant-garde or underground directors who moved to the bigger studios and budgets, and who consequently changed direction thematically, it is clear that each of Cronenberg's films develops a logic that is consistent across his oeuvre. Indeed, a later film such as *Crash* can in many respects be seen as a return to the sparse and minimalist filmmaking of Cronenberg's first output. Another reason for this can be found in Cronenberg's own writing of many of the screenplays for his films, which obviously allows him a great deal of control over material and vision. Steenbeck claims that "Cronenberg is an *auteur;* perhaps more in a European rather than a North American sense. He writes as well as directs most of his material and continues to direct outside systems which threaten to wrest control in any important sense. [This is] a series of movies which began as low budget exploiters and became major motion pictures."[7]

Although Cronenberg is not unique in this, he is part of a rare group of film directors who, in the contemporary setting, can be said to have a genuinely philosophical vision for their films. We will see this philosophical vision when we look in detail at the key themes of his work. As Steenbeck observes, "The director has been encouraged by each movie to progress and refine that experiment—film to film—as part of a lifetime's commitment towards an end; finding the cure to a disease common to us all; it is called mortality."[8] Plato once described philosophy, in the *Phaedo,* as a "preparation for death."[9] Here, we see the authentically philosophical dimension of Cronenberg's vision (which is often occluded in an overemphasis on the sci-fi or "effects" aspects of his cinema). First, Cronenberg is concerned with the experience of mortality, an age-old obsession of philosophers from Plato onward. This is obviously a theme of most science-fiction movies and literature, but in Cronenberg, it most distinctly takes on a more philosophical tendency. Often in his films, attempted solutions or "experiments" run aground, leading to destruction and death, but as Steenbeck notes, "the fact that these alternatives also lead to death and destruction is perhaps less to do with a deep-rooted pessimism or negativity than the need to seek a hard and realistic optimism."[10] Second, his work foregrounds the question of the relationship between mind and body, seeming to critique the view that would radically separate the two. Rather, Cronenberg's work seems to bring about an attempted fusion between mind and body. Third, Cronenberg develops an emphasis on technology and the mutation of the human being, which clearly maps onto similar concerns in some contemporary philosophy.

The experimental nature of Cronenberg's cinema perhaps explains one of the criticisms of his meta-level interpretation of the films that comes from some quarters. According to this viewpoint, Cronenberg is a poor reader of his own work, as what he says about his cinema often fails to correspond to how these films actually work on audiences and critics. But if Cronenberg is a genuine experimentalist, we can say that this applies not simply to the production of his work but also to the interpretation. As we will see with Burroughs also, Cronenberg is conscious of what German philosopher Friedrich Nietzsche called "perspectivism": the view that any and all perspectives are equally valid, as well as the realization that one's perspective is rooted in one's spatiotemporal (or sociopolitical) context.[11] Rather than seeing such perspectivism as grounded in error, (Cronenbergian) experimentalism as a methodology sees such openness of interpretation as endemic, as to be affirmed, if only as a necessary evil. But the criticisms with regard to Cronenberg's experimental approach don't stop there. Some critics are also concerned with the moral dimension of the films, or rather their apparently *amoral* dimension, their refusal to provide ready-made moral answers to dilemmas, and their extremism, in terms of content and direction. This is referred to as "his desire to 'show the unshowable, speak the unspeakable.'"[12] Steenbeck also has something to say about this issue: "The pleasure is in its absolute integrity."[13] In other words, what really seems to matter is less the moralization of content or an ethical or happy ending than the "integrity" of the artistic process. We can see that the respective themes of mortality and perspectivism play a key role in Cronenberg's approach and vision.

There are certainly paradoxes and tensions within Cronenberg's vision of artistry and artistic integrity. His initial films from the 1970s, such as *Shivers* (1975) and *Rabid* (1977), did well at the box office precisely because of their "exploitation" billing.[14] That is, their trailers played on the most sensationalist and pornographic of the elements within the films, and appealed to the transgressive instincts of the audience. Sex sells, and Cronenberg's films have always benefited from his mixing of sci-fi and erotic elements. But rather than see this as a negative aspect, we can perhaps see this as an example of how Cronenberg has succeeded in filtering more intellectual concerns into his work, often under the rubric of exploitation. There may well be comparisons to be made between elements of, for example, Roger Corman's or John Waters's films and those of Cronenberg, but only in the detached or isolated elements of the latter's cinema. Cronenberg's films always self-evidently amount to more than simply exploitation flicks, and it is precisely this hybridization of high and low culture, or cerebral and libidinal, that gives Cronenberg's films their distinctiveness and also their appeal to a wider audience. Cronenberg is not a genre director, but a director who employs genre (e.g., sci-fi) only to subvert it. As Chris Rodley has observed, "One assumes that it was Cronenberg's resiting of horror from the realm of the gothic to the body that thrilled and shocked audiences. Specifically, given *Shivers*' reputation as the first 'venereal horror' movie, it was the films' interest in sex and violent, playful anarchy rather than their disease-obsessed philosophical tendencies, that made them function so well as exploitation movies."[15] This is of course true, but nonetheless, the philosophical tendencies of the films still make Cronenberg's films more than merely exploitation flicks. Whereas exploitation cinema is unashamedly puerile in its concerns, Cronenberg juxtaposes this exploitation dimension alongside the philosophical thematic we have been exploring, and it is precisely this ability to juxtapose otherwise irreconcilable elements that makes his films so unique.

From the Social to the Individual

We can also recognize a shift in Cronenberg's concerns, after *Videodrome* most especially. This film represents "the last of his Canadian tax shelter movies."[16] With *The Dead Zone* (1983), it was the beginning of a new phase of work. Cronenberg moves from the social to the individual level; his focus is "more personalized, claustrophobic, interiorized and affecting cinema; the chaos is chiefly sited in the personal."[17] One way to see this move from social to individual is to view it through a postmodern lens, where Cronenberg would be reinforcing the post-Marxist emphasis on an enigmatic subjectivity and the critique of community as repressive and/or stifling (for example, one gets this emphasis in a thinker such as Jacques Derrida[18]). This is evident in both *Naked Lunch* and *Crash,* as we will see. Yet, it would be wrong to think that Cronenberg has turned his back on social concerns. In both cases, the private relationships constitute a microcosm of what is going on in the wider society, whether it relates to the questions of addiction or the politics of control in *Naked Lunch,* or the relation between sexuality and technology in *Crash.* In both cases, also, we have the sense that what is being foregrounded is a subculture that is some way in advance of the main culture, and thus acts as a symbol (or a cautionary warning, in Ballard's terms) of how things will or might be in the future, with regard to the mainstream culture.

Cronenberg's choice of Ballard's and Burroughs's texts to work on again exemplifies his long-standing interest in literature and its relation to cinema, but also his consistent focus on philosophical ideas. For both these writers, a philosophical vision is central to their art, respective visions that, as we will see, bear both affinities and disaffinities to Cronenberg's own. As with Cronenberg, the philosophical themes in Burroughs and Ballard center on such topics as the relationship between the social and the individual, the experience of mortality, the nature of artistic integrity, and the distinction between morality and immorality.

"A Frozen Moment": Cronenberg, Burroughs, and *Naked Lunch*

If *The Dead Zone* represents a paradigm shift in thematic concern for Cronenberg from more socially focused horror to a more interiorized emphasis, then the film *Naked Lunch* can be seen as intensifying this new emphasis. Cronenberg has often cited Burroughs as the key intellectual and artistic influence on his work (alongside Vladimir Nabokov), and he had been considering the possibility of adapting *Naked Lunch* from the early 1980s. In fact, he had visited Tangier in the 1980s precisely to put the plans in place. However, the production was delayed until 1991 (commercial funding being an issue). As well as the obviously controversial subject matter of *Naked Lunch* (homosexual and "perverse" sex and drug addiction), the complexity and idiosyncrasy of the text made the possibility of an adapted screenplay a very difficult (if not impossible) proposition. A literalist rendering of the text in cinematic terms being an impossibility, Cronenberg settled on a method that employed imagery and some of the enigmatic narrative from the text, with significant autobiographical material from Burroughs's life, alongside themes and images from some of Burroughs's other texts, while also including elements from his own Cronenbergian vision. In effect, Cronenberg, in writing the screenplay, *became Burroughs*. This approach rather appropriately maps onto the renewed focus in Cronenberg's cinema on a more personalized thematic, putting more emphasis on the individual in contradistinction to the social. As Rodley says, "The chaos is chiefly sited in the personal, with little or no impact in reality beyond the context of close, personal relationships."[19] The film thus concentrates on "mental states, this time of would-be writer Bill Lee (Peter Weller)—drug addiction, homosexual sex and violence."[20] Cronenberg refers to being "possessed" by Burroughs, and by a private kind of "chaos": "I tend to view chaos as a private rather than a social endeavor; the chaos that most appeals to me is very private and very personal; you have these little pockets of private and personal chaos brewing in the interstices in the structure of society, which likes to stress its order and control, and that's the collision you see."[21]

A certain qualification has to be made here, however. When one speaks of Burroughs's or Cronenberg's emphasis on the personal, one needs to take account of this precisely not representing a return to some kind of modernist self or personhood, where the self would be seen as rational and self-sufficient (in the case of René Descartes's philosophy, for example[22]). As the historian of the beat movement Ann Douglas has noted, Burroughs was "a leader of postmodern literary fashion in the 60s." His work led him to "discard the humanistic notions of the self; human is an adjective not a noun; his starting point [being] the place where the human road ends."[23] If humanism is the philosophy that optimistically places the human, rational, moral individual at the center of the universe, Burroughs's work rejects what it sees as the hubris of such a philosophical position This antihumanism distinguishes Burroughs from the other beat writers. The beats were a distinct American group of writers, evolving from the 1950s, including Allen Ginsberg, Jack Kerouac, and Gregory Corso. Burroughs's antihumanism was initially directed against the humanism of Ginsberg, linking Burroughs to a different and distinctive tradition within American modernist writing. As Douglas notes: "While he is part of the Beat movement, he also belongs to another literary tradition of *avant-garde* novelists headed by Nabokov, Pynchon, John Hawkes, William Gaddis, John Barth and Don DeLillo."[24] So Burroughs's move from the social to the individual is not a privileging of humanism but rather a foregrounding of a complex and enigmatic subjectivity.

Morality and Immorality

Although the emphasis on a fractured personhood and self links Burroughs very obviously to Cronenberg, a connected emphasis on moral responsibility in his work marks him out from many other postmodern writers and philosophers, and also from Cronenberg. Cronenberg is perhaps a more consistent postmodernist in this respect (in his very amoralism). Here, we can understand postmodernism to mean the break with a modernist emphasis on reason and an isolated selfhood. Mitch Tuchman has, as mentioned earlier, described this important difference between Cronenberg and Burroughs as "Burroughs's impassioned moralism and Cronenberg's bloodless agnosticism."[25]

This "morality" is perhaps best understood as Burroughs's own, independent of his association with the ethics of the beat movement, but it nonetheless also connects to Burroughs's involvement in that movement. Burroughs is certainly paradigmatic in the beat movement, although he later declaimed affinity with beat writers in terms of literary style (despite the obvious personal connections). As Robert Holton notes, the beats were in countercultural resistance to what Robert Lindner called the "centripetal cultural logic of postwar America [that] was ubiquitous from childhood on" and that could be summarized in the phrase "You must adjust," and the beats' mantra might rather be described as "Break out of the cage."[26] At root, the beats were in revolt against what they perceived as the fundamental values of conservative America. Holton refers here interestingly to Herbert Marcuse's seminal text *One-Dimensional Man*.[27] In that text, Marcuse, asks whether alienation becomes obsolete when the individuals of a society identify with the life that is imposed on them. His answer is in the negative: "The result of this identification is not the loss of alienation though, he decides, but actually 'constitutes a more progressive stage of alienation characterized by a loss of the ability to imagine alternatives.'"[28]

The resultant task of the beats, according to Holton, was a moral and ethical one, and this is where we see Burroughs's affinity with the beats over the postmodernists. Here, he quotes Chandler Brossard: "Their task—experienced, really, as an aesthetic/moral obligation—was to create a new sensibility and a new language . . . with which to illuminate the existential crisis of the postwar American in conflict with his society's 'values.'"[29] The ultimate aim of such a sense of moral and aesthetic obligation was personal and cultural "renewal." This is clear in Kerouac's On the Road;[30] but a sense of moral obligation is also present, more elliptically, throughout Burroughs's oeuvre. Certainly, in order to get to this renewal, Burroughs has no difficulty with (indeed, positively affirms) "the privacy of speech and nightmare."[31] This methodology of horror is what joins Cronenberg and Burroughs very closely in spirit. However, whether there remains a tension at the ethical level is a moot point. That is, although both Burroughs and Cronenberg affirm horror, in the former there seems to be an ethics underlying the horror, whereas in the latter, this is far more equivocal.

Where Burroughs breaks with the postmodern position is that, in his fiction, although everyone is in conflict, everyone is also responsible, for everyone is capable of resistance. As Douglas puts it, "There are no victims, just accomplices; the mark collaborates with his exploiter in his own demise."[32] For Burroughs, every individual is responsible for his or her own fate, and in contemporary society, those who claim to be victims must face up to their own complicity in their oppression. This strong notion of responsibility based on a complicity is Burroughsian, and in the adaptation of Naked Lunch by Cronenberg, we can at least say that the emphasis is different. As Rodley makes clear, "in the Cronenberg project—the creation of art must ultimately free itself of political, social and cultural concerns."[33] For Cronenberg, art and morality are often in conflict, if not mutually exclusive. Cronenberg vehemently rejects the idea that art should act as a vehicle for some kind of specific moral or political ideology. We can see this in the way that Cronenberg chooses to emphasize certain aspects of Burroughs's life in the film, most notably his accidental shooting of his wife, Joan. Whereas Burroughs spoke of this event as key to his writing, but also in negative terms as being due to a lapse in his responsibility—allowing a certain kind of "ugly spirit" to overwhelm him[34]—the film adaptation presents the killing in aestheticized terms. In fact, Cronenberg shows the killing twice, in two different scenes, and in the final scene when it reoccurs, it is seen to be the condition of Burroughs's entry into the world of art or creativity. In this final scene, Burroughs is seen to escape from the scene of the killing and then to gain entry into an artists' zone, precisely as an effect of the very act of killing his wife. Although Burroughs always recognized this link between the killing and his creativity, what is lacking from the filmic portrayal is a sense of the ethical dimension that Burroughs brings to his retrospective reading of the event. We can say that this is indicative of Cronenberg's "bloodless agnosticism." That is, Cronenberg is often unconcerned to show any moral or political rationale for the actions of his characters.

It is also arguable that in focusing very much on the personal elements of Burroughs's life—his connection to writer Paul Bowles, for example, in Tangier—Cronenberg emphasizes the personal aspects of Burroughs's art, the autobiographical elements, at the expense of his more sociopolitical concerns. As Douglas notes, Burroughs was a lifelong critic of power, and the misuse of power, perhaps going back to his early understanding of Hitler's regime, and his realization that "everything that Hitler had done was legal."[35] For Burroughs, we are everywhere complicit with power—"to speak is to lie—to live is to collaborate"—but it is arguable that Cronenberg deemphasizes these elements of Burroughs's vision. This, of course, is artistic license, and Cronenberg has spoken of the impossibility of a literalist rendering of *Naked Lunch*. Nonetheless, it also points to tensions within the visions of both artists, so that *Naked Lunch* as a film is distinctly Cronenberg's and not any longer simply the work of Burroughs. In the next section, I will look at how, despite the strong affinities between the two artists, a similar disaffinity can be seen between Ballard and Cronenberg, with regard, for example, to the latter's cinematic adaptation of *Crash*.

"A Cautionary Warning"? *Crash*, Cronenberg, and Ballard

One of the most interesting elements of the relation between Cronenberg and his filmic adaptations of *Naked Lunch* and *Crash* is that it allows us not simply to focus on the relation between Cronenberg and the two writers concerned, but also to foreground the relation between Ballard and Burroughs themselves. Ballard actually wrote the introduction to one of the editions of *Naked Lunch*, and here—in the content of the introduction—we see both the emphasis on an aesthetic of horror that links all three artists and also a distinctive ethical tendency that links Ballard and Burroughs but that distinguishes them from Cronenberg. This emphasis on "impassioned moralism" is also to be seen in Ballard's introduction to the French edition of *Crash*, which he wrote in 1974.[36] For Ballard, "*Naked Lunch* is ... this extraordinary novel ... a comic apocalypse ... a roller-coaster ride through hell, a safari to the strangest people of the strangest planet, ourselves; comic, paranoid, visionary, delirious."[37] However, for Ballard, there is also a philosophical or revelatory imperative in Burroughs's depiction, as this is not simply delirium for the sake of delirium. "A unique world ... is being revealed to us; only later do we realize that this strange city is the one we all inhabit in our waking lives."[38] Ballard here takes Burroughs to be making a comment about the nature of reality, under contemporary conditions. Burroughs is read as providing a two-pronged literary analysis of contemporary humanity's predicament; on the one side, the more personal or intersubjective themes of drug use, homosexuality, and the quest for an "ever-elusive sexual happiness" are explored. But on the other, this more personal or interiorized (even narcissistic emphasis) is balanced by a more sociopolitical exploration of the implications of "addiction": "He sees addiction as part of the global conspiracy by the presiding powers of our world—the media conglomerates, the vast political and commercial bureaucracies, and a profit-driven medical science—which are determined to reduce us to the total dependency of addicts; while teasing us with the mirage of transgressive sex."[39] This last phrase is particularly important—citing the concept of "mirage." Here we have a return to a rather traditional philosophical framework of interpretation that opposes appearance (here, "mirage") to the reality that lies behind. The original reference for this philosophical distinction is in the work of Plato, where Plato sees much of what is taken as reality to amount to a mere image or "mirage" of that reality—for example, in the Allegory of the Cave in *The Republic*.[40]

This Burroughs text, for Ballard, as well as being the "most important and original work of fiction by an American writer since World War II," should not be understood as only a great literary work.[41] *Naked Lunch* is not, as it is often portrayed, a work of literature for its own sake, but rather a literature that has significant ethical and philosophical dimensions. It is these elements that, one might argue, are somewhat occluded by Cronenberg in his adaptation of the book. That is, Cronenberg relegates the ethical dimensions in favor of a focus on the aesthetic. This point is reinforced somewhat even by the title of the book and Ballard's interpretation of its meaning: "Naked Lunch is both the addict's fix, the rush of pure sensation through the brain, and also the stark and unsentimental truth about ourselves, our self-delusions and deceits."[42]

Although Cronenberg undoubtedly does bring some of these elements to the screen, it is nonetheless arguable that the different emphasis is still quite significant. Certainly, we can see the rendering of, for example, the nature of addiction in Cronenberg's depiction of Burroughs's intake of bug powder. The world of Tangier that Cronenberg portrays is decadent in the extreme. Similarly, the depiction of Burroughs's typewriter as a living, grotesque "bug" creature exemplifies the whole hallucinatory nature of Burroughs's vision and text. However, in each of these instances, Cronenberg seems intent on presenting an "aestheticized" picture that disavows any moral or political context for these situations. In relation to what he does see in

Burroughs, we can cite "his long-standing conceptual and visual association with Burroughs's work; but also with his beliefs that writing is a dangerous business; compare imagination to disease."[43] And also, as Cronenberg states, his understanding of the work as "a metaphor for control and addiction": "I understood the metaphorical side. I didn't want it to be a movie about drugs, as Burroughs is more about addiction, manipulation and control."[44] Cronenberg refers here to the very thematic of writing itself, the writing act and the writerly life: "I also knew I wanted it to be about the act of writing."[45]

In addition, as with Burroughs, Cronenberg has always been concerned with morality or death as a paradigmatic issue for his art. If we take, for example, the emphasis on control and manipulation, we can see how this connects with the aforementioned theme of the relation between the social and the individual. In what sense, Burroughs and Cronenberg seem to be asking, can the individual be said to exist in the context of the extraordinarily alienating conditions of contemporary life? We also see how the themes often connect together and supplement each other—thus the themes of immorality, addiction, and death reinforce the theme of the alienation of the individual from society. Here, we undoubtedly see a convergence, but there is a disaffinity also. Cronenberg acknowledges this issue himself, indeed affirming this very difference. And rather than seeing it as a question of Burroughs versus Cronenberg, he sees it rather as a question of a "third thing," as a result of the unpredictable encounter between them: "Of course, it's my version of *Naked Lunch*. . . . I had to abandon the idea of a direct translation . . . create a third thing. . . . What I do is very different from Burroughs."[46] This leads Rodley to conclude that "the emergent film was clearly more Cronenberg than Burroughs."[47] Indeed, Cronenberg even goes so far here as to question the very possibility of bringing a philosophical meaning to bear on the film, or any of his films: "Some people say that movies tend to support or encourage a certain philosophy. . . . Ultimately, that's bullshit. In perspective, you might be able to say something truthful about it; but who has the balance, the magisterial cosmic perspective that he or she can look at a script and say . . ."[48]

What Ballard's reading of Burroughs therefore foregrounds for us is both the affinity and the disaffinity between Cronenberg and the two writers, but it also demonstrates an important convergence in the work of Ballard and Burroughs. Although Ballard's writing started off under the rubric of sci-fi, as with Burroughs, it soon moved to a more individualized, almost uncategorizable area. As we have seen, although Burroughs was associated with the beats, this was not a wholly definitive categorization.[49] It is arguable that Ballard is even less categorizable, and he was never associated with the beats. As an English rather than American writer, Ballard has also never maintained any close connection to his English contemporaries (while nonetheless being eminently respected by all of them as a key figure in the evolution of British fiction in the postwar period).

The same logic that we have seen at work in the Cronenberg-Burroughs encounter can be applied to the Cronenberg and Ballard discussion. A third element does emerge here also, but the question remains of what this encounter can tell us about the differences between the original vision of Cronenberg and those artists' work he is adapting to film. In some respects, Ballard and Cronenberg are closer than Cronenberg was to Burroughs. This is primarily because of the lifestyle issue. Whereas Burroughs sought to live out his vision in real life, Ballard always spoke of a key distinction between the life of the mind and the issue of real existence. Although Ballard does also playfully blur these boundaries—for example, in calling the main protagonists in *Crash* the Ballards—much has always been made of his suburban existence as a single father of three in Shepperton, a suburb of London. In contrast, Burroughs always reveled in the image of a transgressive dandy, which developed even before he started writing, most notably in the creative work of Kerouac.[50] Burroughs may have played the role of dandy, but his life does not always mirror his art. So too with Ballard, whose (suburban) life seems in no way to mirror his (apocalyptic) artistic vision. But Burroughs's life is mythologized across the landscape of beat literature, from Ginsberg to Corso, and it is a moot issue as to the authenticity of this image, its effect on Burroughs's own writing, and his understanding of the relation between his person and his writing.[51] What is worth saying here is that Cronenberg, by his own account, has lived a life more like Ballard's than like Burroughs's, a life of apparent suburban quietness that contrasts sharply with the "body horror" visions of his cinema.[52] Cronenberg comments on this existential affinity between himself and Ballard in an interview and also makes a connecting point to an affinity between the original text of *Crash* and his own screenplay.[53] There seems to have been less reworking of the *Crash* text than in the case of *Naked Lunch*. The adaptation of *Crash* is perhaps, one might say, a more straight adaptation, but as with the case of *Naked Lunch*, I think we can also say that there are issues of tension in the encounter between Cronenberg and Ballard.

In the first case, in terms of Cronenberg's oeuvre, as Rodley has commented, "*Crash* comes on like unrepentant, quintessential Cronenberg.... It represents the director's return to his uncompromising, dangerous roots."[54] *Crash* is a film made on a much smaller budget than *Naked Lunch,* and this is one reason why it reminds one of Cronenberg's early experimental cinema. However, the term "unrepentant" is also significant here. Watching Cronenberg's *Crash*, one is struck by a certain kind of philosophical vision that is being put forward. The initial three scenes of *Crash*, for example, which might be described (for simplicity) as "sex scenes," foreground a certain aestheticism. In philosophical terms, we can see this as linked to a Cronenbergian emphasis on embodiment and pleasure. The fact that these begin the film is itself evidence of Cronenberg's intention to emphasize the aesthetic dimension above all else, which might be viewed as at odds with Ballard's own text. So despite Cronenberg's claims that his adaptation of *Crash* is more faithful to the original, again it is a question of nuance and suggestion.

Here, we can employ Ballard's own reading of his work, in the introduction to the French edition of *Crash* (published in 1974), to contrast with Cronenberg's version and the vision it seems to demonstrate. If there was any doubt as to the intended meaning and significance of *Crash*, Ballard's introduction to the French edition dispels the ambiguity. This introduction is a brilliant précis of the meta-level vision of Ballard's work. What it simultaneously highlights is Ballard's proximity to Burroughs and a significant divergence from Cronenberg. Ballard begins by speaking of an "ever more ambiguous world," and the "spectres of sinister technologies . . . an overlit realm ruled by advertising and pseudo-events, science and pornography."[55] Citing the more optimistic tenor of Marshall McLuhan's readings of new media, Ballard warns that we should, perhaps, pay more attention to Sigmund Freud's profound pessimism in *Civilisation and Its Discontents:* "Voyeurism, self-disgust, the infantile basis of our dreams and longings—these diseases of the psyche have now culminated in the most terrifying casualty of the century, the death of affect."[56] For Ballard, this "demise of feeling and emotion" is linked intrinsically to the framework of "sex as the perfect arena; like a culture bed of sterile pus; for all the veronicas of our own perversions."[57] The tone here is decidedly moral and impassioned, while obviously recognizing both the lure and the inherent ambivalence of meaning associated with many of these contemporary phenomena.

We have already seen Cronenberg disavow the simplicity of philosophical meaning attaching itself to art, but here (albeit polemically), Ballard seems unequivocal in his philosophical pronouncements: "the irrelevancy of the past; the social and sexual philosophy of the ejector seat."[58] He also makes claims for science fiction as the dominant tradition of literary writing in the twentieth century, extending from H. G. Wells through Aldous Huxley to

Burroughs, and aligns himself with this tradition. In fact, he describes this introduction as a defense of "science fiction," and by implication a defense of his own writing and literary vision.[59] Here, he makes an important distinction between the sensibilities of the nineteenth- and twentieth-century novels: the dominant characteristic of the former is "the mood of individual isolation and alienation; but this is the psychology of the 19th century. . . . Yet if anything befits the twentieth century, it is optimism, the iconography of mass merchandise, naivety and a guilt-free enjoyment of all the mind's possibilities."[60] But it is only science fiction that can do justice to this complexity of the twentieth century; "However crudely or naively, science fiction at least attempts to place a philosophical and metaphysical frame around the most important events within our lives and consciousness."[61] Ballard's own particular contribution to this genre he describes as the exploration of what he terms "inner space," that "psychological domain [manifest, for example, in surrealist painting] where the inner world of the mind and the outer world of reality meet and fuse."[62] But this great optimism of the twentieth century is not simply to be affirmed. Castigating early science fiction as "historical romance," Ballard describes the advanced twentieth-century life as "infantile . . . we live in an almost infantile world where any demand, any possibility, whether for life-styles, travel, sexual roles and identities, can be satisfied immediately."[63] Reinforcing the old Platonic distinction between appearance and reality (which he ascribes to the later version propounded by Freud), Ballard refers to the reversal of the roles in the perennial relationship between reality and fiction; now the world has become fiction, and it is the role of the writer to "invent the reality."[64]

Acknowledging the extremism of *Crash* as a novel, Ballard refers to the writer's role as having changed radically: "He has no moral stance . . . his role is that of the scientist . . . faced with a completely unknown territory, all he can do is to devise various hypotheses and test them against the facts."[65] Again, this brings us back to Cronenberg's own vision of his methodology, and there are, of course, powerful affinities between the two artists here. Nonetheless, Ballard is unequivocal in a way that Cronenberg is not on the overall vision of the project: "Throughout *Crash*, I have used the car not only as a sexual image but as a total metaphor for man's life in society today; the novel has a political role quite apart from its sexual content."[66] So what is this political role? For Ballard, it is clearly an ethical injunction, a wake-up call: "Needless to say, the ultimate role of *Crash* is cautionary, a warning against that brutal, erotic and overlit realm that beckons more and more persuasively from the margins of the technological landscape."[67] The term "ultimate" is important here. As with Cronenberg, Ballard is prepared to experiment, to go to the darkest regions of humanity so as to explore meaning. But *ultimately,* this is a cautionary tale, with an ethical message, and also a text with serious sociopolitical concern. It is precisely this ability to draw out to the sociopolitical realm that Ballard locates as a key element of twentieth-century science fiction, and it is this characteristic that distinguishes it, for example, from the nineteenth-century paradigm. Once again, however, we have the concern here that Cronenberg's tendency to focus in on the personal realm, the realm of narcissistic obsession, runs the risk of occluding the more broadly concerned Ballardian conception.

Here we might make a different but related point to the one I made with regard to the *Naked Lunch* adaptation. There, the issue had been one of excessive adaptation, Cronenberg's making *Naked Lunch* his own, the final film being "clearly more Cronenberg than Burroughs." Here, the issue is different. Cronenberg offers a more literalist reading of Ballard's text, his film screenplay apes Ballard's text almost word for word, scene for scene. For example, as I mentioned, the first three opening scenes in the film are sexual: "The movie begins with three sex scenes in a row which replicates the tone of the book which is absolutely unrelenting and confrontational.... In *Crash,* very often the sex scenes are absolutely the plot and the character development."[68] Cronenberg replicates the emphasis in the Ballardian text on the fact that these are not "normal" twentieth-century sexual relationships or love relationships. Most especially, the evolution of technology has changed the relation between sexuality and the world around us, and Cronenberg cites the development of the automobile as a "mobile bedroom."[69] The very nature of sexual contact has also changed, and Cronenberg emphasizes the "non face to face" aspects: "Sex in the movie is rarely face to face . . . the actors looking towards the camera and not at each other. . . . It helped that sort of disconnected thing . . . how do you have sex when you're not quite having sex with each other."[70]

Cronenberg's film would thus seem to remain faithful to the letter of Ballard's text. But it is this very literalness that would seem to be the problem. Taking the text as text, Cronenberg has indeed provided a careful adaptation. According to Ballard, however, this is precisely a text that shouldn't be taken literally; it is a text that beckons beyond its surface to a different reality. *Crash,* in other words, is not what it appears to be. It appears to be a reckless affirmation of so-called postmodern nihilism. In reality, however, it is, at the least, very ambivalent about contemporary developments in terms of societal and personal relationships, and at its strongest, it is quite morally chastening in intent. If the text of *Crash* cannot provide clarity on this, Ballard's aforementioned writings concerning the book are unequivocal.

Conclusion

We have seen in this essay how Cronenberg adapts the work of Burroughs and Ballard in very interesting ways in the films *Naked Lunch* and *Crash*. First, this demonstrates the key influences that both figures have had on Cronenberg, most especially Burroughs. But it also reveals the respective disaffinities between the three artists. That is to say, whereas a close reading of the texts and meta-level interpretation of their work brings Burroughs and Ballard very close together, in the case of Cronenberg, it shows the distance that is not obvious on first inspection. Developing an insight of Mitch Tuchman's, I have attempted to show in this essay how this represents a move from what might be termed the more "impassioned moralism" of Burroughs and Ballard (although this would have to be said with certain qualifications, as we have seen) to the "bloodless agnosticism" of Cronenberg. To say this is not to favor one kind of vision or ideological approach over the other but simply to point to a significant philosophical difference that is rarely cited. It is perhaps this difference, given all the other affinities between the artists, that makes their artistic encounters, resulting in *Crash* and *Naked Lunch* as films, so productive. But it still leaves questions with regard to the ethical and philosophical import of Cronenberg's work. Cronenberg seems to consistently disavow both the ethical and philosophical dimensions of his films, whereas Ballard and Burroughs are happy to embrace these aspects of their literature. Whether this, ultimately, is a matter, as some critics have suggested, of Cronenberg's not understanding the real meaning of his work, or whether rather it points to a genuine philosophical vacuum at the heart of his work, continues to perplex his audience. Perhaps the final word should be left here to Dr. Martyn Steenbeck. Commenting on the ambiguity and conflict of vision in Cronenbergian cinema, he notes: "The pain is in its emergent melancholia ... [and] the pleasure is in its absolute integrity.... Needless to say, the experiment must continue; the cure is elusive."[71]

Notes

1. See William Burroughs, *Word Virus: The William Burroughs Reader*, ed. James Grauerholz and Ira Silverberg (London: Flamingo, 1999).

2. Quoted in Chris Rodley, ed., *Cronenberg on Cronenberg*, rev. ed. (London: Faber and Faber, 1997), 161.

3. Quoted in Rodley, *Cronenberg on Cronenberg*, 157.
4. Foreword to Rodley, *Cronenberg on Cronenberg*, xi.
5. Foreword to Rodley, *Cronenberg on Cronenberg*, xi.
6. Foreword to Rodley, *Cronenberg on Cronenberg*, xii.
7. Foreword to Rodley, *Cronenberg on Cronenberg*, xii.
8. Foreword to Rodley, *Cronenberg on Cronenberg*, xii.
9. Plato, *Phaedo* (London: Penguin, 1961).
10. Foreword to Rodley, *Cronenberg on Cronenberg*, xii.
11. Friedrich Nietzsche, *On the Genealogy of Morals* (New York: Random House, 1967).
12. Cronenberg, quoted in Rodley, introduction to *Cronenberg on Cronenberg*, xvi.
13. Foreword to Rodley, *Cronenberg on Cronenberg*, xiii.
14. Chris Rodley cites Roger Corman's description of an exploitation film as "a movie in which the subject matter alone guarantees an audience, whatever the quality of the film." Implicit here is the assumption that the content of the film will be somehow transgressive, often in a sexual sense. This led to the importance of the sensationalist trailer for the exploitation film, which sometimes was more important than the film itself (Rodley, introduction to *Cronenberg on Cronenberg*, xvi). A recent example of an attempt to resurrect the exploitation (or "sexploitation") genre is Quentin Tarantino's film *Death Proof* (2007).
15. Rodley, introduction to *Cronenberg on Cronenberg*, xvii.
16. Foreword to Rodley, *Cronenberg on Cronenberg*, xi.
17. Rodley, introduction to *Cronenberg on Cronenberg*, xx.
18. Jacques Derrida, *Writing and Difference* (Chicago: University of Chicago Press, 1972).
19. Rodley, introduction to *Cronenberg on Cronenberg*, xx.
20. Rodley, introduction to *Cronenberg on Cronenberg*, xxiii.
21. Quoted in Rodley, *Cronenberg on Cronenberg*, 25.
22. René Descartes, *Meditations* (London: Penguin, 1990).
23. Ann Douglas, "Punching a Hole in the Big Lie: The Achievement of William S. Burroughs," in *Word Virus*, ed. Grauerholz and Silverberg, xxvi.
24. Douglas, "Punching a Hole in the Big Lie," xxvi.
25. Quoted in Rodley, *Cronenberg on Cronenberg*, 157.
26. Robert Holton, "'The Sordid Hipsters of America': Beat Culture and the Folds of Heterogeneity," in *Reconstructing the Beats*, ed. Jennie Skerl (London: Palgrave Macmillan, 2004), 15.
27. Herbert Marcuse, *One-Dimensional Man* (London: Routledge, 2002).
28. Holton, "The Sordid Hipsters of America," 15.
29. Quoted in Holton, "The Sordid Hipsters of America," 17.
30. Jack Kerouac, *On the Road* (London: Penguin, 2002).
31. Rodley, *Cronenberg on Cronenberg*, 17.
32. Douglas, "Punching a Hole in the Big Lie," xxii.
33. Rodley, introduction to *Cronenberg on Cronenberg*, xxiv.

34. Douglas, "Punching a Hole in the Big Lie," xvii.
35. Douglas, "Punching a Hole in the Big Lie," xvi.
36. J. G. Ballard, introduction to William Burroughs, *Naked Lunch* (London: Flamingo, 1993); J. G. Ballard, "Introduction to the French Edition of *Crash* [1974]," reprinted in *Crash* (London: Triad Paladin, 1990).
37. Ballard, introduction to Burroughs, *Naked Lunch*, i.
38. Ballard, introduction to Burroughs, *Naked Lunch*, i.
39. Ballard, introduction to Burroughs, *Naked Lunch*, i.
40. Plato, *The Republic* (London: Penguin, 1990).
41. Ballard, introduction to Burroughs, *Naked Lunch*, i.
42. Ballard, introduction to Burroughs, *Naked Lunch*, i.
43. Rodley, *Cronenberg on Cronenberg*, 168.
44. Quoted in Rodley, *Cronenberg on Cronenberg*, 164.
45. Quoted in Rodley, *Cronenberg on Cronenberg*, 164.
46. Quoted in Rodley, *Cronenberg on Cronenberg*, 164–65.
47. Rodley, *Cronenberg on Cronenberg*, 170. Another contested issue here is sexuality. Cronenberg liberally develops the ambiguity of sexuality in the original *Naked Lunch*, but he undoubtedly emphasises a more heterosexual element than Burroughs did. For example, Cronenberg introduces a sexual attraction and consummation between Burroughs and Jane Bowles when, in fact, their relationship seems to have been far from this level, being rather cold and distant, a relationship of dislike.
48. Quoted in Rodley, *Cronenberg on Cronenberg*, 159–60.
49. Douglas, "Punching a Hole in the Big Lie."
50. Oliver Harris, "Virus-X: Kerouac's Visions of Burroughs," in *Reconstructing the Beats*, ed. Skerl, 203–16.
51. Harris, "Virus-X."
52. Rodley, *Cronenberg on Cronenberg*.
53. Quoted in Rodley, *Cronenberg on Cronenberg*, 164.
54. Rodley, introduction to *Cronenberg on Cronenberg*, xxiii.
55. Ballard, "Introduction to the French Edition of *Crash* [1974]," 5.
56. Ballard, "Introduction to the French Edition of *Crash* [1974]," 5. See Marshall McLuhan, *Understanding Media* (London: Routledge, 2001); Sigmund Freud, *Civilisation and Its Discontents* (London: Penguin, 2002).
57. Ballard, "Introduction to the French Edition of *Crash* [1974]," 5.
58. Ballard, "Introduction to the French Edition of *Crash* [1974]," 6.
59. Ballard, "Introduction to the French Edition of *Crash* [1974]," 6.
60. Ballard, "Introduction to the French Edition of *Crash* [1974]," 6.
61. Ballard, "Introduction to the French Edition of *Crash* [1974]," 6.
62. Ballard, "Introduction to the French Edition of *Crash* [1974]," 7.
63. Ballard, "Introduction to the French Edition of *Crash* [1974]," 8.
64. Ballard, "Introduction to the French Edition of *Crash* [1974]," 8.
65. Ballard, "Introduction to the French Edition of *Crash* [1974]," 9.
66. Ballard, "Introduction to the French Edition of *Crash* [1974]," 9.

67. Ballard, "Introduction to the French Edition of *Crash* [1974]," 9.
68. Quoted in Rodley, *Cronenberg on Cronenberg*, 199.
69. Quoted in Rodley, *Cronenberg on Cronenberg*, 198.
70. Quoted in Rodley, *Cronenberg on Cronenberg*, 199.
71. Foreword to Rodley, *Cronenberg on Cronenberg*, xii.

Contributors

Keith Allen is lecturer in philosophy at the University of York. He was a research fellow at the Institute of Philosophy, London, and studied philosophy at University College London and the University of Cambridge. His research interests include the philosophy of perception, the philosophy of color, and the history of philosophy.

Cynthia Freeland is professor and chair of the philosophy department at the University of Houston. She is author of *The Naked and the Undead: Evil and the Appeal of Horror* (Westview, 1999) and coeditor (with Thomas Wartenberg) of *Philosophy and Film* (Routledge, 1991). Her articles "Feminist Frameworks for Horror Films" and "Realist Horror" have been anthologized several times. Other film articles include "Horror and Art-Dread," in *The Horror Film* (Rutgers, 2004), and "The Sublime in Cinema," in *Passionate Views* (Johns Hopkins University Press, 1999). Freeland has also authored books on topics in ancient philosophy, feminism, and art theory.

Jones Irwin is lecturer in philosophy at St. Patrick's College, Dublin City University. His main areas of research are aesthetics, postmodernism, and philosophy of education. He is the author of *Derrida and the Writing of the Body* (Ashgate, Surrey, 2010), and his next monograph, *Paulo Freire's Philosophy of Education: Origins, Developments, Impacts, and Legacies*, is forthcoming in late 2012 from Continuum.

Peter Ludlow is John Evans Professor of Moral and Intellectual Philosophy at Northwestern University. He has done much interdisciplinary work on the interface of linguistics and philosophy and has also established a research program on conceptual issues in cyberspace, particularly questions about cyber-rights and the emergence of laws and governance structures in and for virtual communities. He has also written on topics in aesthetics that intersect with popular culture, including fan fiction and the ontology of virtual worlds.

Colin McGinn is professor of philosophy at the University of Miami. He has made contributions to various areas of philosophy, most notably in the philosophy of mind. He is the author of *The Character of Mind* (Oxford University Press, 1982), *Knowledge and Reality* (Oxford University Press, 1998), *The Making of a Philosopher* (HarperCollins, 2002), and *The Power of Movies* (Pantheon, 2005).

Daniel Moseley received a PhD in philosophy from the University of Virginia in 2010. He is currently visiting assistant professor in the Department of Philosophy, as well as a clinical assistant professor of psychiatry, at the University of North Carolina at Chapel Hill. He is faculty fellow of the Parr Center for Ethics at UNC, and he serves as a core faculty member in the UNC/Duke University Philosophy, Politics, and Economics program. Moseley's current research focuses on topics at the intersection of moral and political philosophy and the philosophy of mental disorder, including action theory, rationality, and irrationality.

R. Barton Palmer is Calhoun Lemon Professor of Literature at Clemson University, where he also serves as director of the film studies program. Palmer is author, editor, or general editor of more than forty books on various literary and cinematic subjects, including most recently (with Robert Bray) *Hollywood's Tennessee: The Williams Films and Postwar America*, *To Kill a Mockingbird: The Relationship between the Text and the Film*, (with David Boyd) *After Hitchcock: Imitation, Influence, and Intertextuality*, and *Joel and Ethan Coen*. He has contributed essays to many of the volumes in the Philosophy of Popular Culture series and is coeditor, with Steven Sanders, of *The Philosophy of Steven Soderbergh*.

Brook W. R. Pearson received his PhD in 2000 from the University of Surrey, in philosophy, classics, and religious studies (his dissertation was published by Brill in 2001 as *Corresponding Sense*). Formerly senior lecturer in philosophy at Roehampton University, London, he is now teaching in the Department of Humanities at Simon Fraser University in Canada. He is currently editing the unpublished works of the analytic philosopher John

Contributors   219

Wisdom at the Wren Library of Trinity College Cambridge, and is very interested in the relations between philosophy, film, and psychoanalysis.

Duncan Pritchard holds the chair in epistemology at the University of Edinburgh. Previously, he was professor of philosophy at the University of Stirling. His main research area is epistemology, and he has published widely in this area, including *Epistemic Luck* (Oxford University Press, 2005), *What Is This Thing Called Knowledge?* (Routledge, 2006), and *The Nature and Value of Knowledge* (with A. Haddock and A. Millar; Oxford University Press, 2010).

Simon Riches is a researcher at the Institute of Psychiatry, King's College London. He previously taught philosophy at University College London and Heythrop College, University of London. He holds a PhD in philosophy from University College London and has also studied philosophy at the University of Southampton and psychology at the University of East London. His research interests lie in epistemology and the philosophy of psychology. He is a contributing author in *The Philosophy of David Lynch* (University Press of Kentucky, 2011).

Daniel Shaw is professor of philosophy and film at Lock Haven University of Pennsylvania. He is managing editor of the print journal *Film and Philosophy* and has coedited an anthology on the philosophy of horror titled *Dark Thoughts: Philosophic Reflections on Cinematic Horror* (Scarecrow, 2003). He is author of a monograph for the Wallflower Press Short Cuts series, *Film and Philosophy: Taking Movies Seriously* (2008). His new book is *Morality and the Movies: Reading Ethics through Film* (Continuum, forthcoming in August 2012).

Paul F. Snowdon is Grote Professor of Mind and Logic at University College London. He was previously fellow and lecturer at Exeter College Oxford. He has written about the philosophy of mind, metaphysics, epistemology, and the history of philosophy.

Graham Stevens is senior lecturer in philosophy at the University of Manchester. He is author of *The Russellian Origins of Analytical Philosophy* (Routledge, 2005) and has published numerous articles on various topics in philosophy of language, metaphysics, and philosophical logic. He is currently writing a book on definite descriptions.

Index

Adorno, Theodor, 184–86, 189
aesthetics, 3, 9, 13, 16, 21, 26–28, 135–37, 145, 152, 163, 203–6, 209
American Werewolf in London, An, 26–27
Aristotle, 24–25, 34
authenticity, 4, 102–3, 127–37, 208
Ayer, A. J., 81

Bacon, Francis, 176, 184, 189
Ballard, J. G., 1, 4, 36, 122, 159, 175, 177, 198, 201, 205–12
biology, 11, 12, 15–19, 37–42, 45–46, 48–49, 60, 100
body horror, 1, 85, 92–93, 159, 180–85, 198, 208
Bonnie and Clyde, 32
brain-in-a-vat hypothesis, 44, 70–74, 76n2, 145
Brood, The, 119, 120–21, 183
Burroughs, William S., 36, 175, 177, 197–98, 201–12

Carrie, 33
Cartesian dualism, 2
causation, 79–81
Cavell, Stanley, 128–29
Chomsky, Noam, 43
cognitive science, 74

Crash, 1, 24, 48, 76n7, 120, 122–23, 181, 198, 201, 205, 208–12
Crimes of the Future, 158–61, 180, 183
Cronenberg, David: commercial success, 1; on determinism, 118; on film directing, 127; on the human body, 1, 3, 32; on the human condition, 2–3; interest in biochemistry, 36; on literary adaptation, 207; literary influences, 36, 175, 197, 201; on psychology, 1; on science, 49; on tragedy, 118; on violence in his films, 28–32; worldview, 4, 113, 123. *See also titles of specific films*

Dangerous Method, A, 138n10, 172
Dark City, 110n6
Darwin, Charles, 37, 39, 40, 42
Davidson, Donald, 98, 105, 108
Dawkins, Richard, 46, 104
Dead Ringers, 24, 44, 92, 93, 99, 113–19, 121, 155, 176–80, 182, 185, 191–94
Dead Zone, The, 24, 78, 80, 84, 86, 93, 119, 201
Death Proof, 213n14
deception, 30, 73, 92–99, 107, 109
Deleuze, Gilles, 156, 170
Dennett, Daniel, 104–5
Derrida, Jacques, 201

221

Descartes, René, 2, 69, 71, 94, 144, 202
determinism, 113, 118–23, 127
disgust, 10, 12–16, 19–22, 24, 26, 45, 209

Eastern Promises, 1, 25–30, 32–34, 45, 93, 108, 113, 120, 123, 125, 128–29, 133–37, 181
Enlightenment, 100, 176, 179, 181, 184, 186, 189
epistemology, 19, 70, 185
essentialism, 39–46
evolution, 37, 39, 42, 46, 49–50, 104, 108, 178
existentialism, 139n15
eXistenZ, 24, 37, 42–45, 47–48, 69–75, 83, 94, 96, 99, 109, 110n6, 143–44, 146, 149–53, 159
extended cognition, 70, 74–75
extrasensory perception, 77–87, 93

feminism, 193
fictionalism, 145
Fly, The (1956), 12
Fly, The (1986), 1, 12–22, 37, 41–42, 53–65, 76n7, 93, 121, 125–26, 149, 151, 176–80, 182, 185, 188–94
Foucault, Michel, 100
Frankfurt School, 176, 184
Freud, Sigmund, 98, 109, 115–16, 119–20, 122, 156, 158–64, 166–67, 169–72, 177, 183, 209–10
Fromm, Erich, 184

gangster (genre), 125, 128
genetics, 12, 15, 21, 37, 40–41, 45–46, 50, 119, 126, 178, 185, 189–91
Gettier problem, 88–89
Ginsberg, Allen, 202
Guattari, Felix, 156, 170

Halloween, 181
Heidegger, Martin, 139n15
High Noon, 92

History of Violence, A, 1, 25, 28–32, 34, 44, 91–93, 96–97, 99, 101–9, 120, 123, 125, 128–34, 137, 164–65, 167–68, 181
Horkheimer, Max, 184–86, 189
horror (genre), 1, 18–19, 21, 26, 33, 38, 48, 113, 118–19, 122, 125, 175–76, 180–86, 191–92, 198, 200–201, 204–5
human condition, 2–3, 49–50, 177, 192
Hume, David, 69, 83

identity, 24–34, 55–58, 64, 91–93, 96, 105–9, 125–37, 151, 156–59, 167–72, 177–81, 185–88, 191
It's a Wonderful Life, 102

James, William, 79, 83, 89n1
Jung, Carl, 172

Kafka, Franz, 16
Kerouac, Jack, 204, 208
Kripke, Saul, 40, 148
Kuhn, Thomas S., 100

Lacan, Jacques, 155–61, 163–71
Laing, R. D., 104
language, 27, 165, 204
language and linguistics, philosophy of, 40, 43, 47, 64, 143, 145–47, 158, 161, 163, 166–68, 171
Last Tango in Paris, 122
Leatherface: The Texas Chainsaw Massacre III, 130
Lewis, David, 148–52, 154n8
Locke, John, 63
Lord of the Rings, 129
love, 17, 19–20, 25–27, 37, 60–61, 96–97, 102–3, 106–7, 116–17, 123, 157, 162, 193, 211

madness or mental disorder, 44–45, 49, 72–74, 85, 92–96, 99–101, 104, 106,

109n3, 111n31, 115–18, 121, 131, 138n11, 178, 186
mad scientists, 25, 49, 55, 59, 93, 120, 176–77, 180–86, 195n2
Marcuse, Herbert, 177, 184, 203
Marx, Karl, 201
mathematics, philosophy of, 145
Matrix, The, 44, 70, 72–73, 110n6
M. Butterfly, 93, 96–97, 101, 103, 107, 186
McLuhan, Marshall, 209
metaphysics, 36–37, 125–30, 145, 158, 181, 186, 210
mind, philosophy of, 109n2
Moore's paradox, 167
morality, 1, 9, 25–27, 34, 86, 100, 135–37, 138n2, 176–90, 197–98, 200–207, 209–10, 212

Naked Lunch, 1, 24, 49, 83, 95, 119, 158, 181, 197–98, 201–2, 204–8, 211–12, 214n47
narcissism, 20, 117, 136, 160–61, 206, 211
Nietzsche, Friedrich, 166, 199
Night of the Living Dead, 182
Night Porter, The, 122

Omen, The, 181
ontology, 13, 18
Ovid, 158–59

paranormal, 77–81, 85–88
perceptual experience, 78, 81–85, 95
perceptual knowledge, 82–85
personal identity, problem of, 2, 59–65, 86, 125–30
phenomenology, 100
physics, 38, 154n8
Plato, 69, 98, 159, 172–73n7, 199, 206, 210
Pleasantville, 110n6
postmodernism, 45, 201–4, 211

psychiatry, 96, 99, 101, 103–4, 132, 138n11, 169, 183
psychoanalysis, 94, 98, 156–67, 170, 172
psychology, 1, 16, 55, 59, 63–64, 72, 74, 77, 82–83, 87, 89, 92–93, 95–101, 104–5, 108, 110n13, 113, 118–19, 128, 131, 156, 158, 162–66, 172, 180, 182, 185–86, 190–93, 210
psychotherapy, 98, 119–20

Quine, Willard van Orman, 39–40

Rabid, 28, 45, 49, 93, 119, 180, 183, 200
radical skepticism about the external world, 69–75, 94, 96, 110n6, 144–45
rationality, 37, 92–93, 98, 136
relativism, 38, 100–101
Rorty, Richard, 101

Sartre, Jean-Paul, 136, 139n15
Scanners, 1, 24, 37–38, 48–49, 77–80, 85–86, 93, 119, 125, 158, 180, 183
science, 4, 20–21, 36–50, 55–56, 74–75, 83, 100, 176–77, 180–94, 206, 209
science fiction (genre), 1, 18–19, 38, 48, 113, 125–26, 128, 154n8, 175, 182, 199–200, 207, 209–11
self, the, 2–4, 17, 75, 85, 96–98, 104–8, 125–28, 133, 136–37, 156–60, 164–66, 169–70, 173–74n28, 176–79, 186–91, 193, 202–3
self-deception, 50, 96–99, 103–9
semantics, 146–49
sex, 12–18, 24, 26, 28, 29–30, 34, 37, 45–50, 54, 97, 103, 105–6, 114, 116–17, 119–23, 159–61, 163, 177–81, 183, 185, 188, 190–91, 193–94, 200–202, 206, 209–11
Shivers, 1, 24, 37–38, 45–46, 48–49, 92–93, 109n2, 119–20, 125, 127, 158–59, 180, 183, 200
Silence of the Lambs, The, 182
Sixth Sense, The, 26–27

Skinner, B. F., 113
Spider, 24–25, 44, 74, 93–96, 99, 101, 103, 111–12n3, 120, 158–60, 165–66, 168–71, 181, 186
Star Trek, 48
Stereo, 77, 79–80, 85–86, 93, 156, 158–62, 164–65, 169, 197
Stevenson, Robert Louis, 176–79, 185–94
Szasz, Thomas, 104

Taylor, Charles, 136–37
technology, 3, 20–21, 36–37, 42, 48, 74–75, 158–59, 176, 180–91, 194, 199, 201, 209–11
Texas Chainsaw Massacre, 182
Thirteenth Floor, The, 110n6

Total Recall, 74
tragedy (genre), 24, 26, 34
Truman Show, The, 110n6

Videodrome, 1, 28, 42–43, 45, 49, 74, 76n7, 83, 94–96, 119, 125, 152–53, 159, 180, 183, 197, 201
Vienna Circle, 100
"view from nowhere," 38, 48–50

Wild Bunch, The, 32
Wittgenstein, Ludwig, 73, 76n4, 156, 158, 161, 166–68, 171

The Philosophy of Popular Culture

The books published in the Philosophy of Popular Culture series will illuminate and explore philosophical themes and ideas that occur in popular culture. The goal of this series is to demonstrate how philosophical inquiry has been reinvigorated by increased scholarly interest in the intersection of popular culture and philosophy, as well as to explore through philosophical analysis beloved modes of entertainment, such as movies, TV shows, and music. Philosophical concepts will be made accessible to the general reader through examples in popular culture. This series seeks to publish both established and emerging scholars who will engage a major area of popular culture for philosophical interpretation and examine the philosophical underpinnings of its themes. Eschewing ephemeral trends of philosophical and cultural theory, authors will establish and elaborate on connections between traditional philosophical ideas from important thinkers and the ever-expanding world of popular culture.

SERIES EDITOR

Mark T. Conard, Marymount Manhattan College, NY

BOOKS IN THE SERIES

The Philosophy of Stanley Kubrick, edited by Jerold J. Abrams
Football and Philosophy, edited by Michael W. Austin
Tennis and Philosophy, edited by David Baggett
The Philosophy of Film Noir, edited by Mark T. Conard
The Philosophy of Martin Scorsese, edited by Mark T. Conard
The Philosophy of Neo-Noir, edited by Mark T. Conard
The Philosophy of Spike Lee, edited by Mark T. Conard
The Philosophy of the Coen Brothers, edited by Mark T. Conard
The Philosophy of David Lynch, edited by William J. Devlin and Shai Biderman
The Philosophy of the Beats, edited by Sharin N. Elkholy
The Philosophy of Horror, edited by Thomas Fahy
The Philosophy of The X-Files, edited by Dean A. Kowalski
Steven Spielberg and Philosophy, edited by Dean A. Kowalski
The Philosophy of Joss Whedon, edited by Dean A. Kowalski and S. Evan Kreider
The Philosophy of Charlie Kaufman, edited by David LaRocca
The Philosophy of the Western, edited by Jennifer L. McMahon and B. Steve Csaki
The Olympics and Philosophy, edited by Heather L. Reid and Michael W. Austin
The Philosophy of Science Fiction Film, edited by Steven M. Sanders
The Philosophy of TV Noir, edited by Steven M. Sanders and Aeon J. Skoble
Basketball and Philosophy, edited by Jerry L. Walls and Gregory Bassham
Golf and Philosophy, edited by Andy Wible

www.ingramcontent.com/pod-product-compliance
Lightning Source LLC
Chambersburg PA
CBHW030411100426
42812CB00028B/2910/J